Currents in
American History

About the Authors

Terry D. Bilhartz is a professor of history at Sam Houston State University. He also is chair of the History Department, which serves about 4,000 history students each semester. Bilhartz is the author of more than thirty-five articles and book chapters in the fields of American history, psychology, philosophy and religion, and has written scripts for public television documentaries. He is the author of *Urban Religion and the Second Great Awakening,* which was selected by *Choice* as one of the outstanding academic books of 1986. His other books include *Francis Asbury's America: An Album of Early American Methodism* (1984), *Images of Texas in the Nation* (1991), and the popular American history source book *Constructing the American Past* (with Randy Roberts and Elliot Gorn), which is currently in its fifth edition (2004). His comparative world religion textbook, *Sacred Words: A Source Book on the Great Religions of the World* (2006), was recently released. Bilhartz holds degrees from Dallas Baptist College (BS, 1972), Emory University (MA, 1974), and George Washington University (PhD, 1979), and has completed postdoctoral studies in American and world history at Vanderbilt University, Stanford University, the University of Connecticut, the East-West Center at the University of Hawaii, and the Australian National University.

Alan C. Elliott holds an MBA from the University of Texas, Arlington, and an MAS (statistics) from Southern Methodist University. He is a faculty member and has taught at the University of Texas Southwestern Medical Center for over twenty years. Elliott specializes in writing techniques designed to make challenging subjects easy to understand. He has written biographies, a children's book on weather, and books on business and on software usability. He is coauthor of *Statistical Analysis Quick Reference Guidebook* (2006) with Wayne Woodward and author of a forthcoming Texas history book titled *Texas Ingenuity* (2007). Other recent books include *A Little Book of Big Dreams* (2001), and *A Daily Dose of the American Dream* (1998), which contains mini-biographies of innovative Americans whose lives had a significant impact on politics, business, or entertainment. Several of his books have been translated into other languages, including Chinese, Portuguese, Hebrew, Spanish and Indonesian.

Currents in American History

A Brief History of the United States

Volume II: From 1861

TERRY D. BILHARTZ AND **ALAN C. ELLIOTT**

M.E.Sharpe

Armonk, New York
London, England

Library of Congress Cataloging-in-Publication Data

Bilhartz, Terry D.
  Currents in American history : a brief history of the United States /
Terry D. Bilhartz, Alan C. Elliott.
      p. cm.
  Includes bibliographical references and index.
  ISBN 978-0-7656-1821-4 (pbk. : alk. paper)—ISBN 978-0-7656-1817-7
(vol. I : pbk. : alk. paper)—ISBN 978-0-7656-1819-1 (vol. II : pbk. : alk. paper)
    1. United States—History—Textbook. I. Elliott, Alan C., 1952– II. Title.

E179.B595 2007
973--dc22   2006024935

Printed in the United States of America

In loving memory of Lyman Bilhartz and Annette Elliott

Brief Contents

Detailed Contents

Illustrations and Maps

Maps

Acknowledgments

Currents in American History is a testament to the value of friendships. The work was conceived almost a decade ago when Terry Bilhartz, a professor of history at Sam Houston State University (SHSU), called his high school friend, Alan Elliott, a professional writer and biomedical statistician at the University of Texas Southwestern Medical Center, about working together on a history of medicine project. That project never materialized, but from this conversation came an idea to work jointly on a book titled *12 Days That Changed America*. After creating a working manuscript, Terry and Alan contacted another friend, Steve Drummond at M.E. Sharpe. In Steve's able hands, the renamed project evolved into its present form as a brief narrative U.S. history text designed for college students. Steve, we thank you for your vision, creativity, guidance, and support.

We also extend thanks to other networks of friends who helped to make this work possible. Special appreciation goes to SHSU professors Rosanne Barker, Susannah Bruce, Ty Cashion, Caroline Crimm, Yvonne Frear, Jeff Littlejohn, James Olson, Bernadette Pruitt, and Darren Pierson for not only reviewing early drafts, but also for piloting these drafts with their students. We thank the 3,000 SHSU students who participated in these pilot projects, and the 150 high school teachers who offered critiques of the text while attending the U.S. Department of Education Teaching American History Grant summer institutes at SHSU. We also thank Rocky Bilhartz, Lindsey Bilhartz, Teri Bilhartz, Patricia Summey, Betty Gore, Bob and Carole Bogart, Wayne Woodward, William Elliott and Mary Elliott who assisted us as proofreaders and friendly critics. Comments received from these friends, fellow teachers, and students have greatly enriched both the scholarship and readability of this work.

We also thank the academic historians, initially known to us only by their insightful comments, who reviewed early drafts of this work.

Along the production journey, we lost two dear family friends to brain cancer. It is in memory of these family members and friends, Lyman Bilhartz and Annette Elliott, that we dedicate the two-volume edition of this work. Similarly, we dedicate the combined volume edition to our life partners, Patty Ann Bilhartz and E'Lynne Wortman Elliott, friends who not only supported us on this project, but also bring joy to our lives each day.

The M.E. Sharpe
Student Learning Center
to Accompany Bilhartz and Elliott's

Currents in American History:
A Brief Narrative History of the United States

The narrative presented in *Currents in American History* makes for an intriguing story, one that includes drama, personal conflicts, surprise, resolution, and challenge. But what is the method that historians use to construct such a narrative? How and what do they investigate in order to create the story of our nation? The craft of history is based on a historical method of applying rules of evidence to source materials such as letters, speeches, artifacts, and images of different varieties. These primary sources are at the root of every historical investigation and also at the root of the M.E. Sharpe Student Learning Center.

The learning center that complements *Currents in American History* features numerous primary sources that enliven the study of American history, but also serves as a tool to investigate some of the key issues from our country's past. Through your investigation of the learning center, you will find much that tweaks your curiosity and you will utilize your investigative skills to find answers to many of your questions.

Through its browsing and inspection tools, the learning center provides the following resources:

- More than 250 primary sources, including images, videos, audio recordings, maps, and documents, organized by chapter, type, chronology, and key words

- Cause-and-effect exercises to enhance understanding of the currents of change surrounding the key events around which the narrative is organized

- Research folders for organizing, exporting, or presenting online groups of primary sources

- Self-study questions to reinforce the themes and information in each chapter, including drag-and-drop time lines based on the book's innovative "event analysis" methodology.

- Tools for printing, saving, and e-mailing individual primary sources

For all this and more, visit the M.E. Sharpe Student Learning Center at www.sharpelearning.com/history/currents/.

Introduction

The Genesis of America

If you are reading this opening line because you have to and not because you want to, do not fret. This simply means that you are like most first-year American history college students. If we (the authors of this text) do our job right, however, by the time you finish this required reading, you will have discovered a great truth: the story of the United States is a fascinating tale of intrigue and adventure with many surprising twists. You will discover that a journey into the American past not only brings insight into why Americans think and behave as they do, but also is simply a good read.

Our task as textbook writers is not to convert you into becoming a history major. It is, however, to help you realize that you made a good decision when you enrolled for this class. If we succeed, you will be convinced that this slim volume is more gripping, more relevant, and even more entertaining than you would have ever imagined.

Rather than covering just a little bit of everything, *Currents in American History* focuses on the historic ramifications of a handful of essential events that shaped the American past. Shorter than full-length texts, this work describes the causes of a select number of epoch-making events and then examines the short- and long-term consequences of these critical turning point moments. The arrangement of this text makes it possible for students to conceptualize America's complex past by assessing the impact of a dozen or so momentous days that changed the nation. In short, the history of the United States is presented as an intriguing story that includes times of drama, personal conflicts, surprise, resolution, and challenge.

Although you may be familiar with some of the decisive moments detailed in this text, *Currents* does not assume that you have an advanced knowledge of the American past. Even if you do not have a strong background in American history, you will be able to navigate through this volume. As you sail across time and place, you will become familiar with the four Cs of history: continuity, change, cause, and consequence.

Before launching into the first great day that changed America, *Currents in American History* will first introduce you to the craft and method we call "history" and to the idea of becoming an American. Although discussing the meaning of the words *history* and *American* may seem elemental for college-level American history students, be forewarned. These opening pages are probably the most difficult pages in the entire volume. After mastering these concepts, however, you will be ready to delve into the story of how a nation "conceived in liberty" and "dedicated to the proposition that all men are created equal" has struggled to realize its lofty goals.

The History of History

Envision a time before history.

Most of us, when first asked to envision a time before history, create in our minds images of dinosaurs or hairy Neanderthals. These images are accurate, but when thinking these thoughts, we probably are assuming that history means "the past" or, more specifically, "the human past." Although "the past" is indeed a definition of history, it is not the only definition. When students major in history, for instance, they do not major in "the past." Instead, they major in a subject or in a branch of knowledge known as "history."

"History" in this technical sense is not the total past, but rather a perception of the past that has been constructed by following a process known as the historical method. This method involves applying rules of evidence to sources (i.e., letters, speeches, artifacts, etc.) that date to that distant time and place being studied. Historians (meaning students of the past) call these distant sources primary sources. The craft or method of history, thus, is an attempt to understand what life was like in the past by applying reasoned arguments to primary source materials.

When did individuals start trusting the historical method as the most reliable way to make sense of the past? In short, how old is history? Who invented it and why? And how has this approach to the past influenced the way modern Americans think and act? These simple questions have complex answers that may surprise even serious students of the past. Not yet even 2,500 years old, history as a discipline is not as old or as universally accepted as many think. However, its impact upon Western civilization is so profound that many educated Americans find it difficult to approach the past in any other way.

Perhaps there is no better place to begin the search for the origins of history than to investigate the ancient book that opens with the familiar line: "In the beginning God created the heavens and the earth." In this sacred story from the book of Genesis, God speaks, creates, declares the creation to be good, and then calls it evening and morning, the end of day one. God then speaks again, creating more than previously existed, declares the new creation to be good, and then calls it evening and morning, the end of day two. After more creations on days three, four, five, and six, God rests and declares the seventh day to be holy.

The Genesis story continues with the well-known episode involving the characters Adam and Eve. This story, and the subsequent Hebrew sacred stories, make the point that human actions have consequences that can spoil the goodness of creation, but obedience to the God of creation can bring blessings. To these ancient peoples, human decisions and actions were important and carried even sacred, ontological significance.

Although many other ancient peoples also had creation stories, the Genesis account has had the most profound influence on the development of Western civilization. Genesis is important not because scholars consider it superior history or science (indeed, it was composed long before either of these disciplines was invented), but because it takes a novel approach to time and because it gives importance to the consequences of human activity.

Unlike the ancient Hebrews, other ancient peoples often passed down sacred stories that operated outside what moderns would call historic time and place. Many of the great stories of Greek mythology, for example, take place in the skies of Mount Olympus or at the bottom of the sea. In contrast, most of the activities in the Hebrew Bible take place at ground level, in a world that seems mostly recognizable to modern eyes.

More important, to many ancients from both the East and the West, time did not flow forward as much as it moved in a circle like the spinning of a wheel. The sacred stories of many peoples from India to the Americas suggested that just as the sun followed its daily course and the moon, its monthly rhythms, humans also were born, matured, died, and then were returned back into a recycling cosmos. In cultures with sacred myths that viewed time as cyclic, there was less incentive to record daily activities or to fret about daily decisions. In an eternal cosmos with no beginnings or endings, but only transitions, the struggle to improve creation appeared to be an impossible and even an unwanted ideal.

Unlike their contemporaries, however, the ancient Hebrews viewed time linearly and gave credence to the idea of progress. Time flowing forward from the past to the present in a straight line progression did not necessarily imply human progress, since regression also could occur, but it did at least suggest the possibility of improvement.

The sacred stories in the Hebrew Bible are principally theological compositions about the relationship between these people and their God. However, owing to the Hebrew construction of linear time and discussion of cosmic events within earthly space, the ancient Hebrew narratives look more familiar to modern readers of history than many other ancient texts. The Hebrews did not invent the discipline we now call history, but their approach to time and place did lay the foundation for it.

History—that is, the intellectual discipline that uses reasoned evidence from extant sources to make sense of the past—owes its origins not to the Hebrews, but to the Greeks. The evolution of this discipline was slow. In the sixth century BCE, a few Greek thinkers became dissatisfied with the traditional mythological explanations for the creation of the cosmos from the activities of the gods. Trusting observation and reason over their sacred mysteries, these Greeks attempted to explain the natural world without making reference to the supernatural. With these investigations into the physical world, science—or at least a distant relative of it—was born.

About a century later, Herodotus, another Greek intellectual unconvinced by the explanations of the myths, determined to understand how society as he knew it came to be. Specifically, he wanted to understand the causes of the Greek-Persian War, the foremost event that framed the time in which he lived. Herodotus traveled to distant lands, looking for sources—some written, but mostly oral—that could help him find his answers. When his sources offered suggestions that defied observation and logic, he rejected them, demanding instead more reasonable explanations. Herodotus published his findings in a work entitled *The Histories,* a word that literally meant inquiry or research. With this publication, Herodotus invented the genre of history.

Many readers of this book will not embrace the theology of the ancient Hebrews or the philosophies of the ancient Greeks, but most will accept the Hebraic arrangement of linear time and the Greek demand for causation arguments based upon rational analysis of sources. This is because Western civilization has been largely influenced by the ancient ideas of the Hebrews and the Greeks. Like the precursors and creators of the discipline of history, modern Americans view time as a continuous stream of forward moving, nonreversible events, with each event being both a product of previous actions and a force that influences the possibilities of future events.

American History as a Flowing Current

Given this understanding of the relationship of the past to the present, a useful metaphor for explaining how-things-have-come-to-be is the image of currents of flowing water. Consider melting drops of water on top of a snow-capped mountain. The drops gather into a bubble for a while until the pull of gravity breaks them away. The water's unwritten goal is to find a path that leads to the ocean. What path will this journey take? It is impossible to predict. As the trickle of water flows down the mountainside, it encounters barriers—perhaps twigs or rocks. It turns right or left or backs up for a while. One turn influences the next. As the trickle grows to a stream, it gains strength and is now less influenced by small barriers. Momentum builds and the stream grows into a river, pushing past trees, over rocks, perhaps spilling over a cliff to form a waterfall. In time, the power of this flow carves its own path. Its course becomes more predictable and steady, but it still is not unchangeable. Even the path of an immense river can be changed by the convulsions of an earthquake.

The United States was once much like the trickle of water on the mountainside. Its beginnings were fragile. Yet even in its infancy it aspired to lofty goals. Thomas Jefferson articulated such aspirations in the Declaration of Independence, stating that "all men are created equal"* and that government exists to secure the God-given rights to "Life, Liberty, and the pursuit of Happiness." Four score and seven years later, Abraham Lincoln restated these goals, reminding his fellow Americans that the nation "was conceived in liberty and dedicated to the proposition that all men are created equal." Since its founding, the United States, like those pristine drops of water destined for the ocean, has been moving on an epic journey in search of a grand end. The gravitational pull that has guided the currents of America's past has been the quest to secure liberty and establish equality for all its peoples.

Of course, the ongoing pursuit of liberty and equality is not the only theme in American history, but it is a dominant motif that has largely shaped the contours of the American past. This goal has never been fully achieved, but every generation has embraced it as the centerpiece of the American creed. The story of America, thus, can be told as the story of a people in pursuit of an ideal. At times this ideal appears to be within reach; at other times it drifts far away. Like the ebb and flow of water down a mountainside, the currents of American history have not followed a steady, even course. The expansion of liberty and equality sometimes surges forward as powerfully as water over a cliff. At other times liberty confronts obstacles that stop it in its tracks or divert it into unforeseen directions. Each twist in this journey creates a piece of history—a history worth remembering not only for its own sake, but because of its impact on events decades, even centuries into the future.

The best way to understand the cascading flow of events that constitute American history is to follow the journey from its inception, noting the upheavals of each generation and observing how the great events of each era bring the nation into new eras filled with new challenges and opportunities. Although there are many great events in American history, in this volume we focus on a limited number of particular events that stand out as turning points in the stream of time that signaled new ways of thinking and new directions for the American people. Each chapter identifies a turning-point moment and describes how each grand event evolved and was resolved and

---

*For the gender implications of this language, see Chapter 2 below.

how the resolution itself produced unintended consequences that generated future crises. On each of these momentous occasions, events transpired that altered the path of this nation that was "conceived in liberty." This story of America is largely a story of a sometimes divided, sometimes inconsistent nation that nonetheless pursues relentlessly its enduring quest to secure liberty and equality for all its peoples.

Currents in
American History

CHAPTER 7

A NATION DIVIDES

April 12, 1861

Fort Sumter and the Era of the American Civil War

Bombardment of Fort Sumter, Charleston Harbor, April 12 and 13, 1861

(Print by Currier & Ives. 1861. Library of Congress, Prints & Photographs Division, LC-USZ62-2570. 9-29-2006. http://hdl.loc.gov/loc.pnp/cph.3a06242)

TIME LINE

1852	Harriet Beecher Stowe publishes Uncle Tom's Cabin
1854	The Kansas-Nebraska Act revives bitter sectional animosities
1856	Civil War in Kansas
	James Buchanan is elected president
1857	U.S. Supreme Court rejects Dred Scott's appeal for freedom
1858	Abraham Lincoln challenges Senator Stephen Douglas to a series of debates
1859	John Brown attacks Harpers Ferry
1860	The Democratic Party splits
	Northern Democrats nominate Douglas
	Southern Democrats nominate John C. Breckinridge
	Carrying 39 percent of the popular vote, Lincoln wins the presidency
	South Carolina secedes from the Union
1861	Confederates fire on Fort Sumter
	Lincoln calls for volunteers to crush the rebellion
1862	Following the Battle of Antietam, Lincoln announces the Emancipation Proclamation
1863	The Gettysburg Campaigns claims over 50,000 casualties
	Lincoln delivers the Gettysburg Address
1864	Lincoln defeats McClellan to gain reelection
1865	Robert E. Lee surrenders at Appomattox
	Lincoln is assassinated
	Andrew Johnson becomes president
	The Thirteenth Amendment is ratified
1867	Andrew Johnson is impeached for violating the Tenure of Office Act
1868	The Fourteenth Amendment is ratified
	U.S. Grant is elected president
1870	The Fifteenth Amendment is ratified

By the 1850s, the ongoing debate that eight decades earlier had caused the framers of the Declaration of Independence to remove references critical of slavery continued to tear at America's consciousness. For many thoughtful Americans, the slavery issue festered like an unhealed wound, conflicting uncomfortably with other basic American values. Like a giant obstruction in the midst of a river, the troublesome slavery issue threatened to divide the flow of American progress into disparate and opposing directions.

Time and time again over the decades, political compromises had held the volatile issue at bay, but the revolutionary concept that every man was created equal continued to inspire and anger antislavery protesters. By mid-century the growth and influence of the antislavery movement that demanded the prohibition of slavery in the territories raised fear and anger among southern slaveholders and inflamed sectional passions to perilous heights. For growing numbers of southern "fire-eaters"—so named for the heat of their speech—there could be no further talk of political compromise. Something had to be done. Either a southerner's constitutional right to own slaves would be protected by the United States or the South would protect its way of life through secession.

During the decade that preceded the Civil War, slavery questions dominated everyday discourse. Politicians, farmers, clergy, and shopkeepers debated the issue: Was slavery compatible with American values? Should slavery be protected in the newly acquired U.S. territories? Does the Bible condone the institution? Should African-Americans be denied the rights of U.S. citizens?

In *Uncle Tom's Cabin* (1852), a novel that depicted the demeaning nature of slavery, Harriet Beecher Stowe awakened the conscience of millions by suggesting that the moral answer to these questions was simply no. This answer angered southern defenders of slavery like George Fitzhugh, who retorted that the "negro slaves of the South are the happiest, and, in some sense, the freest people in the world." When Dred Scott, a slave who had lived in free territory, sued for his freedom, the U.S. Supreme Court rejected his bid on two grounds. First, the Court ruled that Scott, as a descendant of a slave, was not a U.S. citizen and therefore had no right to sue. Second, the Court said that even if Scott could sue, he still would not be freed since Congress could not constitutionally prohibit slavery in the territories.

This infamous Dred Scott decision, while celebrated throughout the South, inflamed rather than extinguished the slave controversies. In a series of well-publicized debates between Stephen Douglas, a Democrat senator from Illinois, and Abraham Lincoln, his Republican challenger, the two northern senatorial candidates butted heads time and time again over the stands taken by their respective parties. Lincoln, who opposed any expansion of slavery into the territories, insisted that "there is no reason in the world why the negro is not entitled to all the natural rights enumerated in the Declaration of Independence—the right to life, liberty, and the pursuit of happiness." Douglas, however, who favored allowing the white males of each territory to decide whether slavery should be allowed there (an idea known as popular sovereignty), insisted that the "signers of the Declaration of Independence never dreamed of the negro when they were writing that document." Douglas stated, "If you desire negro citizenship . . . if you desire them to vote on an equality with yourselves, and to make them eligible to office, to serve on juries, and to adjudge your rights, then support Mr. Lincoln and the Black Republican party. . . . For one, I am opposed to negro citizenship in any and every form." In 1858, Douglas won the contested senatorial seat, although Lincoln emerged from the campaign as an articulate spokesperson for the new Republican Party, which opposed both the Dred Scott decision and the expansion of slavery into the territories.

In the autumn of 1859 an abolitionist named John Brown led a raid in Harpers Ferry. Authorities captured him quickly and sentenced him to be hanged. From prison he penned an impassioned message: "I am quite cheerful in view of my approaching end, being fully persuaded that I am worth inconceivably more to hang than for any other purpose. . . . I, John Brown, am now quite certain that the crimes of this guilty land will never be purged away but with Blood." This incident, ending in his execution, gave rise to the words of the most popular and widely used marching song of the Civil War:

John Brown's body lies a-moldering in the grave,
His soul goes marching on.

The Road to Disunion

The slavery question tore the Democratic Party (and with it, the nation) into two factions during the presidential election of 1860. Northern Democrats favored "popular sovereignty" as the solution to the slave controversy in the territories. They nominated the "Little Giant," Senator Douglas of Illinois. Southern Democrats, who supported the Dred Scott decision, nominated Vice President John Breckinridge of Kentucky. The remnants of the old and tired Whig Party (renamed the Constitutional Union but called the Do-Nothing Party) fielded a weak candidate, John Bell of Tennessee. The Republicans settled on the lanky, six-foot-four-inch giant called "Old Uncle Abe." Abraham Lincoln's memorable election slogans included "Let us have faith that right makes might," "Slavery is a moral, social, and political wrong," and "Millions for freedom, not one cent for slavery." Although Lincoln managed only 39 percent of the total popular vote, 2 percent in the fifteen slave states, and zero votes in ten southern states, he garnered 59 percent of the Electoral College votes and won the election.

The South had prepared itself for the impending Lincoln victory. South Carolina promised to leave the Union if the "baboon" Lincoln and his "black Republicans" won the election. Senator James Hammond claimed, "The North without us would be a motherless calf, bleating about, and die of mange and starvation." True to its word, on December 20, 1860, the South Carolina Convention voted to secede from the Union. Initial reaction was mild. The influential *New York Tribune* editor Horace Greeley proclaimed, "Let them go," and Mexican War hero Winfield Scott wrote, "Wayward sisters, depart in peace."

Within two months after Lincoln's election, seven lower southern states—South Carolina, Alabama, Mississippi, Florida, Georgia, Louisiana, and Texas—removed themselves from the Union and sent delegates to Montgomery, Alabama, to establish the Confederate States of America. Although these delegates patterned the Confederate constitution after the U.S. Constitution, it contained several notable exceptions: the central government could not impose protective tariffs, subsidize internal improvements, or interfere with slavery in the states; moreover, the new constitution insisted that slavery would be legally protected in the territories. Free states were invited to join the Confederacy so long as they were willing to accept these traditional southern views. Some southerners optimistically predicted that the majority of the states outside of New England that favored these provisions would ultimately join the new nation. These Confederates felt that they were not rejecting the U.S. Constitution; they were merely reforming it under southern direction. Although these "reformers" embraced most of the language of the U.S. Constitution, they were less comfortable with the lofty ideals set forth in the Declaration of Independence. Alexander Stephens, the newly elected vice president of the Confederacy, bluntly articulated the motive for the formation of the government when he stated, "the great truth that the negro is not equal to the white man—that slavery—subordination to the superior race—is his natural condition." To Stephens, the secession movement was a revolution to protect the liberties of white Americans and maintain a labor system that was both constitutional and consistent with the natural order.

President-elect Lincoln, who would not take office until March 1861, watched helplessly as the lame-duck president, James Buchanan, negotiated without success to bring the southern states back into the Union fold. A hopeful Lincoln claimed, "There will be no bloodshed unless it is forced on the government." In fact, many Americans believed that the crisis eventually would be mollified by compromise. Few people realized that a day loomed on the horizon that would transform the country.

Immediately after South Carolina voted for secession, a number of Federal holdings throughout the state were turned over to Confederate hands. But in the port of Charleston, the commander of Fort Moultrie refused to acquiesce. Major Robert Anderson had only recently been assigned to command troops at the ill-protected Revolutionary-era fort on the banks of Charleston harbor. The fortification had been built to withstand an attack from the sea, but not from its own citizens. Even before South Carolina voted to secede, state militias challenged the fort and harassed its occupants. The secessionists built up batteries of guns pointed at Fort Moultrie from nearby Mount Pleasant and on Sullivan's Island. They acquired ladders to scale the walls around Fort Moultrie and made no secret of their intention to take it. However, the secessionist government refrained from actually taking possession of the fort too soon because Buchanan's Department of War (led by a supporter of the secessionist cause) continued to fund significant improvements to this and other local forts. The South Carolinians intended to take the forts once the improvements were complete.

Anderson, a southern sympathizer, feared an imminent confrontation and believed that a battle with the South Carolina militia would ignite a general war. He reasoned that, given time, the U.S. Congress would find another compromise to appease both the southern states and the abolitionists and that all would return again to normalcy. Anderson appealed to Washington for orders but received no clear guidance. Therefore, as a delaying tactic he turned his eye toward an unfinished fort in the middle of the harbor, Fort Sumter. Although still needing work, this fort would be easier to hold than Fort Moultrie.

Six days after South Carolina's vote for secession, on the night of December 26, 1860, Major Anderson unexpectedly informed his officers, "I have determined to evacuate this post immediately, for the purpose of occupying Fort Sumter. I can only allow you twenty minutes to form your company and be in readiness to start." Captain Abner Doubleday, second in command and later of baseball fame,* sent his wife with a few belongings to a local minister's house. He then informed his troops and prepared for the evacuation. This sudden movement of soldiers out of the fort escaped the watchfulness of Confederate spies. Within minutes, Anderson's troops boarded boats that ostensibly had been chartered to move the workers who were improving the forts across the harbor. Two Confederate steamers kept watch on the harbor and one of them spotted the rowboats as they approached Fort Sumter. Captain Doubleday attempted to hurry his boat's progress, but the soldiers had little experience paddling and could not manage much speed. As the steamer approached, he ordered his soldiers to conceal their guns under their coats. The paddle wheels of the steamer stopped about a hundred yards away from Doubleday's boat. In the dark of the evening the soldiers appeared to be simply another crew of workers. The charade worked and they were allowed to pass.

At morning's light the authorities in Charleston learned about the occupation of Fort Sumter. Messengers in town scurried from house to house ringing bells to rouse the populace. At noon, while all of Charleston raged with anger, Major Anderson raised the U.S. flag over the fort. The occupying troops, many of whom were members of a military band, played the "Star Spangled Banner" and a chaplain led the assembly in prayer. In all, eighty-two soldiers and forty workmen occupied the fort.

That afternoon, South Carolina governor Francis W. Pickens sent messengers to Major Anderson demanding that he return his garrison to Fort Moultrie. Anderson replied that while he sympathized with the southern cause, he had determined that his men would be safer at Fort Sumter than in

---

* According to a legend, now generally discarded, Abner Doubleday was the inventor of baseball.

the poorly protected Fort Moultrie and that his action was motivated purely by the belief that it would prevent conflict.

When news of the standoff reached the northern states, the small band of soldiers at Fort Sumter became instant heroes. Northern newspapers carried accounts of their daring escape across the Charleston harbor. In Boston and New York, plays were quickly staged depicting the bravery of these Fort Sumter soldiers. At the same time in Charleston, politicians and newspapers stirred up the public's anger about the situation and pressured the Confederate military to act quickly and with force.

Now cut off from supplies, Anderson waited for orders or help from Washington. Laborers who chose to stay at the fort worked with the soldiers to ready the available guns. On January 9, 1861, a commercial steamer named *Star of the West* approached Fort Sumter. It had been sent by Washington to resupply the fort with food and two hundred and fifty soldiers. However, the Confederates fired on it and since it was not a warship and had no means of defense, it retreated from the harbor without delivering its supplies. Governor Pickens again demanded surrender of the fort, and Anderson again refused.

The standoff continued until Brigadier General G.T. Beauregard of the Confederate army assumed military control of Charleston. A friend of Anderson from earlier days, Beauregard exchanged polite letters with Anderson. Each stated his position and praised each other for valor and gentlemanliness.

On April 11, 1861, Beauregard sent a message to Anderson in response to a direct order from the Confederate government to force the surrender of the fort:

I am ordered by the government of the Confederate States to demand the evacuation of Fort Sumter. . . . All proper facilities will be afforded for the removal of yourself and command, together with company arms and property, and all private property, to any post in the United States, which you may select. The flag, which you have upheld so long and with so much fortitude, under the most trying circumstances, may be saluted by you on taking it down.

Anderson replied:

General: I have the honor to acknowledge the receipt of your communication demanding the evacuation of this fort, and to say, in reply thereto, that it is a demand with which I regret that my sense of honor, and of my obligations to my government, prevent my compliance. Thanking you for the fair, manly and courteous terms proposed, and for the high compliment paid me.

Privately, Anderson told the messengers that he would soon be starved out of the fort anyway and an agreement was made to evacuate the fort by noon on April 15. However, the Confederate government feared that reinforcements would soon arrive to help Anderson, so it ordered Beauregard to attack the fort immediately.

At 3:20 AM on the morning of April 12, a messenger woke Anderson from his sleep and delivered a letter from Beauregard stating that the bombardment of Fort Sumter would commence in one hour. At precisely 4:30 AM a mortar fired from nearby Fort Johnson signaled the Confederate forces to fire. Within minutes, volleys of cannonballs, shells, and hot shot from nineteen surrounding batteries assaulted Fort Sumter in a continuous roar of fire. Anderson's troops did not respond immediately. Amid the bombardment, they assembled in the mess hall for a breakfast of pork and water. The garrison's surgeon, Dr. S.W. Crawford, produced a little farina cereal to supplement the meager breakfast. The troops were calm and almost jovial at the prospect of finally participating in combat. Several hours after the assault began, once the Confederate placements were visible in the morning light, the Fort Sumter garrison responded with cannon fire.

For thirty-four hours the bombardment continued from both sides. The fort's defenders fought with vigor, but could not contain the overwhelming assault of the Confederates. These rebel soldiers now stationed in their old home at Fort Moultrie pounded Fort Sumter with 1,875 shots fired by three eight-inch columbiads, two thirty-two-pound guns and four twenty-four-pound guns. Thousands of shots also blasted the walls of Sumter from other surrounding batteries. Sumter's thick ramparts were soon battered and the wooden structures inside the fort were ablaze. On April 13 at about 1:30 PM a shot from the Confederates hit the fort's flagstaff and brought down the American flag. Several Union soldiers quickly raised it again on a smaller standard, but the action proved hopeless. The battle was lost. With ammunition, food, and strength all exhausted, Anderson raised the white flag in surrender at 2:15 PM. Dr. Crawford described the moment:

It was a scene of ruin and destruction. The quarters and barracks were in ruins. The main gates and planking of the windows on the gorge were gone; the magazines closed and surrounded by smoldering flames and burning ashes; the provisions exhausted; much of the engineering work destroyed. . . . The effect of the direct shot had been to indent the walls, where the marks could be counted by hundreds, while the shells, well directed, had crushed the quarters, and, in connection with hot shot, setting them on fire, had destroyed the barracks and quarters down to the gun casemates.

Miraculously, not one federal soldier had been killed during the assault. The Confederates also claimed no casualties, although there were rumors that a number of bodies had been secretly taken away and buried for fear that a report of the deaths would quell enthusiasm for the Confederate cause.

Southern predictions that northerners would be wary of going to war proved hopelessly wrong. Instead, the news accounts of the fall of Fort Sumter rallied thousands of volunteers in the North and cemented Lincoln's determination to preserve the Union at all costs. Shouts of "Remember Fort Sumter" and "Save the Union" echoed throughout the northern states. Letter envelopes depicting the American flag flying over Fort Sumter and inscribed "Our flag shall wave and none other" were printed and widely used. A coined medal depicting the likeness of Lincoln bore the legend, "The Fall of Sumpter [sic] Will be Avenged and the Rebellion Crushed and the Honor and Integrity of the United States Shall be Maintained." In response, a popular southern song urged,

> *Ye sons of Carolina! Awake from your dreaming!*
> *The Minions of Lincoln upon us are streaming!*
> *Oh! Wait not for argument, call or persuasion,*
> *To meet at the onset this treach'rous invasion!*

The opening volley of cannon shot at Fort Sumter marked in a turning point in American history as the long and tragic American Civil War commenced, with both sides fighting for what they believed was a just and honorable cause.

The Immediate Aftermath: The American Civil War

After the fall of Fort Sumter, President Lincoln asked the states to supply 75,000 volunteers to crush the rebellion against the United States. Citizens from every corner of the Union but one responded immediately to the call. By firing at the flag, the Confederates in a single day had brought a greater degree of unity to the northern states than had been achieved in four generations of political debate. Within a week, tens of thousands of white and black males crammed into enlistment offices to volunteer for duty (although initially only the white recruits were accepted), even as northern women demonstrated their patriotism by organizing relief societies that provided clothing, blankets, and supplies for the troops. Upon witnessing a parade of volunteers marching through the streets of New York, poet and composer George Templeton Strong exclaimed, "My eyes filled with tears, and I was half choked in sympathy with the contagious excitement. God be praised for the unity of feeling here! It is beyond, very far beyond, anything I hoped for."

THE NATION DIVIDES

In border Tennessee, patriotic volunteers also responded to the president's call, even as they mused, "We must not stop to ask who brought about war, who is at fault, but let us go and do battle . . . and then settle the question of who is to blame." In the South, however, Lincoln's call for volunteers fell on deaf ears. Instead, zealous southern crusaders exhilarated by the victory at Fort Sumter trumpeted the cry "On to Washington." Inspired and optimistic, many boldly predicted that the conflict would be over within sixty days. "Just throw three or four shells among those blue-bellied Yankees," crowed one enthusiastic North Carolinian; "they'll scatter like sheep."

The predictions from both sides for a quick settlement proved woefully inaccurate. Within two months after Fort Sumter, however, events transpired that would decisively impact the course of the next four years. During these days before a major military engagement, four additional southern states—Virginia, Arkansas, Tennessee, and North Carolina—joined the Confederacy. With the acquisition of Virginia, the Confederates moved their capital from Montgomery to Richmond, thus audaciously locating their capital only one hundred miles south of Washington, DC.

Equally important, during these critical weeks of decision four other strategically important states—Missouri, Kentucky, Maryland, and Delaware—rejected invitations to join the Confederacy. To keep these states in the Union, Lincoln used a combination of persuasion and force. For example, he gave assurances to Kentucky, Missouri, and Maryland that there would be no tampering with slavery. However, when the security of Maryland appeared threatened, Lincoln responded swiftly by declaring martial law in the region between Washington and Philadelphia, ordering the arrest of known southern sympathizers, and suspending the writ of habeas corpus, an action that allowed the government to arrest suspects and hold them without trial. During this crisis, Lincoln argued that the suspension of certain civil liberties at times was necessary to suppress rebellion. Lincoln was well aware that if these slaveholding states joined the rebellion, the white population (and military manpower) of the Confederacy would be increased by 45 percent and its manufacturing capacity by 80 percent.

Keeping these states in the Union was a major victory for the United States. Without Missouri, the Confederates would not be able to control the Mississippi River and the routes to the West; without Kentucky, they would not control the Ohio River; and without Maryland and Delaware, they could neither encircle the capital of the United States nor control access to Philadelphia and to the northern states. The decision of these states to remain in the Union also tarnished the legitimacy of the Confederate argument that the South was forced to secede in order to protect its constitutional right to own slaves. Although concerns over slavery drove the South toward disunion, the ultimate lineup of the states signified that the Civil War, at least initially, was less a conflict over the future of slavery than a struggle to determine whether the United States was indivisible.

From Saving the Union to Abolishing Slavery

Although vastly outnumbered in population and industrial strength, the Confederates enjoyed several distinct advantages. To be successful, the Confederacy only needed to defend its territories, not invade and conquer another land. Morale and motivation would present no problems since the cause of the South easily could be defined as a defense of the homeland. Southerners knew, or at least believed, that they would make better soldiers than the Yankee clerks and factory workers. Moreover, at least at the outbreak of the war, the Confederates also felt that they held in their hands the ultimate trump card—King Cotton diplomacy. Simply stated, Great Britain and the European continent needed southern cotton. Not only would the Europeans enjoy seeing the expansionist ambitions of their American rivals thwarted, but, according to Confederate optimists, for economic reasons the Europeans also could not afford to allow the United States to shut off their supply of southern cotton. The Confederate hope for victory rested largely on gaining diplomatic recognition by foreign countries and thus securing foreign aid.

Fortunately for the United States, the issue of diplomatic recognition for the South proved more complex than many Confederates imagined. True, Britain depended on southern cotton, but it also imported wheat from the northern states. Economically speaking, neutrality was a safer option than intervention. Furthermore, the strong antislavery sentiment in Britain gave the British leadership good reason to pause before considering Confederate recognition. On the continent, ideological factors also complicated the question of recognition. Conservative European monarchs, themselves threatened by revolutionary elements in their societies, yearned to see the defeat of the United States and its republican form of government. European liberals, however, supported the United States and viewed the American war as part of the general worldwide struggle for the principles of liberty against authoritarian rule.

Even as the Confederacy developed a strategy to defend itself and to secure foreign aid, Lincoln labored to strangle the rebellious states while holding onto the border states and preventing European interference. The war, at least initially, was a fight against the secession movement, not slavery. As casualties mounted and it became apparent that the war would not be brief, Lincoln gradually came to realize that the surest way to keep Europe on the sidelines and to justify the sacrifices being made on the battlefield was to seek a greater war objective. By the summer of 1862, Lincoln made the decision that for the nation to live, slavery must die.

Not wanting this decision to look like an act of desperation, Lincoln patiently waited for a military victory before announcing the new objective. Finally, in September 1862, Lincoln received some good news from the battlefield. The Confederate army under Robert E. Lee invaded Union territory, but its advance was checked by U.S. forces at Antietam under George McClellan. At the end of the day (which is still the bloodiest single day in American history), nearly 25,000 Americans had been killed or wounded. Although the losses on both sides were great, the Union soldiers forced Lee to retreat back into Virginia. If not a resounding U.S. victory, the Battle of Antietam at least gave Lincoln the occasion to announce to the world his Emancipation Proclamation.

The Emancipation Proclamation asserted that if the Confederate states did not return to the Union by the end of the year, the President would, on January 1, 1863, declare all slaves living in rebellious territories to be "forever free." The wording of the proclamation was cautious and politically astute. To keep the loyalty of the border states, where slavery was constitutional, and to secure the allegiance of those areas in the South already occupied by Union armies, Lincoln limited his threat to eliminate slavery to those regions that were in rebellion against the United States. His announcement also gave the rebellious states a hundred days to return to the Union without forfeiting slavery. Thus, when it was announced in September 1862, the Emancipation Proclamation did not liberate a single soul, but ultimately it would fundamentally alter the objectives of the war. From January 1863 onward, the war to save the Union also was the war to abolish slavery in the rebellion states.[*]

---

[*] Slavery in the Union states would forever be abolished by the subsequent ratification of the Thirteenth Amendment to the Constitution on December 18, 1865.

After the terrible and decisive battle of Gettysburg in July 1863, Lincoln consecrated that battlefield by reminding his fellow Americans that the United States was a nation "conceived in liberty and dedicated to the proposition that all men are created equal." For Lincoln, the Civil War itself was a test of the survivability of this great proposition. It was a war that tested the very principles of liberty and national indivisibility. In the end, no European country ever extended diplomatic recognition to the breakaway states. Lincoln's reelection in 1864 over Democrat George McClellan ensured that the Union would continue its fight until victory was won.

Long-Term Consequences: Reconstructing the Nation

Almost four years to the day after the Confederates fired on Fort Sumter, General Lee of the Army of Northern Virginia surrendered his forces to Union general Ulysses S. Grant at Appomattox Courthouse, a town in Virginia. Grant treated Lee's soldiers with respect, giving each man a three-day supply of rations and a parole, which meant that the Confederate soldiers would not be prosecuted for treason.

The price of bringing the rebellious states back into the Union was not cheap. Between 1861 and 1865, 618,000 Americans had lost their lives in what Lincoln called a struggle to determine if "government of the people, by the people, and for the people shall not perish from the earth." The number killed during these four bloody years is only slightly lower than the total number of Americans killed in more than two centuries of other U.S. military engagements from Lexington and Concord (1775) through the war in Iraq (2003). In addition to the number killed, another two-thirds of a million Civil War veterans suffered war injuries. The enormous cost of the war can be visualized by looking at the fingers on one's hand. For every five Civil War soldiers who went to war, three returned safely with only mental afflictions, one returned with serious physical impairments, and one never returned home at all.

Among the last casualties of the war was the president himself. During the war, Confederates and southern sympathizers had conspired to kidnap Lincoln and hold him for ransom, but all these plots had been foiled. On April 14, 1865, however, Lincoln and his wife went to Ford's Theater to see a stage production of *Our American Cousin*. On this night—just five days after the surrender at Appomattox—presidential security lapsed, and the president was shot at pistol-point range by southern sympathizer John Wilkes Booth.* At 7:20 the

---

*April 14, 1865, was Good Friday. Following Lincoln's death, the northern press and pulpit noted the coincidence of the timing of the assassination and drew parallels between the martyrdom of Lincoln and the crucifixion of Jesus.

following morning, a doctor pronounced the death of the president. (Ultimately, eight Americans would be convicted as accomplices in the assassination.) The *New York Times* reported the tragedy with the headline "The Songs of Victory Drowned in Sorrow." Just six weeks earlier Lincoln in his second inaugural address had declared, "With malice toward none . . . let us strive . . . to bind up the nation's wounds . . . [to] achieve and cherish a just and lasting peace among ourselves and with all nations." Yet, on the morning of the fourth anniversary of his call to arms, Lincoln became America's first president to be removed by an act of violence. Ironically, Booth's conspiracy convinced many northerners that harsher measures against the former Confederates would be necessary.

If the cost of the war was great, so were its social benefits. For every death, six slaves were freed. Furthermore, despite the tragic elimination of a generation of young men, the great suffering caused by the war also produced some ameliorating benefits for the widows it created. During the war, tens of thousands of northern women entered factories for the first time, while in the South women ran plantations without assistance from their male relatives. Thousands of other women entered the nursing profession (before the war few women were nurses); many others served as members of the U.S. Sanitary Commission; countless others volunteered their time as fund-raisers for wartime charities. Along with the sorrow and devastation caused by the tragic conflict, the Civil War also forced changes in traditional gender roles and expanded the range of public and economic opportunities for American women.

When the Confederates assaulted Fort Sumter, they also set into motion forces that would fundamentally change the role of the federal government in the life of the nation. For more than half a century before the outbreak of war, southern Democrats had resisted the efforts of the Federalists, the National Republicans, the Whigs, and finally the Republicans to enlarge the powers of the central government. Secession, however, temporarily eliminated southern representation in Congress. Taking advance of the absence of southern opposition, the Republicans during the 1860s enacted a number of federal programs designed to stimulate American business and agriculture. In 1862 alone, Congress enacted a high protective tariff, passed the Homestead Act, which awarded free land to migrants willing to settle the American West, and granted large tracts of public land to railroad companies to support the building of a transcontinental railroad. These and later wartime measures dramatically shifted the relationship between the federal government and private enterprise as Congress jettisoned its pre–Civil War laissez-faire tradition for an activist state that promised to support the efforts of American industry. The Confederate surrender at Appomattox also settled all long-standing questions about the locus of political sovereignty. After decades of heated debate, the war decided once and for all that the central government not only was supreme over the states, but also had broad constitutional powers to act on matters that affected the "general welfare" of the republic.

Another unanticipated, yet enduring consequence of the conflict was its impact on the U.S. Constitution. Before the surrender at Appomattox, more than sixty years had passed since the Constitution had been amended. Within six years after the end of the war, however, three amendments were ratified. The Thirteenth Amendment (ratified 1865) abolished slavery in all U.S. states and territories. The Fourteenth Amendment (ratified 1868) declared former slaves to be U.S. citizens, insisted that no state could deprive U.S. citizens of the rights of "life, liberty, and property without due process of law," and invoked penalties against any state that denied suffrage to adult male citizens. Finally, the Fifteenth Amendment (ratified 1870) forbade states from denying citizens the right to vote on the grounds of "race, color, or previous condition of servitude."

Some reformers were disappointed that these amendments did not do more to change the political landscape of the nation. Susan B. Anthony and many other women, for example, expressed outrage that the Fourteenth Amendment protected only "male" voters and that the Fifteenth Amendment did not add women to the list of groups to whom the states could not deny the vote. Other reformers were disappointed that the Fifteenth Amendment did not prohibit the states from using property ownership or literacy tests to disqualify African-American voters. This measure was blocked by moderates who refused to ban tactics that northern and western states might want to use to deny immigrants the vote. Yet despite these limitations, the three amendments that southern states had to ratify before federal forces would leave their lands promised to extend the civil and political liberties of millions of African-Americans. These constitutional changes raised African-American expectations and aspirations, at least temporarily brought about some degree of badly needed reforms to southern society, and laid the legal foundations for future, albeit belated, efforts to achieve for all American citizens full equality under the law.

Furthermore, in the aftermath of Reconstruction, the U.S. Supreme Court began interpreting the Fourteenth Amendment in novel ways. The assertion, "No State shall make or enforce any law which shall abridge the privileges or immunities of citizens of the United States; nor shall any State deprive any person of life, liberty or property without due process of law," took on new meaning when the courts ruled that business corporations were legal "persons" and therefore were protected against unfavorable state legislation such as regulating railroads and trusts. Thus, one of the most far-reaching and unexpected long-term consequences of the secession movement was that it served as a catalyst for the economic transformation of America from a society of small producers into a nation of large and highly organized corporations. Both the achievements and the problems associated with the late nineteenth-century age of industry can indirectly be laid at the feet of the Confederates who challenged the authority of the United States at Fort Sumter.

Bumps on the Road to Reunion

The cessation of military conflict in 1865 did not mean that sectional peace was restored. The war may have ended on the battlefield, but it persisted in the minds of men and women, North and South. Less than two months after the surrender at Appomattox, an editor for the *New York Times* expressed the thoughts of millions when he reminded his northern readers that "tens of thousands of national soldiers . . . were deliberately shot to death, as at Fort Pillow, or frozen to death as at Belle Island, or starved to death as at Andersonville, or sickened to death by swamp malaria, as in South Carolina." Southerners rejected such accusations, of course, retorting that all the horrors of the prison camps on both sides were caused by the inexorable policy of nonexchange enforced by the United States. Moreover, just as the Yanks seethed at the remembrance of Fort Pillow and Andersonville, Southerners boiled with rage when they recalled the "atrocities" committed by General Sherman's army as it ravaged the countryside during its war-ending march through Georgia and South Carolina. Sherman's march, while demonized in the South, unleashed shouts of pride in the North and was even immortalized in the jubilant song composed by the popular musician Henry Clay Work:

> *Bring the good old bugle, boys, we'll sing another song,*
> *Sing it with a spirit that will start the world along,*
> *Sing it like we used to sing, fifty thousand strong,*
> *While we were marching through Georgia.*
> *Hurrah! Hurrah! We bring the jubilee!*
> *Hurrah! Hurrah! The flag that makes you free!*
> *So we sang the chorus from Atlanta to the sea,*
> *While we were marching through Georgia.*
> *So we made a thoroughfare for freedom and her train,*
> *Sixty miles in latitude, three hundred to the main.*
> *Treason fled before us, for resistance was in vain*
> *While we were marching through Georgia.*

To the men in blue, these celebratory words justified the horrors of the war and affirmed the truth of the biblical adage "all things work together for good to them that love God, to them who are called according to God's purpose." To Southerners, however, the arrogant and jeering tone of "Marching through Georgia" evoked memories of "unspeakable things" that could not be easily forgotten or forgiven. As one ex–Union soldier sullenly wrote following a postwar visit to see a southern family that had befriended him and nursed him to health during the conflict, "They are not us and we are not them. My visit was a bridge across a chasm . . . but it was only a bridge, and neither they nor I ever forgot the void between us." Appomattox ended the war, but more time would have to pass before national harmony would be restored.

Inflaming the sectional wounds caused by the war was the structure of postwar party politics. The Democratic Party had taken a political beating during the war, not only because of the secession of the largely Democratic southern states, but also because growing numbers of northerners had begun to question the patriotism of the party of Jefferson and Jackson. "There is no heavier burden for a political party to bear, than to have appeared unpatriotic in war," stated Carl Schurz, the popular German-born abolitionist and Republican senator from Missouri. Democrats, understanding this truth, consequently wanted the past to be forgotten as soon as possible. Republicans, however, had no reason to allow the past to die. Born in sectional strife, the Grand Old Party had forged an East-West alliance and elected Lincoln without a single southern electoral vote, and then, as the majority party, it had conducted a war that successfully crushed a rebellion, abolished slavery, saved the Union, subsidized the building of transcontinental railroads, and passed a Homestead Act that sped access to the West. Defined by sectional crisis and proud of its wartime accomplishments, the Grand Old Party had no desire to let the past fade into history. By reminding the nation over and over again of the terrible southern beginning and noble Republican Party ending of the war—a technique called "waving the bloody shirt"—the Republicans simultaneously struck the Democrats where they were most vulnerable and united the various factions within their own party. "Waving the bloody shirt" was a powerful political weapon. The Republicans could keep the Democrats on the defensive as long as voters before casting their ballots asked themselves, "Shall the men who saved the Republic continue to rule it, or shall be it handed over to the rebels and their allies?"

Despite the political advantages of the Republicans, the presidential election of 1868 was surprisingly (for the Republicans, alarmingly) close. Lincoln's successor, Andrew Johnson, who spent most of his life as a Tennessee Democrat, was never liked by the congressional Republicans. His postwar leniency toward the South made him even more hated. In 1867, Congress passed constitutionally questionable legislation such as the Tenure of Office Act, which was designed to restrict his presidential power. When Johnson disregarded this legislation, the House of Representatives impeached him, and in his trial in the Senate, Johnson came within one vote of being evicted from office.

Thus, having discarded Johnson, in 1868 the Republicans nominated the popular General U.S. Grant. The Democrats, in turn, nominated the former New York governor, Horatio Seymour, who ran on the slogan "This Is a White Man's Country: Let White Men Rule." Seymour polled 2.7 million votes—only 300,000 votes less than the Republican war hero. Had it not been for the Reconstruction policies passed by the Radical Republicans that deprived three southern states* of the right to vote, disenfranchised another 200,000 white southerners from other former Confederate states, and secured first-time voting privileges for 700,000 freedmen, the Republicans would not have won the election. Moreover, by taking New York and New Jersey, as well as Delaware, Maryland, Kentucky, and Oregon, Seymour carved into some areas previously carried by the Republicans and would have won the presidency had there been a solid Democratic South behind him. Although victorious, the Republicans after the election of 1868 remained fearful that a return to southern politics as usual would undo the social and economic progress that had been secured by Republican war and postwar policies.

Fearing the demise of power every two years in congressional elections and every four years in presidential ones, Republicans would take out "the bloody shirt" and wave it again and again before the electorate. According to standard party-line Republican propaganda, the Democratic Party had "no high aims, no patriotic intentions," was "controlled by the foreign population and the criminal classes of our great cities, by Tammany Hall, and by the leaders of the solid South," and contained "the opponents of the union, . . . men believing in state sovereignty, . . . men contemptuous of equal rights, . . . rebels, repudiators of the war amendments, . . . tools of slavery and secession." There was just enough truth in these accusations to keep the opposition party in retreat. Consequently, throughout the decade that followed the Civil War, the "bloody shirt," coupled with the military occupation of several southern states, kept the Republicans in control of both the White House and Congress.

The Republican monopoly, however, began to wane in 1870 when the Democrats won the majority of the seats in the House of Representatives, the first such election victory in fourteen years. The Republicans regained control of both houses two years later (and also maintained the presidency with Grant's victory over Horace Greeley), but in 1874, for the second time in three elections, the Democrats again took the House. Although still in control of the Senate and the White House, the Republicans approached the election of 1876 with some trepidation. To the faithful, the future of the party, the civil rights of African-Americans, the economic policies (i.e., tariffs, hard currency, railroad subsidies) that had privileged the northern states—all these and more were in peril. To many Republicans, it appeared that the hard-won fruits of the Civil War were in danger of being lost.

---

*Virginia, Mississippi, and Texas were not eligible to vote in the election of 1868. Eight years earlier, some 185,000 Democrats cast ballots in these states.

CHAPTER 8

PRESIDENTIAL BARGAINING

February 26, 1877

The Compromise of 1877 and the Price of National Unity

Is this a Republican Form of Government? Is this Protecting Life, Liberty, or Property? Is this the Equal Protection of the Laws?

(Engraving by Thomas Nast, 1876. Illustrated in *Harper's Weekly*, September 2, 1876, p. 712. Prints and Photographs Division, Library of Congress. LC-USZ62-116355. 9-29-2006. http://hdl.loc.gov/loc.pnp/cph.3c16355)

TIME LINE

1876	The United States celebrates its centennial
	Samuel Tilden wins 184 electoral votes and Rutherford Hayes 165, but twenty electoral votes are disputed
1877	Congress creates an electoral commission to resolve the election crisis
	The Compromise of 1877 is negotiated
	Hayes is inaugurated as president
	The removal of federal troops ends the period of Reconstruction
1881	President James A. Garfield is assassinated; Chester A. Arthur assumes the presidency
1880s–1910s	Rising numbers of eastern and southern Europeans migrate to the United States
1882	Congress passes the Chinese Exclusion Act
1883	The Pendleton Act establishes the U.S. Civil Service Commission
	The Supreme Court rules that the Fourteenth Amendment does not forbid individuals from discriminating against the civil rights of racial groups
1884	Democrat Grover Cleveland defeats James Blaine to win the presidency
1887	Congress enacts the Dawes Severalty Act
1888	The Interstate Commerce Commission is created
	Republicans retake the White House as Benjamin Harrison edges Cleveland in the Electoral College
1890	Harrison signs the McKinley Tariff Act
	For the first time, the U.S. Census reveals more money made in manufacturing than in agriculture
1892	In a presidential rematch, Cleveland defeats Harrison to win the presidency
1893	The Panic of 1893 results in high unemployment
1896	In *Plessy v. Ferguson*, the Supreme Court approves the "separate but equal" doctrine

America's centennial year, 1876, began with great hope and fanfare. After years of regional tensions and war, many Americans wanted to forget the dark moments of their past and remember and celebrate their many grand accomplishments. And celebrate they did. At America's hundredth birthday party, the 1876 Centennial Exposition, proud citizens walked the exhibition halls in Philadelphia gawking at the vast assortment of newfangled gadgets and devices on display. Among the inventions that attracted special attention were the telephone, the typewriter, a colossal 1,400-horsepower Corliss steam engine, sewing machines, and a clasp-lock device that soon became known as the zipper.

Thousands who witnessed these amazing displays had traveled to Philadelphia not by horseback or carriage, as the signers of the Declaration of Independence had arrived a century earlier, but aboard one of the many railroads or steam-powered boats that transported people and goods to and from distant places with amazing speed. To these citizens, the exhibits at the centennial fair offered ample evidence that America was a land of enterprise, vigor, innovation, and progress. The fountain of hope that had gushed forth from Philadelphia a century earlier was still flowing, and despite the many obstacles that had threatened to impede its flow, America at a hundred years old was still a nation on the move that could boast of a dazzling past and an even more dazzling future.

The year that began with hope, however, ended in political turmoil. A controversy over the results of the 1876 presidential election provoked pandemonium over who was the legitimate winner. The brewing political crisis threatened to turn the nation back toward the dark days of sectional war. As the final hours of President Grant's second term wound down, with still no officially recognized successor, the nation approached another moment of decision—a seventh decisive turning point in its history.

Prelude to Compromise: The Politics of Reconstruction

Although the renegade southern states had been brought back into the Union after the Civil War, they did not immediately kiss and make up. The victorious North instituted a program known as Reconstruction, designed to impose by military force the emancipation of slaves and to guarantee for them equal participation in the political process. Troops were stationed at southern state capitals to enforce the law. With the help of the substantial African-American vote, "Lincoln" Republicans were elected all over the South. However, in the early 1870s, the federal government slowly decreased the number of its troops in the South. Without protection, the African-Americans felt threatened and voted less, allowing the Democrats to slowly return to prominence. Thus, as the 1876 election grew near, both Republicans and Democrats saw the southern situation as an important and delicate issue. If African-Americans voted freely, they would help the Republicans retain the presidency, but if growing harassment prevented African-Americans from voting, the Democrats would have the advantage. With this political situation in mind, the two parties selected candidates who had a chance at garnering southern votes. The Democrats selected Samuel J. Tilden of New York and the Republicans chose Rutherford B. Hayes of Ohio.

Tilden, the son of a farmer and storekeeper, had suffered from chronic poor health as a child but eventually graduated from law school at the University of the City of New York. He began his political career writing pamphlets for the Democratic Party, ardently supported the antislavery movement before the Civil War, and became governor of New York in 1874. His record in fighting political corruption won him the Democratic nomination to run for president in 1876. Tilden's presidential campaign condemned corruption in the Grant administration, supported an end to Reconstruction (which African-Americans opposed), advocated tariff reform, and supported an end to federal railroad subsidies.

His Republican opponent, Hayes, was the governor of Ohio. The son of a farmer and distiller, he had earned a law degree from Harvard and married Lucy Webb, a vocal supporter of abolition and temperance. Hayes began his political career as a Whig, but became a Republican in the 1850s because of his opposition to the expansion of slavery into new western states. He served as a major general in the Civil War and as a congressman from Ohio beginning in 1865. In 1867 he was elected governor. During the 1876 presidential election, Hayes faced an electorate that increasingly distrusted the sitting Grant administration because of political corruption and economic depression.

True to the now commonly employed mudslinging tactics in presidential elections, Republicans questioned Tilden's reform image and dubbed him "Slippery Sam" in reference to his association with the politically corrupt Tammany Hall of New York. Popular Republican speakers, including Mark Twain, supported the Hayes campaign with slogans that included "Hurray for Hayes and his honest ways" and "We'll vote for the Buckeye Boy" (Ohio is known as the Buckeye State). Democrats countered with reminders of the current corruption in the Grant White House: "Turn the rascals out," "Hayes, hard money and hard times," and "Grantism means poor people made poorer." To influence the election in favor of Tilden, organizations such as the Ku Klux Klan stepped up their threats and violence to prevent blacks from voting. The following Republican rhyme lambasted the Southern Democrats' harassment of blacks:

> *Sing a song of shotguns,*
> *Pocket full of knives,*
> *Four-and-twenty black men,*

Running for their lives;
When the polls were open,
Shut the nigger's mouth,
Isn't that a bully way
To make a solid South?

When Election Day arrived, early results clearly favored Tilden. On the strength of these returns, the *New York Tribune* and other influential newspapers proclaimed Tilden the victor. Dismayed Republicans languished in certain defeat. However, some Republicans would not give up so easily. When Daniel Sickles, a former Union general and congressman, decided to check on the returns at Republican headquarters at midnight on November 7, 1876, he discovered a flaw in Tilden's claim of victory. The electoral count showed Tilden still one vote shy of the needed votes to win, with the counts from Florida, Louisiana, and South Carolina yet to be finalized. Sickles concocted a bold scheme. He telegraphed Republican leaders in the three outstanding states, urging them to do whatever possible to secure the votes for Hayes. By 3:00 AM he received his first answer. South Carolina governor Daniel Chamberlain responded, "All right. South Carolina is for Hayes. Need more troops."

Since Republicans held the majority on the election commissions in these three southern states, they were able to hold the line on declaring the vote for Tilden while they created a strategy to question the results. This delay gave Republicans a glimmer of hope and spread uncertainty within the Democratic Party. Overwhelming historical evidence shows that both Republicans and Democrats used illegal tactics during and after the election, including bribery, violence, and fraud. For example, in an effort to fool illiterate African-Americans, Democrats printed ballots that looked like the Republican ballots (including a prominent picture of Abraham Lincoln), but when used actually cast a vote for Tilden. To counter this and other wrongs, the Republicans, who controlled the slates that certified the election returns in these states, threw out thousands of votes (just enough to carry the elections) that they claimed were a result of Democratic fraud.

When the nationwide popular votes were tabulated, Tilden clearly won with 4.2 million (51 percent) votes to Hayes's 4.0 million (48 percent). However, the electoral vote, which would ultimately determine the election, remained in dispute. Tilden had secured 184 unchallenged electoral votes, still one vote shy of victory. Hayes had garnered 165 votes. Twenty votes remained up in the air—four for Florida, eight for Louisiana, seven for South Carolina, and one for Oregon. In the three southern states, both sides claimed victory and sent to Washington conflicting outcomes. In Oregon, the Republicans won the popular vote, but when it was discovered that one member of the Electoral College did not constitutionally qualify to serve as an elector, the Democratic governor of the state appointed in his place the next highest vote getter, a Democrat, thus giving the Democrats claim to a lone vote in an otherwise Republican state. In this case, it was the Republicans who cried foul. Thus, even two months after the voters had gone to the polls, the election of 1876 was up for grabs with the electoral scoreboard still blinking: Tilden 184, Hayes 165, Undecided 20.

According to the U.S. Constitution, the members of the Electoral College vote in their respective states and then send the certified results of their voting to the nation's capital, where "the President of the Senate shall, in the presence of the Senate and House of Representatives, open all the certificates and the votes shall then be counted." If a candidate receives a majority of these votes, a president is elected. If not, the election will be decided in the House of Representatives.

But who should do the counting? The answer to this piece of what normally would be trivia is not detailed in the Constitution. If the president of the Senate (at the time, a Republican) alone counted the returns, then Hayes would receive all the disputed votes and be elected. If, on the other hand, the two houses acting jointly did the counting, then the election would go in favor of Tilden since the Democrats controlled the House by a greater margin than the Republicans controlled the Senate. Or, if all of the disputed ballots were thrown out and thus no majority was obtained for either candidate, then the election would be decided in the House of Representatives, which the Democrats controlled.

To forestall a constitutional crisis, in late January 1877, Congress passed an electoral commission bill that created a fifteen-member commission to study the disputed returns and determine the legitimate winner in each of the contested states. According to this law, the decisions of the commission would be considered legally binding unless overridden by both houses of Congress, an unlikely scenario. Ultimately, when eight Republicans and seven Democrats were placed on this commission, the stage was set for a showdown. A strictly partisan vote would (and did) give the Republicans the White House, but carrying the election in this way brought grave dangers. Deeply ingrained in everyone's memory was the southern reaction to Lincoln's legitimate election victory just sixteen years earlier. How would the nation respond to the seating of Hayes through such nefarious methods? Some people warned that there were fifteen states with Democratic forces composed of war veterans making preparations to move on Washington. Other more moderate Democrats threatened to stage a fierce filibuster to prevent the theft of an election by the shenanigans of a corrupted commission. In describing the crisis, the chairman of the Democratic National Committee, Abram Hewitt, recalled: "Business was arrested, the wheels of industry ceased to move, and it seemed as if the terrors of civil war were again to be renewed." President Grant even felt the need to announce that he would counter "any warlike concentration of men" with a declaration of martial law. The Republicans had the cards to win the hand, but to play that hand would threaten the social fabric of the nation.

As Grant's term wound toward a close, the candidates tried to stay above the fray and on the sidelines. Tilden refused to take an active role in the controversy, secluding himself in his library where he worked on a legal brief to support his claim of victory. Hayes also kept a low profile by remaining in Ohio during the turmoil. Privately, however, he kept in close contact with his supporters, who were busily engaged in finding a solution that would bring Hayes to the White House without invoking national calamity. Both parties, as well as isolated factions within each party, were willing to negotiate to find a solution that would achieve some of their objectives without thrusting the nation into disarray. Even as threats publicly were shouted from the floors of Congress, intense private negotiations were taking place in proverbial smoke-filled rooms. After weeks of arguing and posturing, a compromise began to take shape.

The Wormley House Agreement: February 26, 1877

Among all this backroom bargaining, the negotiations in a crowded room in the Wormley Hotel in Washington stand out. Early on Monday morning, February 26, 1877, a representative of the Louisiana Democrats, Edward Burke, was summoned to the White House. President Grant said that he agreed with Burke that most Americans no longer wanted federal troops in Louisiana. Grant's dilemma, however, was that he did not want to undercut Hayes by pulling out the troops. Armed with this knowledge, Burke scurried back to Capitol Hill to meet with some of Hayes's closest advisers. After locking themselves into a cloistered committee room, Burke told Hayes's men of a plan that could break the impasse. All Hayes had to do was to convince Grant that withdrawing troops from Louisiana would not embarrass him. With assurances that Reconstruction would come to an end, either immediately under Grant or soon under Hayes, southern Democrats, who wanted self-rule more than they wanted Tilden, would break the threatened filibuster and allow Hayes to be certified as president. After listening to the scheme, Ohio senator John Sherman* insisted that more assurances would be needed before Hayes would agree to the scheme. To discuss such details, a meeting was set for that evening at the Washington residence of the Republican chief

---

* John Sherman was the brother of the famous (in the South, infamous) William Tecumseh Sherman, the Union general who had helped end the Civil War by destroying southern land and property as he marched his troops through Georgia and the Carolinas in 1864.

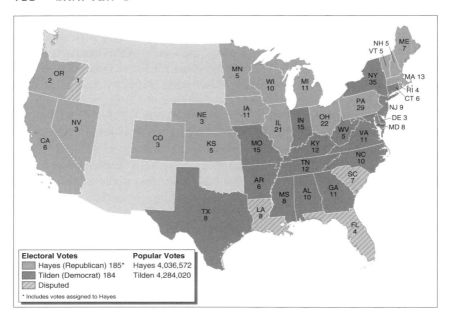

Electoral Votes

Hayes (Republican) 185*
Tilden (Democrat) 184
Disputed

Popular Votes

Hayes 4,036,572
Tilden 4,284,020

* Includes votes assigned to Hayes

THE ELECTION OF 1876

counsel before the electoral commission and former U.S. attorney general, William Evarts.

Evarts resided in the Wormley Hotel, a small, discreet establishment on the corner of H and Fifteenth streets that was owned and managed by a pioneering African-American entrepreneur named James Wormley. The Wormley Hotel was among the city's most elegant houses, offering its patrons a world-class cuisine, an elevator, and one of Washington's first telephones. The site was ideal for the meeting, not only because of its cozy sophistication and convenient location just a mile or so from Capitol Hill, but also because it was one of the few hotels in town where visitors would be sure not to find southern patrons engaged in late-night, high-stakes poker games. The only southerners who would be at Wormley's on the shivering, wintry night of February 26 would be those warm to a horse trade—the presidency for southern self-rule.

On the last Monday night of Grant's second term, a full moon illuminated the clear Washington sky as several horse-drawn carriages arrived at the Wormley Hotel. A dozen of the capital's influential men, both Democrats and Republicans, gravitated to Evarts's room. Joining Burke were his congressional colleagues William Levy and E. John Ellis of Louisiana. The Ohio faction included Governor William Dennison, Senator John Sherman, and Congressman and future U.S. president James Garfield. Garfield's presence particularly was uneasy, since as a Republican member of the electoral commission, he already had voted that Hayes had carried Louisiana. Now, at a secret meeting in a smoked-filled hotel room, he was in effect acknowledging that that verdict was not legitimate.

The dozen power brokers removed their coats and top hats and sat together around a table to work out a compromise acceptable to both parties. The southerners wanted assurances that notwithstanding Hayes's refusal to publicly announce the withdrawal of federal troops, Hayes would as president indeed support the end of Reconstruction. In contrast, the Ohio Republicans wanted pledges that the Democrats would uphold black civil rights in the "redeemed" southern states and that the new Louisiana legislature under Democratic control would not elect a long-term Democratic senator until after March 10, so as not to provoke Republican hostilities toward Hayes that could threaten confirmation of his cabinet nominations. Once these assurances were made, the parties struck a deal. The Republicans agreed to appoint a southern Democrat to the cabinet and to abandon the two remaining Republican governments in the South, thus enabling the Democrats to reestablish control over Louisiana and South Carolina. The Southern Democrats, in turn, agreed to work toward the defeat of their party's filibuster and to support a peaceful succession of Hayes into the White House.

Immediate Consequences: The Inauguration and Administration of Hayes

The following day, February 27, the electoral commission completed its work by announcing the verdict for the state of South Carolina. While important, this final action of the commission was anticlimactic, since on three previous occasions this group of eight Republicans and seven Democrats already had revealed its inclinations. By strictly party line 8–7 votes, the commission had awarded the state of Florida to Hayes on February 9; on February 16, it gave Louisiana to Hayes; and on February 23, it gave the disputed vote in Oregon to Hayes. Then, on Tuesday the 27th, the commission by the same 8–7 vote gave South Carolina to Hayes. By awarding all twenty disputed votes to Hayes, the commission determined that Hayes had won the Electoral College with a 185–184 majority.

This announcement, however, did not make Hayes president. Congress still had to confirm the electoral votes. For the next three days, passions flared in the halls of Congress with members even mounting their desks to express their disgruntlement. Democrats shouted, snarled, fumed, and pouted, but in the end, after Wormley Hotel negotiator William Levy rose to announce that he had "solemn, earnest, and, I believe, truthful assurances" from both Hayes and Grant regarding "a policy of conciliation toward the Southern States," enough Democrats backed down from their rebellious protests to end the filibuster.

Finally, at 4:10 AM on March 2, 1877, Congress confirmed Hayes as president-elect. Later that day, President Grant told Burke that he had dispatched an order stating that federal troops no longer could be used to uphold the Republican regime in Louisiana. With the count complete, President-elect Hayes arrived in Washington on March 2 in a private car provided by the Pennsylvania Railroad. Because of concern about possible violence surrounding the Republican victory, Hayes took the oath to become the nineteenth president of the United States at a private ceremony in the White House on March 3, 1877. Two days later he retook the oath at the official public inauguration celebration.

The Compromise of 1877 signaled the beginning of a new era. For a generation following the outbreak of the Civil War, America's two major political parties had viewed each other less as merely political opponents than as deadly enemies to be destroyed. The Republican Party, with no southern base to appease, took credit for saving the Union, eliminating slavery, and protecting the civil rights of freed slaves. Determined not to allow the past to be forgotten, the Republicans "waved the bloody shirt" by reminding the electorate over and over again of the despicable sins of the southern rebels and the northern Democrats who sympathized with them. Democratic Party appeals to the constitutionality of the states' rights tradition won few converts in this postbellum period. In both high-brow literature and low-brow reporting, northern writers villainized white southerners and depicted the African-American freedmen as heroic freedom fighters. By the time of the Compromise of 1877, however, the mood of the nation was beginning to change. As the storms of the past stilled and the political winds shifted, the North and the South gradually exited an age of divide and entered into a new era that would be marked by reunion and economic expansion. To some, this emerging industrial era would be known as America's Golden Age; to others, the new America was not golden, but only gilded.

As promised, shortly after taking office, President Hayes ended Reconstruction by ordering the remaining federal troops to be withdrawn from the southern states. He also appointed, and the Republican-controlled Senate confirmed, the ex–Confederate general David Key as postmaster general. With a southerner and a Democrat as postmaster general, the South not only had a voice in the cabinet, but Democrats north and south were assured that some of the jobs to be awarded by the postmaster general would be theirs. To further balance his cabinet, President Hayes selected William Evarts, the host of the Wormley Hotel meeting, as secretary of state and the anti-Grant liberal Republican Carl Schurz as secretary of the interior. Keeping the old guard party regulars happy with such a diverse cabinet proved a difficult task. After serving one term as president, Hayes would not receive his party's nomination in the election of 1880. The next president, while still a Republican, would be James Garfield, a compromise candidate deemed to be more acceptable to the diverse wings of the badly splintered Republican Party.

Long-Term Consequences:
Reunion and the Rise of the New South

As the generation that had been too young to fight in the Civil War reached maturity, a new type of southerner arose from the ashes of the tragic conflict. Earlier, a great chasm had separated the regions of the nation. The South, with its holy trinity of agriculture, aristocracy, and decentralized authority, stood in marked contrast against the North, with its holy trinity of machine industry, democracy, and centralized authority. The war and the elimination of slavery, however, removed the cornerstone of the antebellum South. Free labor transformed plantations into small farms and shifted the focus of the southern economy from wholesale to retail. It also stirred ambition among some people who formerly would have accepted their lot as part of the lower order. In the Old South, the ideal of the southern gentleman provided dignity to the life of leisure, but it also brought contempt toward manual labor. In the New South, however, it was the idler, not the worker, who was viewed as the social outcast. In this new age, Yanks and former Rebs no longer seemed to be from different human species.

Although still largely an agrarian society, by the 1880s the land of Dixie was beginning to shed its heavy dependency on agriculture. Between 1880 and 1890, railroad mileage in the former Confederate states increased by 100 percent, timber productivity by 200 percent, cotton mill products by 300 percent, and pig iron production by 400 percent. After the invention of a cigarette-rolling machine in 1880, cigarette factories sprang up near the tobacco fields, soon producing 400,000 cigarettes a day. The northern press recognized and applauded these changes. "The old 'Solid South' of slavery and Bourbonism is dead," wrote an editor of the *International Review* in 1881.* "A new South is rising from the ashes, eager to keep step with the North in the onward march of the Solid Nation." A *Harper's Weekly* cartoon also published in 1881 echoed this same sentiment. In the full-page spread, the cartoon pictured Louisiana and New York shaking hands before a smiling Uncle Sam, with Columbia proudly writing on a map of the United States, "No North! No South! But the Union!"

Moreover, with the rise of the New South, a new southern ideology emerged that challenged some of the assumptions of the antebellum years. No longer bound to spend their intellectual energies defending the institution of slavery, southern thinkers were freed to shift their focus to the problems of small farmers and small businessmen. By the 1880s, southerners were expressing themes that a generation earlier would have been considered heresy. "It is

---

*Bourbonism is a pejorative label that refers to outdated social and political beliefs.

the white man of the South more than the black," asserted W.F. Tillett, "that has been freed by the Civil War." Woodrow Wilson, the southern-born future president, concurred. "Because I love the South," Wilson wrote in 1880, "I rejoice in the failure of the Confederacy."

Jim Crow and the Limits of Southern Progress

Unfortunately, the advance of industry did not translate into significant improvement in the quality of life for many southerners. Wages for southern workers always lagged behind the wages of northerners doing similar work. Southern textile workers, for instance, received only about one-half the wages of New England textile workers. Moreover, although some African-American men found work with the railroads and others gained skilled positions as bricklayers, carpenters, and painters, most African-Americans who left the fields found employment only in unskilled, low-paying jobs. In the newly built textile mills and cigarette factories, white and black workers performed segregated tasks. For the most part, the African-Americans worked the janitorial jobs, and rarely stood side by side with the whites who operated the machines. White-only unions were formed to enforce the segregated work policies. Only on rare occasions did southern workers unite behind a common cause.

At the end of the nineteenth century, most employed white southern males earned more than the $300 per year deemed necessary to maintain a household, but most southern black males survived only at this subsistence income level. Meanwhile, the average southern white woman made about $220 annually—poverty wages, but still more than the $120 average yearly income of southern black women. During the final decades of the century, the New South was being transformed, but its progress was slow and the benefits of this transformation were not universal.

If the economic advance in the New South was slow, so was the movement toward the realization of full civil liberties for all southern citizens. Following the Compromise of 1877, whites regained political dominance in the South, and with this ascension the short-lived era of political parity for African-Americans abruptly ended. Even though the negotiators of the Compromise of 1877 received verbal assurances that black civil rights would be protected, such promises were never delivered. Ironically, the bargain struck at the black-owned Wormley Hotel adversely affected the lives of blacks for over a hundred years. Not until the civil rights movement of the mid-twentieth century would southern African-Americans regain the degree of civil liberties that they enjoyed before the end of Reconstruction.

In the post-Reconstruction era, southern whites used the power of law to maintain the white supremacist ideologies that had permeated southern society since colonial times. New state and local laws mandated separation of the races in public places—railroad cars, city parks, hotels, theaters, and schools. Some local ordinances even went so far as to demand separate water fountains for whites and blacks. These forms of legal discrimination against blacks were known as Jim Crow laws, named after the antebellum minstrel show character Jim Crow.

Despite protests from the African-American community, the Jim Crow system received little opposition from whites north or south. The U.S. Supreme Court contributed to this attitude with a series of late nineteenth-century rulings that upheld the constitutionality of Jim Crow. In 1883 the Court ruled that the Fourteenth Amendment forbade only states, not individuals within the states, from discriminating against the civil rights of racial groups. Later it ruled that states could constitutionally enforce racial segregation on public transit systems. In the famous (or infamous) *Plessy v. Ferguson* case in 1896, the Court, asserting that "legislation is powerless to eradicate racial instincts," established the "separate but equal" doctrine that justified segregation policies so long as facilities offered to blacks and whites were of equal quality. Two years later in *Williams v. Mississippi,* the Court again defended the right of the states to establish their own racial policies when it approved Mississippi's plan for depriving African-Americans of the franchise.

By the turn of the century, the prevailing northern opinion regarding race relations was captured by the editor of the *New York Times* who casually observed, "Northern men . . . no longer denounce the suppression of the Negro vote. . . . The necessity of it under the supreme law of self-preservation is candidly recognized." Historian C. Vann Woodward in his landmark study *The Strange Career of Jim Crow* describes the period about 1898 in these words:

> At the very time that imperialism was sweeping the country, the doctrine of racism reached a crest of acceptability and popularity among respectable scholarly and intellectual circles. At home and abroad biologists, sociologists, anthropologists, and historians, as well as journalists and novelists, gave support to the doctrine that races were distinct entities and that the "Anglo-Saxon" or "Caucasian" was the superior of them all.

In one of history's many ironies, as the New South after the Compromise of 1877 became more northern in its economical aspirations, the North became more southern in its racial attitudes. National unity was achieved, but it came at a price largely paid by African-Americans.

The Emerging Industrial North: Immigration and Urbanization

Why northern Republicans in the late nineteenth century retreated from their earlier defense of the civil rights of blacks and even embraced traditional southern attitudes toward race relations is a complex question with many answers. One factor that no doubt influenced northern acceptance of the "doctrine of race" was that region's reactions to the rapid influx of "new immigrants" who arrived in America during the latter decades of the century. From the day the first English settlers arrived in the New World, America was a land of immigrants. During the last quarter of the nineteenth century, however, industrial expansion transformed the pace and the form of migration to America, altering both the physical and mental environment of the industrializing nation.

Before 1880, the overwhelming number of immigrants to the United States came from northern or western Europe. Most of these immigrants were Caucasians who worshipped in Protestant churches, spoke the English language, migrated from countries with democratic traditions, and settled in rural areas where they employed the same agricultural skills that they carried with them from the Old World. Although newcomers to America, these "old immigrants" had much in common with the white, Anglo-Saxon Protestants (WASPs) who dominated nineteenth-century American culture. Equipped with useful language, political, and economic skills, the old immigrants had little difficulty assimilating into American life and gaining entrance into the American middle class.

After 1880, however, increasing numbers of immigrants fleeing oppression and depression came from southern and eastern Europe. Many of these "new immigrants"—Italians, Poles, Russians, Bohemians, Hungarians, and Slavs—were Roman Catholic or Jewish, not Protestant. These peoples often came from non-English-speaking and nondemocratic countries, and although farmers in the Old World they settled in America's cities where they had to learn new skills before being employable. In comparison with the old immigrants, the new immigrants were at a distinct disadvantage and consequently found assimilation into America's great melting pot much more difficult.

Many late nineteenth-century American WASPs, however, attributed the slower transition of the new immigrants into the American middle class not to social factors but to flaws in their genetic makeup. According to a popular late nineteenth-century American myth, the United States was a land of unlimited opportunity for anyone who worked hard and was thrifty. Failure to rise in the United States, therefore, was considered the consequence of flaws within one's individual character. Thus, according to this logic, the poverty of large numbers of people in a given racial or ethnic group signified the genetic inferiority of that group. In the late nineteenth century, many Americans from all regions and parties were prone to embrace these false assumptions that attempted to give a degree of scientific respectability to the doctrine of race.

Of course, the reason so many new immigrants came to America in the late nineteenth century was the job opportunities that awaited them in the great cities. As a consequence of industrialization and the expansion of America's rail system, by the end of the nineteenth century 90 percent of all manufacturing took place in urban areas. Though the jobs were dangerous and the wages meager, immigrants swarmed by the millions into America's great manufacturing centers. At the end of the Civil War, only one in six Americans were urbanites; three decades later, about one in three lived in cities.

To Josiah Strong, a well-known Protestant clergyman and author, the metropolis was the nation's "storm center," the place where "luxuries are gathered—everything that dazzles the eye, or tempts the appetite." Strong and other observers also noted, however, that the great cities were also places of abject poverty where millions survived on the margins of society, living in squalid, overcrowded, infested tenement houses run at great profits by absentee landlords. The immigrants who survived these living conditions were fortunate, for thousands of the less fortunate perished weekly on the streets from disease and starvation. Economic advance in America's industrial age was real, but it came at a price. In a laissez-faire political environment that advocated few governmental regulations on business initiatives, progress and poverty often went hand in hand.

Party Politics: Choosing Between Tweedledee and Tweedledum

The political détente that resulted from the Compromise of 1877 also had an impact on presidential party politics. True, in election after election the Republicans still tried to "wave the bloody shirt" and the Democrats continued their complaints against Republican cronyism and corruption. The shrillness of their castigations, however, did not signify substantial policy differences. At least to those outside the political mainstream, a popular nursery rhyme aptly described the late nineteenth-century relationship between America's two major political parties:

> *Tweedledum and Tweedledee*
> *Resolved to have a battle,*
> *For Tweedledum said Tweedledee*
> *Had spoiled his nice new rattle.*
> *Just then flew by a monstrous crow,*
> *As big as a tar barrel,*
> *Which frightened both the heroes so,*
> *They quite forgot their quarrel.*

In 1880, the Republicans offered a balanced ticket by nominating the moderately reform-minded General James A. Garfield for president and the conservative or "Stalwart" Republican Chester A. Arthur for vice president. The Democrats, in turn, nominated a war hero and political lightweight, General Winfield Hancock. Other than their standard differences on the tariff

(Republicans favored high tariffs and Democrats low tariffs), no pressing issues separated the candidates. Both party platforms, for example, favored legislation to restrict Chinese immigration and gave lip service to efficient, responsible government. The popular vote was evenly split, but, as usual, the Republicans won in the Electoral College.

On the morning of July 2, 1881, only four months into his presidency, Garfield arrived at Washington's Sixth Street Station to board a train on his way to a college reunion. As he passed through a waiting room, Charles J. Guiteau, a mentally deranged Stalwart Republican who wanted Arthur to be president stepped up to Garfield and fired two shots. The first shot grazed Garfield's arm, but the other lodged in his back. After lingering for about two months, Garfield died of the bullet wound and Arthur assumed the office. Much to the dismay of the Stalwarts, who favored old cronyism and political patronage, the "new Chester Arthur," like Garfield, stubbornly supported a civil service system that would make federal jobs more dependent on what you knew than on who you knew. With congressional support from the Democrats and reform-minded Republicans, Arthur secured passage of the Pendleton Act (1883), which established the U.S. Civil Service Commission to administer a federal employment system based on merit and not political connections. Arthur's other noteworthy act was signing into law the Chinese Exclusion Act, a bill that banned Chinese laborers from the United States for ten years. Future administrations would extend this prohibition, and the ban against Chinese immigrants would not be lifted until 1943.

The presidential election of 1884 was an unusually muddy, fiercely fought contest, but the ferocious campaign centered less on public policy differences than on attempted character assassinations. Rejecting the controversial Arthur, the Republicans nominated James Blaine, a longtime congressional leader whom the Democrats portrayed as a corrupt politician who had accepted bribes from nefarious railroad interests. Meanwhile, the Democrats nominated Grover Cleveland, a no-nonsense New York governor known for his crusade against governmental waste and corruption. Although Cleveland had no political skeletons in his closet, he did have a well-known personal, private indiscretion. Cleveland had fathered an illegitimate son—a fact that the Republicans touted at every opportunity, routinely interrupting Democratic rallies by shouting from the rear the sarcastic catcall, "Ma, Ma, where's my pa?"

At the end of the campaign, the Republicans made a tactical mistake at a New York City rally by branding the Democratic Party as the party of "rum, Romanism, and rebellion." This condemnation offended many Roman Catholic New Yorkers, who turned out in large enough numbers to give the state to Cleveland. By carrying New York, Cleveland took the Electoral College and thus became the first Democrat since the Civil War to win the White House. Democratic newspapers celebrated the victory by adding a new line to the Republican campaign accusation:

Ma, Ma, where's my pa?
Gone to the White House, ha! ha! ha!

Although Cleveland did sign into law the Dawes Severalty Act (1887), which allowed the dispersal of tribal lands to individual Native American families and the sale of the remaining acres to Anglo settlers, and the Interstate Commerce Act (1888), a very weak federal attempt to regulate the powerful railroads, Cleveland is more remembered for his 414 vetoes than for any particular legislative accomplishment. A fiscal conservative who lived by his motto "No Special Favors," in four years Cleveland vetoed more than twice the number of bills than all of his predecessors combined. No matter what group approached Cleveland with a request, his answer was the same. To farmers who sought a drought relief bill, to veterans who demanded a pension bill, or to businessmen who expected higher protective tariffs, Cleveland gave the same two-letter reply—No!

In the election of 1888, Cleveland faced Republican Benjamin Harrison. This lackluster campaign generated little heat, except the usual party debates over appropriate tariff rates. As in previous years, the election was close. Cleveland won the popular vote, but by carrying the most populated states, Harrison won the presidency in the Electoral College. As president, Harrison pushed for and secured the McKinley Tariff Act (1890)—legislation that raised tariff rates to historically high levels. Under Harrison, Congress also opened the public till to an assortment of special interest groups and for this generosity picked up the nickname "The Billion Dollar Congress." However, public reaction to the McKinley Tariff Act and to the high level of public spending was unfavorable. In 1890, Republicans lost control of Congress, and in 1892, in a rematch between the incumbent Harrison and ex-president Cleveland, the fiscally conservative Democrat won a return to the White House. Also receiving over a million votes in 1892 was James Weaver, the candidate of the newly formed People's (or Populist) Party. To a small but growing number of reformers and minority groups not satisfied with mainstream politics, this election, like the others of the era, only signified that Tweedledee had defeated Tweedledum.

Whether Golden or Gilded, America Comes of Age

American economic achievements during the last quarter of the nineteenth century are legion. With an abundance of natural resources, a rapidly growing cheap labor supply spurred by increased immigration, and a Congress and Supreme Court friendly to industrial development, the United States moved from the fourth-largest to the greatest producer of goods on the planet. In 1890, for the first time in the nation's history, Americans made more money in manufacturing than in agriculture. Americans were making about four times more in manufacturing than they had made only a generation earlier. Most, but not all, of these benefits went to the few rather than to the many. In 1900, the largest 2 percent of the corporations in America produced more than 50 percent of the goods, and 90 percent of American wealth rested in the hands of the top 10 percent of the population, while the average American laborer worked a sixty-hour week to take home about $450 per year—an amount barely sufficient to keep a household above the poverty line. Moreover, with prejudice and legal discrimination denying many Americans full citizenship privileges, America had not yet achieved its lofty goals of securing liberty and justice for all its people. At the time of the Compromise of 1877, eight African-Americans were serving in the House of Representatives, but when the new century opened, no blacks sat in Congress because poll taxes and literacy tests had virtually disenfranchised African-American voters in eight former Confederate states. Nonetheless, the United States had emerged as the greatest economic power on earth and, if it wished, could become a major player in world affairs.

During the prosperous 1880s, many people predicted that the regional and class inequities that remained in America soon would disappear. After a depression hit the nation in the early 1890s, however, fewer Americans embraced such an optimistic worldview. The Panic of 1893—the worst economic crisis to hit the nation in more than a century—created class tensions that sometimes, as in the Pullman strike of 1894, exploded into violence. President Cleveland, the first Democrat in the White House since before the Civil War, responded to this railroad strike much as his Republican predecessors had responded to other threats against American corporations. Claiming that the railroad strike was disrupting the delivery of mail, the Cleveland administration issued a blanket injunction against the strikers, sent federal troops to operate the railroads, and arrested the leaders of the American Railway Union. Cleveland ended the strike, but his decisive actions did not quench the bitter debates over what role the federal government should play in stimulating economic growth and in resolving conflicts between management and labor.

In this last decade of the century, as national leaders reflected on what America would be like in the twentieth century, more and more citizens began to argue that the nation needed more foreign markets to ensure its future prosperity. In a moment of economic difficulties and growing class and racial antagonisms, many viewed the acquisition of an overseas empire that would provide raw materials and markets for American industry as the best medicine for the domestic ills that were threatening the tranquility of the nation. As America approached the twentieth century, it was being primed for another turning point that would propel it into a new national era.

CHAPTER 9

THE SINKING OF THE *MAINE*

February 15, 1898

The Spanish-American War and the Emergence of America as a World Power

USS Maine is Destroyed by Explosion in Havana Harbor, Cuba, February 15, 1898

(Artwork copied from the publication *Uncle Sam's Navy*. U.S. Naval Historical Center photograph #NH 61236. http://.navsource.org/archives/01/maine.htm)

TIME LINE

1890   The Sherman Antitrust Act is passed

1893   Hawaii's Queen Liliuokalani is overthrown

1896   William McKinley defeats William Jennings Bryan to win the presidency

1898   The USS *Maine* explodes in Havana Harbor

The United States passes the Teller Amendment and declares war on Spain

1899   The Senate ratifies the Treaty of Paris

1900   McKinley defeats Bryan in a presidential rematch

1901   McKinley is assassinated; Theodore Roosevelt assumes the presidency

U.S. forces leave Cuba after the signing of the Platt Amendment

1902   Roosevelt intervenes to settle a coal strike

1904   Roosevelt defeats Alton Parker to win reelection

The Roosevelt Corollary to the Monroe Doctrine is announced

1906   Congress passes the Meat Inspection Act and the Pure Food and Drug Act

1908   William Taft defeats Bryan to win the presidency

1910   Progressives become disenchanted with President Taft

1912   Taft wins the Republican nomination; Roosevelt bolts from the party

Woodrow Wilson wins the presidency carrying only 42 percent of the vote

1913   Wilson secures passage of the Federal Reserve Act

1914   Archduke Francis Ferdinand is assassinated and World War I begins

1915   The sinking of the *Lusitania* results in 1,200 deaths

1916   Running on the slogan "He Kept Us Out of War," Wilson narrowly defeats Charles Evans Hughes to win reelection

1917   Wilson leans about the Zimmermann Note

The United States enters World War I

1918   Wilson announces the Fourteen Points

Germany signs an armistice ending the fighting in World War I

For over a hundred years the United States expanded westward toward California and the Pacific coast in its quest to fulfill its manifest destiny. However, as the nineteenth century neared its end, the American West reached its natural boundary. The North American frontier had largely been settled and tamed. Still, Americans itched for expansion. American farmers and rapidly growing American industries needed new markets to sell their goods. This pent-up demand for growth swelled like the backed-up waters of an obstructed river. As the turn of the century grew nearer, America stood on the verge of bursting forth into the world as a new and formidable economic power. In 1898, Senator Alfred Beveridge captured the sentiments of many when he remarked:

> Today we are raising more than we can consume. Today we are making more than we can use. . . . Therefore we must find new markets for our produce, new occupation for our capital, new work for our labor. . . . Ah! As our commerce spreads, the flag of liberty will circle the globe and the highway of the ocean—carrying trade to all mankind—will be guarded by the guns of the republic. And as their thunders salute the flag, benighted peoples will know that the voice of liberty is speaking, at last, for them . . . that civilization is dawning at last, for them.

A popular theory of the time known as Social Darwinism argued the case for extending the reach of America. This theory, a sociological adaptation of Charles Darwin's "survival of the fittest" biological theory, asserted that America's laissez-faire capitalist tradition outperformed other, inferior economic systems and that therefore, according to American jingoists of the period, the world would benefit if "American culture, morality and democracy" supplanted the "barbarous" and often despotic rule of "less fit" nations. The benefits to American industry of such expansion were considered a serendipitous outcome of a win-win situation. Although some American reformers condemned the racial overtones and the secular values implicit within Social Darwinism, by the late nineteenth century these critics were lone voices crying in the wilderness.

Meanwhile, around the world expansionist Americans searched for opportunities to extend "democracy" in the name of social progress. The concept initially found root in the island kingdom of Hawaii. American settlers had arrived on the islands in the early 1820s. Although the Americans originally arrived with Christian missionary objectives on their minds, by 1890 a sizable number of the descendants of these missionaries owned and operated many of the businesses on the islands. However, when Hawaiian queen Liliuokalani attempted to reduce American influence on the island with a campaign proclaiming "Hawaii for the Hawaiians," the Americans rebelled and helped fund a revolution that overthrew the monarchy. They declared a provisional "democratic Hawaiian government" on January 17, 1893, and immediately appealed to the United States for annexation. Although lame-duck Republican president Benjamin Harrison was warm to the idea of annexation, incoming president-elect Grover Cleveland had strong reservations about taking over another independent country. When Cleveland took office, he withdrew the Senate treaty of annexation that Harrison had submitted for consideration. During Cleveland's administration, the Democrats forestalled the taking of Hawaii. However, after Republican William McKinley defeated Democrat William Jennings Bryan in the election of 1896, the expansionists won out. In July 1898, the Hawaiian Islands became an American possession. With this acquisition in the mid-Pacific, American businesses looked even farther west—to Japan and the Philippines. The growing American presence in the Pacific would become an important factor in future American expansion into Asia.

Brewing Troubles in Cuba

Another island, this one off the southern coast of Florida, also interested expansionist Americans. The residents of Cuba had long opposed colonial rule by Spain. Secessionists such as José Martí, called "the apostle of independence," led Cuban uprisings against Spain, but the Spanish army prevailed against them. The first Cuban insurrection lasted from 1868 to 1878. Americans watched with interest and American newspapers made the most of the conflict, most often siding with the revolutionaries.

One particular incident turned American opinion firmly against Spain. On October 31, 1873, the Spanish ship *Tornado* captured the side-wheel steamer *Virginius* off the coast of Jamaica. Virginius, a filibustering ship that fraudulently displayed the American flag, carried supplies for Cuban insurgents, fifty-two crewmen, and 103 passengers (including sixteen Americans and nine Britons). Spanish general Don Juan de Burriel took the captured crew to Santiago de Cuba and treated them as pirates, staging several brutal public executions. When British and American ships arrived in Cuba to register a protest, Spain apologized and paid restitution to the families of the slain crew members. The crisis subsided without further American protest as President Ulysses S. Grant chose to apply the golden rule to diplomacy. During the American Civil War, Spain had not intervened on the side of the rebels. Consequently, during Grant's administration, the United States also would refrain from official intervention in Spain's civil war in Cuba.

Hostilities between the Cubans and the Spanish authorities smoldered for a while, but in 1895 the flame of rebellion gained renewed strength. By this time decades had passed since the American Civil War, and Americans no longer felt morally bound to a noninterventionist policy toward Spain. At the very least, the rebellion in Cuba interested American newspaper readers. Media giants printed sensational stories about the events in Cuba. As Americans read these stories, more and more called for U.S. military intervention. A poem published in the *Rural New Yorker* echoed this rising sentiment:

> *Off yonder in the ocean blue*
> *Fair Cuba strives in freedom's battle,*
> *She has a right to look to you,*
> *For manly words—not idle prattle.*

Furthermore, American businessmen and their political allies saw the Cuban situation as an opportunity to expand American markets. The civil war in Cuba disrupted normal commerce with the Spanish colony. If Spain, however, were out of the picture and if peace were restored, would not the Cubans purchase most of their goods from the United States? In 1896 Massachusetts senator Henry Cabot Lodge commented on the Cuban situation, "The only thing that can remove this threat of danger to business stability is the settlement of the question and the restoration of peace to the island and this can only be brought about by firm and decisive action on the part of the United States." Fellow senator John Thruston of Nebraska, whose farmers stood to gain by an expanded Cuban market, concurred. In 1897 he argued, "Why should we not act? . . . There is no nation . . . upon the face of the earth with which we have such immediate, such direct, such important commercial and other relations. . . . We have lost the advantages of the Cuban market."

Even though the already cash-strapped and beleaguered government of Spain could ill afford to administer Cuba, it refused to grant the Cubans independence. Giving concessions to the rebels in Cuba, Spain felt, would simply encourage rebellions in other Spanish colonies, from Puerto Rico to the Philippines. Therefore, Cuba must be held. To maintain control, Spain sent General Valeriano Weyler y Nicolau to quell the uprising. Under his brutal leadership, Spanish troops rounded up 100,000 Cubans for detention. A large number of them died from starvation and disease. American newspapers claimed that as many as one-fourth of all Cubans died as a result of Spain's harsh rule. These harsh Spanish measures momentarily crippled the rebellion, but they also outraged the American public into calling for immediate action to liberate the people of Cuba.

In 1896, newspaper publisher William Randolph Hearst sent popular illustrator Frederic Remington to Cuba to capture the Cuban struggle in pictures. When Remington telegraphed back, "There is no war, request to be recalled," Hearst is reported to have responded, "You furnish the pictures and I'll furnish the war." Remington stayed and produced a number of sensational illustrations to back up the stories of Spanish atrocities against the Cubans. One illustration, created in New York after Remington had returned to the

United States, showed Spanish soldiers strip-searching a naked woman on an American steamship. The headline read,

DOES OUR FLAG SHIELD WOMEN?
Indignities Practiced by Spanish Officials On Board American Vessels
Richard Harding Davis Describes Some Startling Phases of the Cuban
Situation—Refined Young Women Stripped and Searched by Brutal
Spaniards While Under Our Flag on the Ollivette

What the readers did not know was that the searches were always performed by female attendants, not the surly, mustached Spanish males portrayed in Remington's illustrations.

Both Hearst and his rival, Joseph Pulitzer, used these kinds of sensational headlines, along with illustrations and stories about the atrocities (real and fictitious), to sell newspapers. These barely credible stories were soon labeled "yellow journalism," a name originating with a popular cartoon called "The Yellow Kid"; the term was first applied to Hearst's newspapers and eventually to all sensational newspapers. These newspapers told only the Cuban side of the war and managed to turn American opinion decidedly against Spanish rule.

When Cuban protests and riots erupted in Havana in January 1898, President McKinley feared for the safety of Americans on the island. Under pressure from Congress, he sent the battleship USS *Maine* from Key West to the Havana Harbor. When it arrived on January 25, 1898, its captain, Charles Sigsbee, found Spanish government officials suspicious but courteous. To avoid provocation, Captain Sigsbee did not allow his sailors to go ashore. Days passed without incident as the *Maine,* with its gleaming white hull and two mustard-colored smokestacks, sat peacefully in the harbor. Its presence seemed to bring calm to the tense situation in the city.

Meanwhile, back in the States, public sentiment toward the Spanish was anything but calm. In December of the preceding year, while in Washington, DC, a Spanish ambassador, Enrique Depuy de Lôme, penned a personal letter to a friend in Cuba. In this private letter, the Spanish minister commented that President McKinley was a "weak" and "low politician" who catered to the "rabble" in order to "stand well with the jingos of his party." Somehow, the Cuban rebels intercepted this private note and wisely saw that it fell into the hands of William Randolph Hearst. On Wednesday, February 9, 1898, the front page of Hearst's *New York Journal* featured a sensational story about the de Lôme letter. The commentary about this two-month-old, unofficial, private note was introduced with large, boldface print and the headline "The Worst Insult to the United States in Its History." In the late nineteenth century, news did not travel at Internet speed, but scoops such as this juicy, international scandal quickly circulated from newspaper to newspaper throughout the country. For the next week, Americans expressed outrage toward the Spanish minister who dared to call into question the integrity of President McKinley. The public uproar became so great that de Lôme resigned in an attempt to still the protest.

Even as Americans back home were simmering at the indiscretions of the Spanish minister, the sailors on the USS *Maine* sat in boredom on the decks of their ship planted in Havana Harbor. On the moonless evening of February 15, 1898, however, boredom broke with a sudden flash. Captain Sigsbee remembered taps sounding at 8:45 in the evening as he sat in his quarters finishing a letter to his wife. As he later wrote,

> I laid down my pen and listened to the notes of the bugle, which were singularly beautiful in the oppressive stillness of the night. . . . I was enclosing my letter in its envelope when the explosion came. It was a bursting, rending, and crashing roar of immense volume, largely metallic in character. It was followed by heavy, ominous metallic sounds. There was a trembling and lurching motion of the vessel, a list to port. The electric lights went out, then there was intense blackness and smoke. The situation could not be mistaken. The Maine was blown up and sinking. For a moment the instinct of self-preservation took charge of me, but this was immediately dominated by the habit of command.

A nearby passenger liner, *City of Washington,* and the Spanish cruiser *Alfonso XII* rushed to rescue the crew. Many of the crew members died in their bunks and went down in the twisted wreckage. In all, 254 seamen died; fifty-nine were wounded and eight of those later died.

American newspapers rushed to the streets with a frenzy of provocative headlines claiming that Spain had deliberately torpedoed and sunk the *Maine* in an act of war. Captain Sigsbee refused to jump to that same conclusion. He wired the secretary of the navy that "public opinion should be suspended until further report." However, the public, the press, and Congress were in no mood for patience. They spoke with one voice: "Remember the Maine. The Hell with Spain." At that moment, most Americans agreed—Cuba must be liberated. America must break away from its continental borders and take its brand of democracy and its "superior culture" to the "barbarous world."

President McKinley had seen battle. He had experienced the horrible price of death during the Civil War and he hesitated to bring that kind of suffering upon Americans again. Furthermore, the American army and navy were ill prepared for conflict. They had progressed little in technology and tactics since the Civil War and their numbers were significantly less than what they had been thirty years earlier. McKinley sought for options other than declaring war. For such "peace-mongering," McKinley was branded as "Wobbly Willie." Theodore Roosevelt called him a "white-livered" coward who did not have "the backbone of a chocolate éclair."

With the reelection season only two years away, McKinley realized the futility of pursuing peace while the nation clamored for war. Ultimately, he yielded to the public frenzy that had been fed for years on a daily diet of yellow journalism. Two months after the sinking of the *Maine,* McKinley sent a war message to Congress asking for armed intervention to free Cuba. In accepting this request, Congress also adopted the Teller Amendment, a proviso that promised the world that the United States would liberate Cuba from Spanish misrule, not annex it as an American possession. This declaration of war against Spain resulting from the sinking of the *Maine* would unleash America's pent-up expansionist energy and permanently change the direction of American foreign policy.

Consequences of the Spanish–American War

Before the war with Spain, previous American military conflicts had lasted an average of four years. Fortunately, this war lasted only about four months. Fighting erupted on May 1 with a stunning U.S. naval assault against the ten-fleet Spanish armada in Manila Bay in the Philippines. Never suspecting that America's war to liberate Cuba would be launched on the other side of the world, the Spanish were caught by surprise and decisively defeated. In this early morning battle, Spain lost some 400 sailors while not one American was killed. Following the easy victory, Commodore George Dewey allegedly told the American sailors, "Men, let's retire for breakfast."

After the battle at Manila Bay, most of the fighting occurred in Cuba. In all, 5,462 Americans would perish in this war, but only 379 died from enemy fire. The remainder died from disease and from food poisoning that resulted from contaminated rations the government sent to feed its troops. The high death rates from disease and poisoning ultimately cost Secretary of War Russell Alger his job after the war when Americans demanded a scapegoat for the sanitary blunders that incapacitated American troops into an unceremoniously labeled "army of convalescents."

By August 1898, Spain sued for peace, promising not only to liberate Cuba, but also to cede the Spanish colonies of Guam and Puerto Rico to the United States. President McKinley added one more item as a condition for peace. In addition to the above terms, he pressured Spain into selling the Philippines to the United States for $20 million. During the war, Filipino rebels had cooperated with the Americans, trusting that after Spain was defeated, they, like the Cubans, would be liberated. They did not expect a transfer of colonial rule from Spanish to American hands. McKinley later told the American people that in a moment of prayer, he came to the conviction that the United States had an obligation "to educate the Filipinos, and uplift and civilize and Christianize them." The irony in this statement is that most Filipinos already were

Christian, although as Roman Catholics, they differed from most American Christians, who, like President McKinley, were Protestant.

Almost as intense as this "splendid little war" (the name Secretary of State John Hay called it) was the Senate battle over the ratification of the Treaty of Paris that would end the conflict. Those arguing in favor of the colonial acquisitions adopted talking points featuring the alliteration of D-words: *duty, defense, destiny, dollars.* According to this argument, possession of the Philippines would not only improve the standard of living of the Filipino peoples and improve America's military defense, but also give the United States a toehold in the great untapped China market. As one historian mused, "God directs us—perhaps it will pay." Others were more crass. "If this be commercialism," shouted industrialist Marcus Hanna, then "for God's sake, let us have commercialism."

Not all, however, embraced these arguments. Patriotic Americans, including notables such as industrialist Andrew Carnegie, unionist Samuel Gompers, humanitarian Jane Addams, Yale academician William Graham Sumner, reformer Carl Schurz, and author-humorist Mark Twain, condemned the treaty for violating the spirit of America's Declaration of Independence. To these anti-imperialists, it was inexcusable for a nation founded on the principle that legitimate governments derive "their just powers from the consent of the governed" to force people into colonial subjugation against their will. Other anti-imperialists used less lofty arguments to oppose imperialism, including the racial warning that U.S. expansion into Asia would bring "inferior" peoples into the nation.

In early February 1899, about one year after the tragedy of the sinking of the *Maine,* the Senate voted by a slim one-vote majority to ratify the Treaty of Paris. With this vote, the United States acquired Puerto Rico, Guam, and the Philippines. Moreover, despite the Teller Amendment, the United States had no intentions of leaving Cuba before ensuring that the Cubans were capable of self-government. American forces remained in Cuba until 1901, exiting only after the Cubans agreed to accept the provisions of the Platt Amendment. The terms of this agreement restricted Cuba's autonomy in diplomatic and financial matters, guaranteed the United States the right to build naval bases on the island, and allowed the American military to intervene in Cuba if disorder was ever threatened. As General Leonard Wood, the American military governor in Cuba, acknowledged, "There is, of course, little or no independence left in Cuba under the Platt Amendment."

With these developments at the turn of the new century, the U.S. flag proudly waved around the world from Cuba and Puerto Rico to Hawaii, Guam, and the Philippines. Like it or not, the old European powers had to acknowledge that America had finally emerged as a colossal world empire. The Spanish-American War served as a giant coming-out party for the United States. It not only announced to the world America's new status as a superpower, it also eased the regional tensions between northern and southern Americans that had lingered since the days of the Civil War.

Unfortunately, the official end to the war against Spain also launched an undeclared war against the Filipino insurrectionists who opposed American rule just as much as they had opposed Spanish rule. Over the ensuing three years, the United States sent four times as many soldiers into the Philippines as it had sent into Cuba during the Spanish-American War to crush the rebellion. Heavy government censorship on war news prevented most Americans from learning about this undeclared war, but Filipino soldier and noncombatant casualties were exceedingly high. When one reporter alleged that American troops were slaughtering "men, women, and children, prisoners and captures, active and suspected people, from lads of 10 and up," another California newspaper justified such actions with the rejoinder, "Let us all be frank. WE DO NOT WANT THE FILIPINOS. WE DO WANT THE PHILLIPINES. . . . The more of them killed the better. It seems harsh. But they must yield before the superior race."

In the U.S. presidential elections of 1900, Democratic candidate William Jennings Bryan denounced the annexation of the Philippines and promised to free the Filipinos if elected. Following the custom of the day, incumbent president McKinley refrained from public speech-making during his reelection campaign, leaving this task to his energetic vice presidential running mate, Theodore Roosevelt, the rough riding war hero who had recently been elected governor of New York.

Notwithstanding Roosevelt's celebrity status, placing him on the ticket created some stir in Republican circles. McKinley himself was lukewarm toward Roosevelt, in part because the president's trusted adviser, Marcus Hanna, hated Roosevelt's arrogance and independence. However, Republican bosses in New York, leery of a governor that they could not control, connived with party officials to place Roosevelt on the ticket. Following his nomination, a dismayed Hanna commented, "There's only one life between that madman and the Presidency." Yet on the stump, the popular and energetic Roosevelt worked his magic. "If you choose to vote for America, if you choose to vote for the flag for which we fought," Roosevelt cried, "then you will vote to sustain the administration of President McKinley." When the results poured in, McKinley carried 53 percent of the popular vote to Bryan's 47 percent. Despite intense opposition, the majority of American voters clearly embraced the policies of President McKinley, including his expansionist foreign policy.

Roosevelt, Progressivism, and Progressive Foreign Diplomacy

McKinley had little time to enjoy his reelection. Only six months into his second term, an anarchist named Leon Czolgosz shot McKinley at point-blank range with a .32-caliber revolver while the president greeted people in a reception line at the Pan-American Exposition in Buffalo. After lingering for eight days, McKinley died on September 14, 1901. When Hanna learned that his worst nightmare had come true, the Ohio industrialist bemoaned, "Now look, that damn cowboy is President of the United States." In that era, justice toward the assassin was quickly rendered. Within six weeks, Czolgosz was charged, brought to trial, convicted, and executed for the murder of McKinley.

Replacing the mild-mannered McKinley, a president renowned for his courtesy, conservatism, and deliberate decision making, the brash and boastful, Harvard-educated, forty-two-year-old war hero Theodore Roosevelt took Washington by storm. Considered by some party bosses to be a bull in a china shop, Roosevelt was a testosterone politician before scientists discovered the existence of testosterone. His restless energy made even coffee nervous. An apostle of what he called "the strenuous life," Roosevelt urged Americans not to seek a life of ease, but rather a "life of toil and effort, of labor and strife":

> The man must be glad to do a man's work, to dare and endure and to labor. . . . The woman must be the housewife, the helpmeet of the homemaker, the wise and fearless mother of many healthy children. . . . When men fear work or fear righteous war, when women fear motherhood, they tremble on the brink of doom. . . . As it is with the individual, so it is with the nation. . . . happy is the nation that has a glorious history. Far better it is to dare mighty things, to win glorious triumphs, even though checkered by failure, than to take rank with those poor spirits who neither enjoy much nor suffer much, because they live in the gray twilight that know not victory nor defeat.

A man of great wealth, intellect, action, and passion, Roosevelt lacked little except humility. Mark Twain called him "the Tom Sawyer of the political world," an egotist "always hunting for a chance to show off." Even Roosevelt's own son admitted that the president had to be "the bride at every wedding and the corpse at every funeral." Yet whatever demands he placed on others, he placed more on himself. He was an intellectual, a poet, a historian, a prolific writer, an avid bird-watcher, a cowboy, a boxer, a sailor, and a soldier. Moreover, as a politician, he never shied away from duty, but embraced any power within his grasp in order to respond to the nation's needs. "I did not usurp power," he once remarked about his presidency, "but I did greatly broaden the use of executive power." Indeed, the consolidation of power within the executive branch ranks as one of Roosevelt's most significant legacies.

Turn-of-the-century reformers who supported the use of power to eliminate perceived social evils were known as progressives. Progressives were found in every party and often disagreed among themselves, largely because sighting "evil" often depended on the eye of the beholder. To some, progressivism meant woman suffrage or joining the temperance crusade. To others, progressivism was synonymous with anti-imperialism. During his presidency, Roosevelt cared little for these reforms, but in other areas like trust-busting, railroad regulation, public health initiatives, and conservationism, Roosevelt was the consummate progressive.

Moving beyond the conservative instincts of his predecessor, Roosevelt believed that government must be powerful enough to take on the money trusts that exerted tremendous clout over the nation's economy. Recognizing the advantage of large-scale corporations, Roosevelt generally favored regulating the trusts rather than dissolving them. Only monopolies guilty of chronic and malignant misbehavior should be eliminated. To assist the powerless against the unfair business practices of one gigantic trust, however, in 1902 Roosevelt dusted off the little used Sherman Antitrust Act of 1890. He used it to take on the powerful Northern Securities Company, a holding company that held a virtual monopoly on the railroads in the Northwest. Before Roosevelt, no president had been successful in dissolving a major trust, but the president's legal team persuaded the Supreme Court that Northern Securities had to go. For this, Roosevelt acquired the nickname "trustbuster," although the number of trusts he actually dissolved during his presidency was quite small. Roosevelt also broke precedent when he intervened as a friend of the workers in a coal strike in 1902. After months had passed without a settlement, Roosevelt threatened to take over the coal mines if the owners did not reach an agreement with the striking workers.

By the time of the election of 1904, Roosevelt had already won the hearts of many reformers. His campaign promise for a "Square Deal for Labor" obviously appealed to the public because he defeated his Democratic rival, Alton Parker, by the widest margins of any candidate since the popular vote was tabulated in presidential elections.

During his next four years, Roosevelt continued his pursuit of progressive reforms, securing, for example, the passage of the Hepburn Act, which regulated the railroads, and the Meat Inspection Act and the Pure Food and Drug Act, which empowered the federal government to launch public health initiatives. In addition to these domestic accomplishments, he also used his clout to achieve foreign policy goals—protecting the newly acquired colonies, securing U.S. naval bases around the globe, enlarging and modernizing the navy, and securing permission to build a canal through Central America that would simultaneously improve the nation's military readiness and promote greater marine trade with the Far East. In each of these areas, Roosevelt achieved remarkable success. For instance, when the nation of Colombia balked at the terms that the United States offered to build a canal through its Panama territory, Roosevelt fomented a revolution in the region, acknowledged the existence of a new republic of Panama, and then forced the new government to consent to U.S. terms. Although critics complained about

Roosevelt's ruthless methods for securing permission to build in Panama, Roosevelt himself was pleased with the results of his "big stick" diplomacy, smugly commenting, "While Congress debated, I took it."

Roosevelt also demonstrated his willingness to use a "stick" to secure foreign policy objectives in other areas of the world. When Venezuela defaulted on its debt to Germany and England and the World Court in The Hague ruled that the European powers could use military means to secure debt repayment, Roosevelt announced his Roosevelt Corollary to the Monroe Doctrine. According to the Roosevelt Corollary, the United States would not allow any European nation to intervene in the Americas; if Latin American nations misbehaved by defaulting on their debts, thereby making intervention necessary, the United States would serve as the policeman of the Americas and intervene on behalf of the offended parties. Roosevelt first acted on this doctrine in 1905 when he sent the U.S. Marines into the Dominican Republic to guard its custom house from foreign creditors. This would be the first of dozens of occasions that Roosevelt and future U.S. presidents would invoke the Roosevelt Corollary in order to justify military intervention in Latin America.

Under Roosevelt's tutelage, the United States also intervened in international affairs in Europe and the Far East. In 1905, Roosevelt arbitrated a settlement that ended the Russo-Japanese War, winning for himself the Nobel Peace Prize. In 1906, the United States for the first time intervened in European diplomatic affairs by engaging in a conference that was called to settle a crisis in Morocco. The ensuing year Roosevelt negotiated a "gentleman's agreement" with Japan. In this agreement, Roosevelt promised to convince the school board in San Francisco to desegregate its schools, thus allowing Japanese children to attend classes with Anglos. In return, Japan agreed to stop issuing visa permits to laborers who wished to immigrate to the United States. Later in his administration, Roosevelt sent America's newly built navy, known as the Great White Fleet, on a world tour intended to show off the military prowess of the United States. During the decade that followed the Spanish-American War, America emerged as a confident, ambitious nation that expected and demanded that other people recognize its elite status as a world power.

From Progressivism to World War

Although Roosevelt decided not to seek reelection in 1908, he virtually handpicked his successor by endorsing William H. Taft for the presidency. With Roosevelt's backing, Taft won the Republican nomination and then easily defeated William Jennings Bryan—the longtime leader of the progressive wing within the Democratic Party—in the general election. For the third time in his life, Bryan lost a race for the White House. His only comfort was that many of the reforms that he had initiated, such as a federal income tax, lower tariffs, antitrust legislation, and labor protection, eventually would be incorporated into American life. Later he quipped that he was the only politician in history who could rule the nation by losing the presidency.

Although Taft was exceedingly bright (he graduated second in his class at Yale), even at more than 300 pounds he looked like a dwarf when placed in Roosevelt's shadow. His willingness to accommodate to conservatives in his party made him an easy target of progressive Republicans and Democrats alike. Although he actually busted twice the number of trusts and secured the passage of even stronger railroad regulation than his predecessor, by the end of his term, only the conservative wing of the Grand Old Party supported Taft. After concluding that Taft's presidency was a failure, Roosevelt came out of political retirement and announced that he would accept the Republican nomination in 1912. The conservative party leaders, however, refused to dump the incumbent, and at the Republican convention, Taft was renominated.

Never a good loser, Roosevelt bolted from the party to create his own Bull Moose or Progressive Party. His platform, which he called "New Nationalism," was more progressive than anything he had advocated while serving as president. In contrast to the pro-business platform of the Republican Party, Roosevelt's Progressive Party supported woman suffrage, a federal income tax, workers' compensation laws, child labor laws, lower tariffs, and the creation of strong regulatory agencies to control business excesses.

Meanwhile, the Democrats responded by nominating Woodrow Wilson, an untested rising star with an unusual political pedigree. Holding a PhD from Johns Hopkins University, Wilson had spent most of his career as a professor of government and president of Princeton University. Ideologically progressive, Wilson taught and wrote about government, but he did not seek political office himself until he was in his mid-fifties. In 1910, in his first political outing, he was elected the governor of New Jersey. A staunch Presbyterian and the son of a clergyman, Wilson was intelligent, moralistic, articulate, and stubborn. These defining traits were his chief liabilities as well as his foremost strengths. The platform he ran on in 1912, which he called "New Freedom," promised tariff reform, stronger antitrust laws, better banking laws, and no labor injunctions. Unlike the Bull Moose Progressives, however, Wilson and the Democrats did not advocate a constitutional amendment supporting woman suffrage or social legislation such as federal child protection laws.

The campaign of 1912 was wild and woolly. In Milwaukee a deranged saloon keeper shot Roosevelt just before he gave a stump speech. With a bullet wound in his chest, Roosevelt insisted on finishing his address before going to the hospital. The bullet did not fell the "Bull Moose," but it did close his campaign for a few days. Displaying good sportsmanship, the other candidates also limited their campaign appearances during his convalescence. In the end, after a vigorous campaign, 15 million Americans went to the polls. With traditional Republicans splitting their votes between Taft and Roosevelt, Wilson carried 42 percent of the popular vote and won the election, becoming just the second Democrat in more than fifty years to win the White House. The election signified not so much the popularity of Wilson or the Democratic Party, but the popularity of the reform movement, as three in four voters cast their ballots for progressive candidates. The lone quasi-conservative candidate, the incumbent president, could do no better than a third-place finish.

Although endorsed by just over four in ten voters, President Wilson proved to be effective in getting his progressive reforms through Congress. His political prestige soared when he secured the passage of the Underwood Tariff Act, the first significant downward revision in tariff laws since before the Civil War. Later, he signed into law the Federal Reserve Act, which created the federal reserve system with its twelve district banks controlled by the Federal Reserve Board, authorized with the power to alter interest rates; the Federal Trade Commission (FTC) Act, which created the FTC with power to issue cease and desist orders to any firm guilty of unfair business practices; and the Clayton Antitrust Act, which, among other things, prohibited interlocking directories, made CEOs liable for illegal actions of the corporation, and exempted labor unions from antitrust legislation. Samuel Gompers, the founder and longtime president of America's largest labor union, rejoiced at the passing of the Clayton Act, calling it the "magna charter" for labor unions.

After fulfilling the promises of his "New Freedom" program, Wilson moved further to the left, signing into law social legislation like the Adamson Act, which established an eight-hour workday for railroad workers, and the Keating Owen Act, which prohibited the interstate sale of goods made by children under fourteen years of age. During Wilson's presidency, the authority of government expanded as progressive reformers sought through federal legislation to protect the weak from the excesses of the strong.

Outside of America, however, all was not well. In 1914, the assassination of Archduke Francis Ferdinand, the heir to the throne of the Austro-Hungarian Empire, ignited a war blaze that soon consumed all the major world powers, except the United States. Even as the world divided up for the fight—Germany, Austria-Hungary, Turkey, and Bulgaria versus Britain, France, Russia, Belgium, Italy, and Japan—the United States under Wilson's leadership maneuvered to remain neutral in this Great War. A century earlier, before the outbreak of the War of 1812, the United States in its infancy discovered the difficulty of remaining neutral during a global war. Notwithstanding America's new superpower status, remaining neutral in the twentieth century would prove as difficult.

In the American hemisphere, Wilson never shied away from using military force to achieve his foreign policy objectives. During his first term he sent U.S. troops into the Dominican Republic, Haiti, and Mexico, although unlike his immediate predecessors in the White House, Wilson's justification for military action was not protecting American property abroad, but rather forcing brutal regimes to embrace democratic ideals and self-determinism. Wilson's interventions in the Americas produced at best mixed results, but they did demonstrate the president's willingness to use the "big stick" whenever he felt that the cause was noble. In regard to the Great War, however, for almost three years Wilson refrained from military involvement, attempting to deal with both sides according to international law, which sought to regulate relations between neutral and belligerent nations. In his high-minded hope, he reasoned that from a position of detached neutrality, he could forge a negotiated settlement. In time, however, all such efforts would prove futile.

Even while Wilson proclaimed America's neutrality and refrained from military interference, the nation's economy weighed in on the side of the Allies. Before the Great War erupted, U.S. trade with Britain, France, and Russia stood at twice the level of its trade with the Central Powers of Germany, Austria, and Turkey. By the end of 1916, this trade imbalance had increased from about two to one to more than 1,000 to one. Moreover, when the Allies no longer had the cash to purchase U.S. goods, Wilson offered generous loans. During the months of official neutrality, the United States granted $2.3 billion in loans to the Allies and only $27 million to the Central Powers. Notwithstanding Wilson's proclamations, the United States never fully embraced complete neutrality during the Great War.

Wilson's military hesitancies, peacemaking initiatives, and obsession with rules of fair play galled many Americans like Theodore Roosevelt, who felt that the alleged German atrocities in Belgium deserved swift punishment. Pressure for military action increased after May 7, 1915, when a German submarine sank the British passenger ship *Lusitania,* killing 1,200 civilians, including 128 Americans. Many Americans at this time agreed with the *New York Times* editor who prophesied, "The nation that remembered the sailors on the *Maine* will not forget the civilians of the *Lusitania.*" Meanwhile, Wilson moved slowly with military preparations, gradually increasing the size of the nation's army and navy, even while holding to the hope that world peace could be achieved without U.S. military involvement. In the presidential election of 1916, the Democrats rallied behind the incumbent president, using to their advantage the slogans "Reasonable Preparedness" and "He Kept Us Out of War." He faced a strong challenger in the distinguished, longtime progressive Republican Charles Evans Hughes. However, Wilson managed to carry the election in the Electoral College by the margin of 277–254. A few thousand more votes for Hughes in California, however, would have given the White House back to the Republicans.

Waging War and Peace:
Ending the War to End All Wars

Rejoicing in victory, albeit a razor-thin one, Wilson launched one final peace initiative. In January 1917, the president asked the belligerent nations to accept a "peace without victory" and to embrace his vision of a world order that was based on self-determinism, arms reduction, freedom of the seas, and an international league that would ensure world peace. Once again, Wilson's offer found no suitors. By the end of the month, Germany announced its intentions of unleashing its submarines against all ships, neutral or belligerent, found in the war zone. Wilson promptly broke diplomatic ties with Germany and ordered armed U.S. ships to shoot at German submarines on sight.

In the ensuing weeks, even as shots were being exchanged between Americans and Germans in the Atlantic, two international events grabbed Wilson's attention and assuaged his conscience. First, he learned that Germany's foreign minister, Arthur Zimmermann, sent a telegram encouraging Mexico to ally itself with Germany, promising in return to ensure that Mexico would recover its lost territory in Texas, New Mexico, and Arizona. Second, a revolution in Russia overthrew the undemocratic czarist regime and established a democratic provisional government. At this moment, the major Allied powers were democracies, while the Central powers were autocracies. To the moralistic Presbyterian president, the Great War had developed into a crusade of good against evil.

On April 2, 1917, Wilson delivered a war message to Congress. In this address, he stated that Germany's submarine "warfare against mankind" made neutrality no longer possible. The United States, thus, must join the war, fighting not for "conquest or domination" but for "the ultimate peace of the world and for the liberation of its peoples." Simply stated, "The world must be made safe for democracy." After a passionate debate, the Senate and House concurred, voting 82–6 and 373–50, respectively, for a declaration of war.

With war finally at hand, Wilson insisted that lessons must be learned from the irrational bloodbath, and declared that this Great War must be "a war to end all wars." To clarify his expectations, he refined his "peace without victory" speech into an idealistic list, the Fourteen Points, that pointed all nations, Germany included, in the direction of a better world. This list of international goals included assurances of "self-determinism" for all peoples, freedom of the seas, open diplomacy, and the creation of a general association of nations that would work together to prevent future wars. To encourage a quick end to the war, leaflets containing the Fourteen Points were dropped by air into the cities of Germany.

Most Americans responded enthusiastically to the war effort with conservation, economy, and self-sacrifice. Americans planted vegetable plots known as "victory gardens." Daylight savings time was instituted to save energy. And young Americans from farms and cities donned green fatigues to join the fighting in France. The author of this tongue-in-cheek rhyme noted the contributions that Americans made to social service organizations, which funneled the benefits to the troops:

My Tuesdays are meatless,
My Wednesdays are wheatless,
I'm getting more eatless each day.
My coffee is sweetless,
My bed is sheetless,
All sent to the YMCA.

For the great majority of Americans, however, sacrifice and patriotism rose above personal feeling. Between April 1917 and November 1918, Democrats and Republicans alike raised the flag against the common enemy, and their efforts produced the desired effects. American intervention tipped the scales toward the Allies, and on the eleventh hour of the eleventh day of the eleventh month of 1918, Germany, the sole remaining Central Power, put down its arms. The starting point for negotiating the treaty of peace was the Fourteen Points. For some, Wilson's vision of a better world echoed an American sense of fairness, forgiveness, self-rule, and self-determination. The war-hardened leaders of the European Allies, however, saw things differently. They demanded quick, unsympathetic, and uncompromising revenge against Germany.

CHAPTER 10

THE SILENCING OF WOODROW WILSON

September 25, 1919

Peace, Normalcy, and the
Rise of American Isolationism

Will You Have a Part in Victory?
(Print by James Montgomery Flagg, 1918. Prints and Photographs Division, Library of Congress, LC-USZC4–10232. 9-29-2006. http://hdl.
loc.gov/loc.pnp/cph.3g10232)

TIME LINE

1918	Wilson drafts the Fourteen Points
	U.S. army recruits at Camp Funston contract the swine flu
	Republicans win control of both houses of Congress
1919	The Treaty of Versailles is negotiated
	The Red Scare causes anxiety across America
	Wilson collapses in Pueblo, Colorado
	The Senate rejects the Treaty of Versailles
1920	Women gain the right to vote with the ratification of the Nineteenth Amendment
	Advocating a "return to normalcy," Warren Harding is elected president
1921	Congress formally ends the war with a simple joint resolution
1922	The Five Power Naval Treaty is negotiated
1923	Harding dies; Calvin Coolidge assumes the presidency
1924	Immigration restrictions placed on southern and eastern Europeans
	Calvin Coolidge is elected president
1928	The U.S. embraces the Kellogg-Briand Pact
	Herbert Hoover defeats Alfred Smith to win the presidency
1929	The stock market plummets and the Great Depression begins
1930	Hoover signs the Hawley-Smoot Tariff Act
1932	Bonus marchers are expelled from Washington, DC
	Franklin Roosevelt defeats Hoover to win the presidency
1933	During Roosevelt's first "Hundred Days," Congress enacts the CCC, FERA, CWA, PWA, HOLC, and TVA
1936	Roosevelt wins a landslide victory over Alf Landon

President Woodrow Wilson's train rumbled into a sweltering station in Pueblo, Colorado, shortly before 3:00 PM on Thursday, September 25, 1919. Less than ten months had passed since Armistice Day, but to the president, it must have seemed like ten years. Looking older than his sixty-two years, the exhausted president had spent a restless night. Now, on the twenty-second day of a grueling speaking tour, Wilson suffered almost constant headaches. He had barely slept for days. His wife, Edith, alarmed by his ever-increasing infirmity, begged him to take a rest, but he refused. He felt he could not disappoint the thousands waiting to hear his message about the importance of the League of Nations and how it could prevent future wars. According to this idealistic humanitarian, the world's best hope for preventing another tragedy like the late Great War lay in the establishment of this League. That evening Wilson ascended the steps to a speaker's podium. What happened next would have an enormous impact on the future course of American history.

The year that preceded this Pueblo speech had not been kind to President Wilson or, for that matter, to millions of others across America and around the world. About one year earlier, in early October 1918, the world entered the fiftieth month of what seemed to be a never-ending bloodbath. Already more than 10 million people had perished in World War I bloodbath, including 6 million civilians. Unfortunately, a pestilence that was even deadlier than the battlefield swept across the world. The Spanish influenza killed millions. This new and dangerous virus jumped from birds to swine and at last to humans. First noticed in the spring of 1918 when it infected U.S. army recruits at Camp Funston in Kansas, this infection engulfed the world with unprecedented speed and virulence, taking in its wake as many as 20 million victims. In the United States, where the influenza infected more than one in five citizens, the epidemic reached its zenith in October 1918. In this single month, 200,000 Americans died of the flu.

If the October days of 1918 were darkened by war and pestilence, they also flickered with rays of hope. Aided by nearly 2 million American doughboys in Europe and spurred by the promise of millions more on the way, the Allies saw fresh victories. They disabled Bulgaria and Austria-Hungary, penetrated the German lines in France, and reduced German troop strength by 600,000 men. Although few military advisers expected an immediate end to hostilities with Germany, in early October the German government flinched. It revealed that it would cease hostilities based on Wilson's personal peace plan, the Fourteen Points which he had designed to bring the war to a quick diplomatic conclusion.

Wilson had drafted these Fourteen Points the previous January. He produced the document largely to restore the war's moral footing after the Russian Bolsheviks released for world inspection the secret treaties that promised to divide among the Allies the territories and wealth of the conquered Central Powers. By publishing these secret agreements from the czar's archives, the Bolsheviks hoped to encourage laboring masses around the world to repudiate the war as an imperialistic venture that masqueraded its nefarious intentions with moral pretensions. To blunt the impact of this news, Wilson formulated the Fourteen Points as an alternative peace plan that viewed the war as a crusade for international justice, not a sordid scramble of greedy nations for new territories. His plan promised a future characterized by open (not secret) national covenants, the freedom of all nations to navigate on the open seas, national disarmament, an impartial adjustment of colonial claims based upon the principle of self-determination, the redrawing of European boundaries along largely ethnic lines, and the establishment of an international assembly of nations that would maintain the future peace. Wilson proposed a "peace without victory," the same idea he had advocated even before the United States had entered the war. In his idealistic mind, he could justify war only if it brought about a moral and lasting peace. Therefore, he prayed that his Fourteen Points would convince the Central Powers to sue for an early peace to end the Great War.

From the time of Wilson's proposal until Germany offered to accept it, however, another 50,000 American soldiers lost their lives fighting the un-repentant Central Powers. Therefore, by October 1918, Wilson's idealistic hopes for a quick peace had taken a beating. He balked at Germany's belated promise to accept a peace based on the lenient Fourteen Points. Indeed, Wilson flatly rejected the German offer, stating that Germany also must demonstrate assurances that it had "reformed"—a veiled request calling for the abdica-tion of the kaiser, Wilhelm II. However, despite Wilson's initial rejection of Germany's offer, he continued to carry on negotiations.

Other political leaders in America took a decidedly different view of how to end the war. They demanded complete military victory. As word of Wilson's "peace without victory" negotiations reached American newsstands, former presidents Theodore Roosevelt and William Taft, Senator Henry Cabot Lodge, and other Republicans critical of the "softness" of Wilson's war-ending agenda insisted that Germany's unconditional surrender be the only basis for peace. These critics urged voters to elect a Republican Congress in the upcom-ing November elections in order to safeguard America's national interests. Alarmed by these attacks, Wilson consulted the leaders of his party and on October 25 released the following statement to American voters: "If you have approved of my leadership and want me to continue to be your unembarrassed spokesman in affairs at home and abroad, I earnestly beg that you will express yourselves unmistakably to that effect by returning a Democratic majority to both the Senate and the House of Representatives."

Wilson's risky appeal for Americans to give him a Democratic majority so he would have free rein to shape postwar policy severed the tenuous truce that had existed between the parties during the war. True, in 1898, President McKinley had issued a similar plea for voters to give him a Republican con-gressional majority to assist him in securing the treaty terms he wanted to end the Spanish-American War. Wilson's decision, however, was wrought with more danger, since the slim Democratic hold on Congress in the normally Republican majority country rested more on disunity within Republican ranks than on the numerical strength of the Democrats. During the final ten days of the campaign, both parties engaged in a bitter contest over control of Congress.

Indignant Republicans accused the president of questioning their patriotism and expressed outrage at the blatant partisanship of his foreign policy. They branded him "Kaiser Wilson."

Historically, parties that hold the White House often lose seats in midterm elections. The elections of 1918 were no exception. Numerous factors, many of them more local than national, influenced voters' decisions. When the American voters went to the polls on November 5, they elected more Republicans than Democrats, thus placing both houses of Congress into Republican hands. Just four days later, Kaiser Wilhelm abdicated, and the Germans formed a new republican government. Wilson welcomed this development with renewed hope for his plan for peace. He forwarded the German request for peace to the Allies, who accepted the preconditions for an armistice with two modifications: Great Britain reserved the right to restrict the meaning of Wilson's point concerning "freedom of the seas," and France insisted that Germany must compensate for "all damages done to the civilian population of the Allies." On November 11, an armistice based on the Fourteen Points with these two modifications was signed. The Great War was over. Americans celebrated in the streets. What would have happened in the midterm elections if Armistice Day had come one week earlier is a "what if" question that the discipline of history cannot answer. What is clear, however, is that the stunning 1918 Republican victory propelled Henry Cabot Lodge into two strategically vital posts, Senate majority leader and chair of the Senate Foreign Relations Committee. With these posts, Wilson's old nemesis would be well positioned to challenge the president's foreign policy at every turn. The outcome of this political struggle between Wilson and Lodge would shape American foreign policy for decades to come.

Negotiating the Treaty of Versailles

Undaunted by this thrashing at the polls, Wilson soon announced that he personally would lead the delegation to France to negotiate the terms of the peace settlement. This concerned some Americans who held to the old view that presidents should not leave the country during their term of office. Critics also cried foul when Wilson announced that his team of advisers would include Secretary of State Robert Lansing; General T.H. Bliss, a member of the Supreme War Council; Wilson's close friend and trusted adviser, Colonel Edward House; and Henry White, an experienced diplomat and Republican, but not a major leader in his party. Although this bipartisan team consisted of men of talent, none was a member of the Senate that ultimately would be asked to ratify whatever treaty the delegation delivered.

Opposition to Wilson's internationalist inclinations and postwar agenda began immediately. Before Wilson left American soil, ex-president Theodore Roosevelt interpreted the midterm elections for the European nationalists by stating, "Mr. Wilson has no authority whatever to speak for the American people at this time. His leadership has just been emphatically repudiated by them. . . . Mr. Wilson and his Fourteen Points . . . have ceased to have any shadow of right to be accepted as expressive of the will of the American people." Within a week of Wilson's arrival in Paris, Senator Henry Cabot Lodge repeated the same message. In a speech to the Senate, Lodge advised the Allies that what Europe did to Germany was of no concern to the United States, that no attention need be paid to Wilson's principles regarding the redrawing of European boundary lines, and that all talk of constructing a League of Nations should at least for the moment be postponed.

Despite these criticisms, the stoic Presbyterian president remained confident, even arrogantly confident. Wilson believed that if he could bring Europe to accept a just peace based on the principles of charity and self-determination, then in time the opposition in Congress would be dissolved by the sheer force of public opinion. He had overcome early congressional opposition to his reform efforts in the past, and if he held firmly to this righteous cause, he believed, he would do so again.

Upon his arrival in Europe, crowds greeted Wilson as a conquering hero. Before the peace conference opened, Wilson spent a month visiting Allied cities, although he purposely chose not to visit the areas most devastated by the war. "I don't want to get mad," he told a reporter. "I think there should be one man at this peace table who hasn't lost his temper." Wherever he went, masses lined the streets to shout hurrahs to the popular American who had promised to "make the world safe for democracy." In later speeches, Wilson poignantly described his memories of these days: "Delegations from all over the world came to me to solicit the friendship of America. . . . They frankly told us that they were not sure they could trust anybody else, but that they did absolutely trust us to do them justice and to see that justice was done for them." These emotional outpourings convinced the president that the peoples of Europe were counting on him to help them build a better world. To critics at home and abroad, Wilson was an egomaniac with a messiah complex, but to others and perhaps to himself, Wilson was like Atlas, the one appointed by Zeus to carry the weight of the world on his shoulders.

When Wilson sat down at Versailles with the other leaders of the Allied and Associated Powers,* he quickly discovered that few were interested in his vision of a morally just ending to the war. While the United States had lost about 115,000 men in the Great War, taken together the three other members of the "Big Four" (France, Britain, and Italy) had lost about 3 million lives.

---

*Since the United States entered the war not to defend the Allied nations but to protest German violations of American neutrality, President Wilson insisted on calling the United States an Associated Power rather than an Allied Power.

Given these enormous losses, it is understandable that the priority of the Allied leaders was to punish Germany for its sins, not to honor the idealistic aims reflected in the Fourteen Points. French premier Georges Clemenceau captured the sentiment of many when he reportedly quipped, "Moses gave us the Ten Commandments and we broke them. Wilson gave us the Fourteen Points. We shall see."

And break them (or at least bend them) they did. In negotiations that lasted on and off for nearly six months, Wilson won fewer concessions than he would have liked from the other protagonists at the bargaining table. Most significantly for Wilson, he persuaded the delegates at Versailles to create a League of Nations and to include its constitution within the general peace treaty. In quintessential Wilsonian language, the covenant of the League would require all nations to pledge to respect the territorial integrity of other nations. Also embodied in the agreement was the idea of collective security, whereby League nations would consider an attack against one as an attack against all, hence binding all nations to cooperate to enforce and preserve the peace. Wilson's influence in these areas, however, was offset by the concessions that he was obliged to make to the Allied leaders, who knew all too well of his willingness to trade all his cards for that one ace of diamonds, the creation of the League. It is true that without Wilson, the treaty would have been even more punitive toward the Germans and less open to the principles of self-determination than the treaty that emerged from the Paris conference. It also is true, however, that the final settlement was badly flawed, was exceedingly harsh toward Germany, and fell far short of the promise to provide a "free, open-minded, and absolutely impartial adjustment of all colonial claims."

During the difficult negotiations, Wilson could not understand the mind-set of his peers. Over time he grew to see them as narrow-minded, ruthless, and implacable madmen. His frustration rose to such intensity that his personal physician, Dr. Cary Grayson, begged him to step aside for a while and rest. Wilson refused to slow his pace until a terrible coughing fit seized him on April 3, 1919. His temperature rose to 103 degrees, and he suffered an excruciating headache and experienced twitching on the left side of his face. Rumors flooded Paris that Wilson had been poisoned. After the acute crisis passed, a physically weakened and mentally exasperated Wilson returned to his labors. When the negotiations finally ended, the treaty had little resemblance to Wilson's original hope of "peace without victory."

In May, German delegates received a draft of the treaty and, upon studying it, expressed outrage that it was not the peace of justice they had been promised. It imposed devastating punishments on Germany and even included a humiliating guilt clause accusing Germany of starting the war. Count Ulrich von Brockdorff-Rantzau, leader of the German delegation at Versailles, railed against the Allied demands. He stated in part,

> Under the terms of the peace treaty, Germany is to give up her Merchant Marine and vessels now under construction suitable for foreign commerce. . . . Moreover, Germany must renounce her Colonies; all her foreign possessions, all her rights and interests in the Allied and Associated countries. . . . When the territorial clauses of the Peace Treaty go into effect Germany will lose in the East the most important regions for the production of wheat and potatoes, and this would be equivalent to a loss of twenty-one percent of the total harvest of these foodstuffs. . . . Those who sign this treaty will sign the death sentence of many millions of German men, women and children.

Under a threat of an Allied march on Berlin, however, Germany reluctantly accepted the treaty. The signing date was set for June 28, 1919, the fifth anniversary of the assassination of Archduke Francis Ferdinand that sparked the Great War. Premier Clemenceau formally opened the ceremonies with a brief address that warned the Germans to respect the provisions of the treaty. The French hosts then gave to President Wilson the honor of being the treaty's first signatory.

The Treaty of Versailles did include provisions for a League of Nations, which to Wilson was the hope of the world. When Wilson returned to the United States, he delivered the treaty to the Senate, naturally downplaying its flaws and focusing instead on its one redeeming quality—the covenant for an international body with the power to prevent future wars. Once established, Wilson insisted, the League would be able to review the details decided in Paris and iron out whatever imperfections remained.

Many senators who were responsible for approving the treaty, however, were not enamored with the document. As early as March 1919, Senator Lodge presented Wilson with a list of thirty-nine senators opposed to the League as proposed. Within this number were about fourteen "irreconcilables," avid isolationists who swore never to support any League under any circumstance. Public opinion at the time supported the League of Nations overwhelmingly, but without some of these senatorial votes, no treaty could be ratified. In assessing the situation, Lodge told the irreconcilables that "any attempt to defeat the Treaty of Versailles with the League by a straight vote in the Senate, if taken immediately, would be hopeless." Concurring with that political assessment, the irreconcilables agreed to cooperate with Lodge in a delaying tactic by supporting for the moment amendments to the treaty that Lodge would offer. Much to Wilson's chagrin, Lodge asked the Senate Foreign Relations Committee to study and revise the treaty before bringing it to the Senate floor for a vote. To ensure the outcome, Lodge packed the committee with opponents of the League. In fact, six of the ten Republicans on it, enough to shape the outcome, were among the irreconcilables. If Wilson could pack the peace negotiation team, critics said, then Lodge could pack the committee that would review its work.

Just as Lodge hoped and Wilson feared, as the Senate hearings dragged on and an endless list of amendments were presented and debated, public enthusiasm for the League waned. To save his League from defeat, Wilson decided to take the case directly to the American people, just as he had done on other occasions when his reforms were stalled in the Senate. Wilson remained optimistic. After all, thirty-three governors and thirty-four state legislatures had endorsed the League. Moreover, history was on his side. The Senate never before had rejected a peace treaty.

Wilson's Last Speech: September 25, 1919

Although his headaches that had begun on April 3 continued, Wilson ignored his wife's pleas to take some time off. The treaty was too important. Therefore, he made plans to embark on an ambitious, 9,981-mile speaking tour that would take him by train from the Canadian border to near Mexico. His task was to use his greatest talent—the power of persuasion—to raise a tide of public protest that would unloose the Senate from the quagmire of opposition.

On September 3, 1919, a seven-car presidential railroad train rolled away from Washington, DC, with Mayflower, the blue presidential railroad car, in tow. An enthusiastic Wilson stopped in dozens of small towns, giving impromptu speeches from the rear platform of the car. On most days after entering a large city, he left the Mayflower to present his case to crowds at civic auditoriums and churches. Without air conditioning or microphones, Wilson often had to shout his message to sweltering crowds. The exhausting speeches and endless handshaking took their toll on the health of the already ailing president. Edith Wilson and his doctor continued to warn him to slow down and take a few days of rest. Wilson's vision, however, spurred him onward.

Enthusiastic crowds cheered him at every stop. With masterful oratory, Wilson rebutted point by point the standard arguments of the critics of ratification. To those, for instance, who said that the treaty violated America's isolationist tradition, Wilson rejoined, "The isolation of the United States is at an end, not because we chose to go into the politics of the world, but because . . . we have become a determining factor in the history of mankind, and after you have become a determining factor you cannot remain isolated, whether you want to or not." To those who said that the United States should disavow the treaty because it contained some unfortunate concessions, such as the concession that gave Japan the right to economically control China's Shantung Province, Wilson quipped that refusing to join the League would "accomplish nothing for China" but would neuter America's opportunity to become "a determining factor in the development of civilization."

At times, Wilson's remarks appeared prophetic. In commenting about the new nation-states created in the treaty, Wilson warned,

> The formula of pan-Germanism, you remember, was Bremen to Bagdad—Bremen on the North Sea to Bagdad in Persia. These countries that we have set up as the new home of liberty lie right along that road. If we leave them there without the guarantee that the combined force of the world will assure their independence and their territorial integrity, we have only to wait a short generation when our recent experience will be repeated. . . . If Germany had known that England would go in, she never would have started [World War I]. If she had known that America would come in, she never would have dreamed of it. And now the only way to make it certain that there never will be another world war like that is that we should assist in guaranteeing the peace and its settlement.

Also spliced somewhere in every speech was Wilson's passionate plea: "My fellow countrymen . . . you must make up your minds, because, after all, it is you who are going to make up the minds of this country."

Twenty-two arduous days into the campaign, the presidential train turned toward Pueblo, Colorado. Wilson's health had deteriorated considerably since the beginning of the trip. The headaches in the back of his head now felt as if they were in the center of his brain. On its passage from California to Salt Lake City, the presidential train rumbled through miles of hot, raging forest fires. At times flames nearly lapped against the side of the train. For hours the unair-conditioned railroad cars were choked with smoke and noxious gas, particularly when the train passed through numerous long tunnels. At night, neither Wilson's doctor nor his wife, Edith, could help him find a comfortable way to sleep. Yet his tenacious resolve urged him forward.

As his train entered Pueblo, Colorado, even the indomitable President Wilson looked for relief from the ever-demanding mobs that met him at the station. When he discovered that he was expected to stand in his automobile for a two-mile parade, he exploded into anger at whoever had made such arrangements. Told that he had given personal approval to the plan, he remarked that any "fool who was stupid enough to approve such a program has no business in the White House." Wilson made the open-topped car trip in blistering heat and entered the civic auditorium to the sounds of applause. However, as he stepped onto the stage, he stumbled. As an aide rushed to help him, he recovered and stepped to the podium. The stifling heat and stale air of the auditorium railed against the throbbing pain in his head. He spoke in a weaker than usual voice. "Mr. Chairman and Fellow Countrymen: It is with a great deal of genuine pleasure that I find myself in Pueblo . . ." Attempting to proceed, he found himself stumbling over sentences that he had delivered on scores of occasions: "Germany must never be allowed . . ." He began again. "A lesson must be taught to Germany . . ." He stopped and stood still for a moment. Edith Wilson looked up to her husband with terror in her eyes. He spoke again, "The world will not allow Germany . . ." This time he continued, but in a soft and fragile voice. The speech he knew by heart was no less effective than when he had given it dozens of other times. He spoke with emotion about American soldiers who went to France and who would now never come home. Tears filled his eyes and the eyes of those who could hear him as he ended the speech:

> There is one thing that the American people always rise to and extend their hand to, and that is the truth of justice, and of liberty, and of peace. We have accepted that truth and we are going to be led by it, and it is going to lead us, and through us the world, out into pastures of quietness and peace such as the world never dreamed of before.

This would be the last public speech President Woodrow Wilson would deliver. As he stepped down from the podium, his head almost burst open with pain. By the time he arrived back at his train car, his steps were labored and he required help. After leaving Pueblo, Wilson relaxed. The train stopped for a while and he walked with Edith and felt reinvigorated. But that evening near midnight, as the train rolled through Kansas, Wilson called out to his wife, "Can you come to me, Edith, I'm terribly sick." Edith and Dr. Grayson were horrified to find him in a state of debilitating pain. They pleaded with the president to cancel the remainder of the tour and return to Washington. Wilson's answer was mumbled and hard to understand: "I must go on. I should feel like a deserter." He tried to stand, but his left side was nearly paralyzed. Unable even to dress himself, the president could not go on. Reluctantly, his personal secretary told reporters, "The tour's off." Admiral Grayson, his friend and physician, filled in for Wilson in Wichita, greeting a crowd of 50,000. Trying not to create an alarm, Grayson read a statement that the president suffered from "nervous exhaustion" that resulted from overwork and was returning to Washington for a well-deserved rest.

The greatest advocate of the League of Nations was silenced. That day, although not yet obvious to the world, saw the birth of a new generation of American nationalism that would supplant Wilson's idealistic hope for American leadership in world peace.

The Convalescence of President Wilson

After Wilson's speedy return to Washington, Edith kept a watchful eye on him. Then, on the morning of October 2, Wilson, feeling stronger, rose from his bed and went into his bathroom to shave. After a few minutes, Edith heard him fall to the floor with a cry and a moan. She found him with blood gushing from his nose, which had hit against the sink as he fell to the ground.

The president had suffered a serious stroke. Edith called his doctor, and Wilson was immediately confined to bed. For six months, the president was incapacitated. For seven and a half months, he would not hold a cabinet meeting. Protected from visitors by his wife and doctors, Wilson maintained only limited contact with friends or foes on the Hill. Sometimes barely able to communicate, Wilson passed what instructions he had about state affairs through Edith. She took over a number of routine tasks of the government, turned other responsibilities over to heads of departments, and forbade the doctors from fully disclosing the state of the president's health. Although she recalled in her memoirs that she never made any major decisions, some scholars disagree, saying that on occasion she made significant decisions and signed the president's name on important papers. Some even have called her the first female president.

One thing is certain. Wilson no longer had the stamina or the charisma to bring victory to his cause. Following his collapse, Wilson's stubbornness became accentuated. On November 13, the Republican-controlled Senate approved a set of reservations to the treaty offered by Lodge that asserted that the United States would not be obligated to defend other League members without the approval of Congress. Wilson instructed his supporters to oppose the treaty with the Lodge reservations. Without Democratic support, the Senate rejected the revised treaty, 55–39. When the reservations were eliminated, another vote was taken with similar results: 53–38 (including only one Republican voting in favor).

In early 1920, when the League of Nations held its first sessions, the European hosts lamented the absence of American representation. Meanwhile, back in the States, moderate senators from both parties worked on a compromise that could secure ratification of the treaty. Again, Wilson opposed these efforts, insisting that revisions be considered only after the United States had ratified the treaty and joined the League of Nations. In response to pressure, in March the Senate agreed to reconsider the treaty one more time. Additional Lodge reservations were added to clarify that the treaty would not supersede the Monroe Doctrine. When the vote was taken, a number of Democrats broke with the president by approving the treaty with these reservations. A 57–39 majority approved the revised treaty, but this tally was still seven votes short of the two-thirds majority required for ratification. Even at this date, Wilson refused to give up hope that his League would be accepted. By now able to walk with a cane, Wilson looked to the election of 1920 as a national referendum on the issue and, notwithstanding his deteriorating health, volunteered himself as the Democratic standard-bearer.

By now, however, Wilson's hopes no longer reflected the mood of America. While the bitter partisan debate over the merits of collective security soured sentiment toward both parties, the rising apathy and disillusionment over the treaty hit hardest the Wilsonian idealists who had made promises they could not keep. During the last year of Wilson's presidency, the nation drifted like a rudderless ship on the open seas. Wilson could no longer unite the members of his own party, much less the national electorate. Unlike Midas, everything he touched turned to rust. He wanted the treaty, but, insisting on all or nothing, got nothing and was left, as his critics bemused, with "not a League to stand on." He did not want federal prohibition of alcoholic legislation, yet Congress passed over his presidential veto of the Volstead Act that prohibited the manufacture, transportation, and sale of alcoholic drinks. At the Democratic Convention, the divided party, passing over both Wilson and his son-in-law William McAdoo (Wilson's former secretary of the treasury), nominated the wealthy and energetic Governor James Cox of Ohio, whose attributes included few ties to the president. The Democratic platform supported approving a treaty without any crippling reservations, although clarifying reservations were not prohibited. In the upcoming campaign, Cox would support the League of Nations, but not make it the centerpiece of his campaign.

Meanwhile, the Republicans, smelling a victory if they could avoid a major catastrophe, bypassed the controversial irreconcilable Senator Hiram Johnson of California and nominated the amiable, if mentally unsophisticated, former newspaper editor and Ohio senator, Warren G. Harding. Shrewdly, the Republican platform was ambivalent toward the League of Nations, opposing Wilson's organization, but leaving open the possibility of embracing an acceptable one. Republicans who supported the League assured voters that Harding's election would bring the United States into the League, while irreconcilable Republicans promised the opposite. The election of 1920 would be many things, but it would not be a national referendum on the League of Nations.

Returning to Normalcy: The Election of 1920

In the aftermath of the Great War and in the absence of Wilson's passionate, moral, and now all but silenced voice, the fires for domestic and international reform cooled as wearied Americans expressed concerns about more personal issues like rising prices, labor strikes, and the fear of a Bolshevik revolution. This last obsession, called the "Red Scare," spurred government agencies to take action to eradicate the alleged communist conspiracy. The Department of the Interior, for instance, joined with motion picture executives to promote motion pictures that would combat the infiltration of "ultraradical" tendencies. Meanwhile, the Department of Justice, under the leadership of Attorney General A. Mitchell Palmer, raided alleged communist cells in thirty-three cities, arresting in its dragnet 3,000 accused communists. With approval of the secretary of labor, noncitizens accused of communist ties were deported without jury trial.

Even as Americans were busy chasing communists, Congress ignored Wilson's advice and enacted over his veto the Volstead Act, a prohibition law made possible by the ratification of the Eighteenth Amendment. Although the law did reduce per capita alcohol consumption, it also caused the equivalent of hangover headaches to enforcement officers around the nation. The final reform of the Progressive Era was realized in August 1920, when Tennessee became the last state necessary to ratify an amendment giving women voting rights in all states. The ratification of the Nineteenth Amendment, which ended an eighty-one-year struggle for female suffrage, succeeded in part because of the constant pressure applied by protesting women determined to rid the democratic nation of the hypocrisy of male-only suffrage. Even more important than the picket lines of the protesters, however, were the selfless sacrifices carried out by American women during the Great War. After the war, even old guard, conservative males had to acknowledge that the patriotic participation of women in the war effort had earned them the right to vote. For years antisuffragists had argued that woman suffrage would dramatically alter the political complexion of America, since women would follow their nature and select soft candidates lacking in the manly virtues. The election of 1920 would be the first election to test this widely held, but unproven hypothesis.

The campaign itself was rather drab and listless, made interesting on occasion only by the presence of a federal prisoner on the ballot. Eugene Debs, running for the fourth time as the Socialist Party candidate, conducted his campaign from cell number 2253 at the Atlanta Penitentiary, where he was imprisoned for speaking against American participation in the Great War, a violation of the wartime Espionage Act of 1918. The major candidates, Harding and Cox, covered little new ground during the campaign. To many voters, the choice was not really between these two men and their ambiguous attitudes toward the League of Nations. Rather, it was a referendum on whether to sustain the highbrow, idealistic, self-sacrificing moralism associated with the age of Wilson or to move forward (or backward) into a quieter age that would allow Americans to relax and be whomever they wanted to be. Harding expressed his longing for the latter option with the words: "America's present need is not heroics, but healing; not nostrums but normalcy; not revolution but restoration; . . . not surgery but serenity." No gender gap influenced this election, but at the polls American women and men shouted their decision in unity. Carrying over 60 percent of the popular vote, Harding won the presidency by the widest margins of any candidate since the popular vote was recorded.

As a postscript to this story, Woodrow Wilson died three years after leaving office, ironically surviving Harding, who died unexpectedly of a stroke in August 1923. Wilson, more respected than loved in life, died a shattered man with shattered dreams. Before his death he told a friend, "I am a broken piece of machinery. When the machinery is broken . . . I'm ready." At his death, hundreds gathered in the snow outside his Washington home to pay final

THE SILENCING OF WOODROW WILSON, SEPTEMBER 25, 1919   165

respects. To these admirers, Wilson was a martyred saint. Others disagreed profusely, while to some, like journalist William Allen White, who penned these lines, Wilson left a mixed legacy:

> *God gave him a great vision.*
> *The devil gave him an imperious heart.*
> *The proud heart is still.*
> *The vision lives.*

The Leave-Me-Alone Decade: America in the Twenties

America was ready to party. The decade of the 1920s has been dubbed with many labels—roaring, Republican, conservative, elegant, narcissistic, hedonistic, iconoclastic, racist, isolationist, and lost. Each of these terms describes a version of the truth. The twenties sprang onto the American scene as a decade of new tastes, new ideas, and a new individualism, each allowed because the dominant passion of the times was simply "leave me alone." It was a decade characterized by unabashed political conservatism, social experimentation, organized crime and government corruption, and isolationism in foreign affairs. Harding's "return to normalcy" victory in 1920, an emphatic rejection of the crusading collectivism of prewar America, was just the first of three national elections that signaled America's comfort with the principle "live and let live."

As more citizens for the first time lived in cities than on farms, a revolution against the mores and morals of the past engulfed Main Street America. And the rebellious troops challenging the old order were not Bolsheviks but die-hard capitalists bent on increasing their wealth and having a good time doing it. "The same disillusion which had defeated Woodrow Wilson," Frederick Lewis Allen wrote, " . . . furnished a culture in which the germs of the new freedom could grow and multiply." The new freedoms to which he referred included, among other things, the enjoyment of short skirts, short hair for women, radio, rayon, lipstick, cigarettes, dance marathons, flagpole sitting, jazz, petting parties, and speakeasies. It included gate-crashing at dances, discussing Freud in public, idolizing athletes and movie stars, and necking or more in the privacy of the new, fully enclosed automobiles.

One curious exception—the imposition of Prohibition—defied the trend of throwing out restraints. Although associated mostly with the 1920s, this "noble experiment," as it was called by Herbert Hoover, actually was a Progressive Era movement that succeeded largely because of the wartime association between brewers and German-Americans, whom many regarded as dubiously loyal citizens. However, the law was largely ignored and often flagrantly and officially repudiated in the great cities. Where enforcement was attempted, the effort to control alcoholic consumption was justified as a patriotic attempt to maintain American rural values and factory productivity as much as a way of improving public health.

"America: Love It or Leave It" did not appear on bumper stickers of the automobiles coming off the assembly lines in the 1920s, but the idea certainly was in the air. Owing largely to the disillusionment that followed the peace settlement, antiforeignism was popular in the postwar era. Harding was only two months in the White House when he signed a stopgap immigration measure designed to slow the flood of unwanted immigrants into the country. "Refuse the refuse" was the slogan of the moment. Efforts to keep foreigners out and to protect the ethnic complexion of America did not cease with this law. Three years later, President Calvin Coolidge signed a more thorough immigration law that limited the number of immigrants from various nations to no more than 2 percent of the number of residents from that nation who lived in America. To reduce further the numbers admitted from southern and eastern Europe, these quotas were not based on the most recent U.S. census, but on the 1890 census, when the population of the United States was overwhelmingly Anglo. The 1924 law also created the U.S. Border Patrol and the Immigration and Naturalization Service (INS) to enforce these limits.

Anti-immigrant sentiment, as well as prejudices against blacks, Catholics, Jews, and labor unions, also contributed to the revival of a radical racist organization called the Ku Klux Klan. This body grew rapidly during the twenties as its appeal escaped the confines of the South to become accepted in small towns across America. With 5 million dues-paying members, at the time about 8 percent of the adult population, the reconstituted Klan wielded potent political influence. Returning to normalcy did not reduce prejudice. It had the opposite effect. It accentuated xenophobic intolerance against foreigners abroad and ethnic minorities at home.

The will to promote America first, second, and last also was manifested in the nation's economic and foreign agendas of the 1920s. In foreign affairs, one of Harding's first concerns was to undeclare war. Having refused to ratify the Treaty of Versailles, Congress in 1921 passed a simple joint resolution saying the war was officially over. Soon thereafter, it approved separate peace treaties with Germany, Austria, and Hungary. These agreements awarded America with all the advantages of the unratified treaties, but with none of the obligations and responsibilities. Following the lead of the Republican irreconcilables, Harding avoided the League of Nations, although he did send unofficial observers to its headquarters in Geneva to keep an eye on its activities.

To assuage Republican guilt for rejecting the League, Washington hosted a disarmament conference that although unable to make any progress with disarmament on land, did produce the Five Power Naval Treaty of 1922. This agreement between the United States, Britain, Japan, France, and Italy slowed the naval arms race by imposing limits for ten years on the number of battleships and aircraft carriers for each nation. Since no restrictions were placed on cruisers, destroyers, or submarines, the conference results received mixed reviews, both by contemporaries and by later historians. Harding's naval conference, however, has received more scholarly applause than the peacemongering of his successor. In 1928, President Coolidge gave his approval to the famed Kellogg-Briand Pact, an agreement that would be ratified by sixty-two nations. This pact "outlawed" war as an instrument of national policy, although it did permit defensive wars. Since no nation ever admits to instigating nondefensive wars, this toothless pact prevented no wars, although in some instances it did abolish formal declarations of war.

The Politics of Prosperity

More important to most Americans in the twenties than foreign affairs was the health of the U.S. economy. The economic guru of the decade was Andrew Mellon, the secretary of the treasury for Harding, Coolidge, and Hoover. A fiscally conservative, multimillionaire industrialist, Mellon believed that the formula for economic growth included raising tariff rates to protect American industry, cutting fixed expenses, reducing the debt service by paying down the national debt, and lowering taxes out of the surplus revenues. Before the Great Depression broke the economic boom of the 1920s, the Mellon plan seemed to be the perfect manure to grow the American economy. As new tariff legislation raised the average cost of foreign imports about 45 percent, income taxes, which at that time were levied primarily on wealthy Americans, dropped precipitously. For instance, in 1921, the tax bite on an annual income of $1 million was $663,000; by 1924, the tax on this amount was $200,000, resulting in a savings of over $400,000 that could be reinvested in stocks. Meanwhile, the national debt was slowly being reduced. When Secretary Mellon first took over the Treasury Department, the U.S. debt was above $25 billion. When he left, the debt was at $21 billion, although at one point during his tenure it had been reduced as low as $16 billion. During the Harding, Coolidge, and Hoover years, Mellon's popularity followed the same pattern as the Dow Jones average, which for most of the decade was soaring into the stratosphere.

Unfortunately, other Harding appointments earned more shame than fame. Veterans' Bureau head Charles Forbes resigned under suspicion, fled the country, and later would serve two years in Leavenworth for bribery and corruption. Similarly, Harding's attorney general, Harry Daughtery, was accused of selling pardons and profiteering from an illegal sale of government alcohol supplies, although, unlike Forbes, Daughtery escaped prison. Less fortunate was Harding's secretary of the interior, Albert Fall. After leasing federal oil reserves at Teapot Dome and Elk Hills to private companies, Secretary Fall received a $400,000 loan from oil friends. After being convicted for accepting bribes, Fall made history by becoming America's first cabinet member to be imprisoned for crimes committed in office.

Scandalous talk also dirtied the reputation of President Harding. Nan Britton, the attractive author of America's first kiss-and-tell book, *The President's Daughter*, confessed that she and Harding carried on a clandestine affair in disreputable hotels, the Senate Office Building, and even in the coat closet of the White House. Britton's baby daughter, she asserted, was fathered and financially supported by the president. The veracity of these statements still remains open to question.

Following Harding's sudden death from a stroke in August 1923 and Vice President Coolidge's elevation to the presidency, however, few Americans other than partisan Democrats took great interest in the allegations of financial or sexual misconduct of Harding and his appointees. In the election of 1924, when the conservative Democratic candidate, John Davis, tried to make political capital of the Harding scandals, most Americans considered his remarks in bad taste, since whatever shortcomings Harding may have had, these indiscretions had nothing to do with Coolidge or his party.

Unsatisfied both with the Democrats and with the conservative drift of his own party, the longtime progressive Republican Robert La Follette broke from the GOP to run independently on the Progressive Party line. Even with this minor split in Republican ranks, Coolidge won reelection easily by carrying 54 percent of the popular vote. What a difference a dozen years can make! In 1912, three in four American voters favored progressive candidates; twelve years later, three in four Americans favored staunchly conservative ones.

At mid-decade, normalcy still ruled, and it would continue to rule under the leadership of "Silent Cal," the dour-faced New Englander described by ex-President Roosevelt's daughter Alice as a man "weaned on a pickle." Renowned for his integrity and frugality, Coolidge is less remembered for the legislation he signed than for the witty maxims that expressed his conservative, no-nonsense philosophy. "The business of government is business," he asserted. On another occasion this high priest of business remarked that "the man who builds a factory builds a temple." As the economy steamed forward, critics complained that Coolidge got credit for doing nothing, but that is precisely what the president wanted to do. When asked about his presidency, Coolidge remarked, "One of the most important accomplishments of my administration has been the minding of my own business."

Hoover, the Great Depression, and the Coming of the New Deal

The popular Coolidge easily could have won the Republican nomination in 1928, but instead he told his party he would not seek reelection. The Republicans thus turned to the star-studded Herbert Hoover. Although he had never been elected to a public office, Hoover's credentials were impeccable:

farmer, Stanford alumnus, businessman, and public servant. Hoover had achieved national fame during the early stages of the Great War by serving as head of the Commission for Relief in Belgium. President Wilson then picked Hoover to head the U.S. Food Administration, and after the war he directed the American Relief Administration, which fed 350 million people in twenty-one countries. Then for eight years Hoover served loyally as Harding's and Coolidge's secretary of commerce. A compassionate Quaker, able administrator, and self-made man, Hoover represented the best that rural America could produce.

Challenging Hoover in 1928 was his mirror image, Democrat Alfred Smith of New York. Unlike Hoover—the Protestant prohibitionist from the farms of Iowa—Smith was Catholic, the grandson of an immigrant, and an anti-prohibitionist from the Irish ghettos of Manhattan. For the first time in history, the radio played a major role in an election. Neither candidate used the new medium to its fullest advantage, but Hoover's statesmanlike promotion of "rugged individualism" played better on the air than Smith's wisecracking aphorisms spoken with his heavy East Side accent. Religious bigotry, expressed in slogans like "A Vote for Al Smith Is a Vote for the Pope," also influenced voters despite Hoover's attempt to eliminate the smear campaign. Ultimately, it was not religion but economics that most influenced voters. The Republican promise that Hoover would put "a chicken in every pot, a car in every garage" seemed plausible to Americans enjoying the benefits of prosperity. By a 58 percent majority, the Republicans for the third time in the decade sent an apostle of normalcy to the White House.

Unfortunately for Hoover, however, the prosperity of the times was less deep and more tenuous than most people acknowledged. Despite the stock market surge and the phenomenal growth in the new automobile, radio, motion picture, and electrical appliance industries, there were a number of unnoticed trouble spots within the economy. One major defect was the decline in overseas trade, which dipped from about $9 billion annually at the opening of the decade to about $4 billion at its closing. This problem was aggravated by the high retaliatory tariffs placed on American goods by European countries upset at high U.S. tariffs. Efforts to negotiate lower tariff rates during the 1920s failed, largely because the United States insisted on linking tariff reductions to repayment of war debts, which most former Allies refused to pay.

A second dark spot in the economy was the plight of American farmers, who found it increasingly difficult to survive after Congress removed the agricultural price supports that had aided farmers during the war years. At mid-decade, the suffering farmers lobbied for and won passage of a bill to re-establish price supports. President Coolidge vetoed this act, insisting that price supports were too expensive and violated America's laissez-faire tradition.

Just as the prosperity of the 1920s never reached American farmers, neither did it trickle down to American laborers. Even before the bubble burst and the so-called good times ended, only one in six American families owned a car, only one in five lived in houses with running water or electric power, and only one in ten had a telephone. The average American salary before the crash of 1929 was about $1,500 per year, which was under the estimated $1,800 per year that was required to keep a family of four out of poverty. The increasing inequality of wealth was a dangerous development for everyone, not just for the poor, since it prevented millions of Americans from being able to purchase the new appliances and gadgets that industrial America was spewing out. The problem of the late 1920s was not that the market for new goods had been saturated, but that too few consumers had the purchasing power for goods that businesses could sell essentially only in America.

By the summer of 1929, inventory levels were triple the levels of the previous year. Fewer workers were needed, but laying off workers meant fewer consumers able to purchase the goods already produced. The deadly cycle had begun. In October, stocks began to fall swiftly, losing 40 percent of their value within a month. This was only the beginning of bad times. After a brief recovery of stock values in early 1930, the market took another sudden fall in the spring of 1930 and would continue this downward trend for the next three years. By 1933, stocks were about 80 percent below their 1929 highs. As prices fell, business failures soared, and with them, so did unemployment. Eventually, one in four households had no breadwinner.

As secretary of commerce, Hoover had advocated self-regulation of business through trade associations rather than governmental regulation through federal agencies. A free enterpriser in mind and soul, Hoover staunchly believed that government should intervene only as a last resort. Consequently, as president, Hoover first responded to the deteriorating economic conditions by asking businessmen for voluntary pledges not to cut workers and counseling farmers to agree among themselves to lower production levels (and thus, by reducing supply, raise farm prices and profits). To encourage Americans to buy American goods, the president also supported the passage of the Hawley-Smoot Tariff Act, which established the highest protective tariff in peacetime history, with average duties 59 percent the value of the product. As the times grew more desperate, Hoover reluctantly supported the creation of the Reconstruction Finance Corporation (RFC), which would loan taxpayers' dollars to the railroad and banking industries to keep these necessary businesses from collapsing. Hoover, however, drew the line at giving public relief to individual citizens. "No dole," Hoover asserted, arguing that welfare to individuals would destroy the incentive to work.

Among those hard-hit by the Great Depression were the veterans of World War I. In the summer of 1932, thousands of these men, who had been promised a pension at retirement, marched on Washington to demand an early down payment on their bonus. When Congress rejected their pleas, riots erupted in the camps of the protesters. To protect the city, Hoover ordered U.S. Army general Douglas MacArthur to move in with bayonets, tear gas, and fire hoses to evict the protesters. Driving heroes of the Great War out of town brought additional public condemnation of the besieged president. The man who had promised "a car in every garage" now was viewed as the heartless soul whose policies had put "two families in every garage."

Even as MacArthur and his troops were pointing fire hoses at the bonus marchers, in Chicago Republican delegates were gathering to renominate Hoover for a second term. Failure to do so would have been tantamount to repudiating the cherished doctrines of the last three presidents. Meanwhile, the Democrats turned to their rising star, Franklin D. Roosevelt, who, like his fifth cousin Theodore Roosevelt, was well-bred for political life. Both Roosevelts had been born into wealthy New York households, attended Harvard, served as assistant secretary of the navy and as governor of New York, and received vice presidential nominations from their parties at early ages. Theodore clearly bested his younger cousin in body build and athleticism, largely because Franklin was stricken with polio at age thirty-nine. What Franklin Roosevelt lacked in body, however, he made up for in charm. His zest for life and uplifting voice could bring hope that would lighten a darkened room. Unlike Hoover, an ideologue bound to his conservative philosophy, Roosevelt was a nondogmatic pragmatist, a try-anything-once politician who loved to experiment and break traditions. These assets gave him insurmountable advantages over his Republican foe, an incumbent in depressed times whose best argument for reelection was "It could have been worse."

But the Depression reigned in the minds of Americans. In October 1932, popular singer Bing Crosby recorded a song penned by E.Y. Harburg and J. Gorney called "Brother, Can You Spare a Dime?" It captured the frustration of the Hoover era and the desire for the kind of new hope promised by the Democrats.

> *They used to tell me I was building a dream. And so I followed the*
> *   mob*
> *When there was earth to plow, or guns to bear I was always there,*
> *   right on the job.*
> *They used to tell me I was building a dream, with peace and glory*
> *   ahead,*
> *Why should I be standing in line, just waiting for bread?*
> *Once I built a railroad, I made it run, made it race against time.*
> *Once I built a railroad, now it's done. Brother, can you spare a dime?*
> *Once I built a tower, up to the sun, brick, and rivet, and lime.*
> *Once I built a tower, now it's done. Brother, can you spare a dime?*
> *Once in khaki suits, gee we looked swell*
> *Full of that Yankee Doodle Dum,*
> *Half a million boots went sloggin' through hell,*
> *And I was the kid with the drum!*

Say don't you remember? they called me Al; it was Al all the time.
Why don't you remember? I'm your pal. Say buddy, can you spare a
dime?

(Song copyright Warner Bros., Inc.)

Before the Depression, in 1928, Hoover won by a landslide; four years later, he lost by one. The 1932 Democratic victory demonstrated Franklin Roosevelt's popularity, but not as much as it revealed Hoover's unpopularity. Democrats regained solid control of both houses of Congress, picking up thirteen senators and ninety seats in the House, a mere foretaste of the congressional majorities that the party would enjoy for most of the next generation. Normalcy had been dethroned, and in its place was a reinvigorated party committed to delivering a "New Deal" for the American people. Democrats sang aloud "Happy Days Are Here Again," but even as they celebrated in the streets, the economy continued to putrefy. By the day of Roosevelt's inauguration, 80 percent of the banks in America had closed their doors and 15 million Americans were unemployed.

Roosevelt's New Deal promised to provide Americans with the three Rs: relief for the unemployed, recovery of the economy, and reform of the system so that the country never again would suffer from such a great depression. After giving assurances in his inaugural address that "the only thing we have to fear is fear itself," Roosevelt plunged ahead to deal with the banking crisis. He declared a nationwide banking holiday to stop the runs on banks and called Congress into a special session to deal with the emergency. Within days, Congress passed an emergency banking law, which provided for the opening of all sound banks (allowing the weak ones to fall) and took the United States off the gold standard. Eight days into his presidency, in the first of many "fireside" chats broadcast on the radio, Roosevelt reassured citizens that it was now safer to keep their money in banks than under their mattresses. Soon, 90 percent of the banks were reopened and a billion more dollars were back in circulation.

Roosevelt next concentrated on providing work relief for the millions of unemployed. In his first "Hundred Days," he set a standard of accomplishment that never has been equaled. The measures passed and programs created during these days read like the letters in a can of alphabet soup:

- CCC (Civilian Conservation Corps)—employed 3 million young men from destitute families to work on parks and natural resources for $30 per month
- FERA (Federal Emergency Relief Administration)—provided $3 billion in relief funds to the states to distribute to the unemployed
- CWA (Civil Works Administration)—provided temporary employment for 4 million unemployed workers

- PWA (Public Works Administration)—sent federal funds to private construction firms to hire workers for heavy construction projects in order to provide unemployment relief and stimulate economic recovery
- HOLC (Home Owners Loan Corporation)—provided federal loans to mortgage holders faced with the threat of losing their homes
- TVA (Tennessee Valley Authority)—built dams and hydroelectric plants in the Tennessee River Valley that would provide flood control and cheap electrical power to the impoverished region

Later, the Works Project Administration (WPA) would be created to employ millions of workers in a variety of jobs, from beautifying city streets with murals to constructing schools, parks, dams, roads, and sidewalks.

Congress also drafted laws designed to jump-start the economy. The Agricultural Adjustment Administration (AAA), for instance, was created with the power to pay subsidies to farmers willing to reduce the amount of acreage in production. The National Recovery Administration (NRA) was empowered to work with representatives of business and labor to create codes of "fair practice" (i.e., no child labor, maximum hour and minimum wage provisions) designed to stabilize the economy through cooperation and planning. Reform measures also were passed, including the Glass Steagall Banking Act, which regulated the banking industry and established the Federal Deposit Insurance Corporation (FDIC) to insure bank deposits up to $5,000 per customer; the Security Exchange Act, which created the Securities Exchange Commission (SEC) to regulate stock exchange; and finally, the climax of the New Deal reforms, the Social Security Act, which provided old age insurance funded by equal taxes contributed by workers and employers.

The New Deal was not without its critics. Fiscal conservatives opposed the deficit spending that raised the national debt by $12 billion in just four years. Other conservatives opposed the government interference in the economy, saying that such actions violated the Constitution and gave too much power to the president and to labor unions. Small businesses complained that the New Deal encouraged monopolies and drowned them in paperwork. Other critics attacked the New Deal from the left, saying it did too little for the poor and was simply a sop that perpetuated the exploitation of capitalism.

For the great majority of Americans, however, the New Deal was just the medicine that the nation needed. In the presidential election of 1936, Roosevelt demolished the Republican Alf Landon, carrying 61 percent of the popular vote and all but eight electoral votes. Riding Roosevelt's political coattails, Democrats also were swept into local, state, and national offices across the country. After the election of 1936, Democrats controlled 79 percent of the Senate and 75 percent of the House, a far cry from the Republican ascendancy of the Harding and Coolidge years. The New Deal did not immediately cure the economy or restore full employment, but its popularity did transform the political complexion of the nation.

Although the domestic progressivism of the era of Theodore Roosevelt and Woodrow Wilson had been revived, one legacy of the age of normalcy survived intact. Americans in the thirties, as they had in the twenties, still insisted that the United States should refrain from foreign entanglements. While most supported promoting international trade with lower tariffs, the hard times of the Depression years reminded Americans that they had enough everyday problems to deal with at home without being preoccupied with the problems of the world. According to opinion polls, a 70 percent majority of Americans during the 1930s thought that the Great War was a result of national and corporate greed and that the United States was wrong to have entered it. Moreover, to ensure that these mistakes would not be repeated, Congress passed a series of neutrality acts that prohibited selling arms or extending credit to nations at war, warned U.S. citizens not to travel into war zones, and allowed nonmilitary goods to be exchanged with belligerent nations only on a cash-and-carry basis that effectively prohibited U.S. ships from entering war zones. The House of Representatives even considered, but narrowly rejected by a 202–200 vote, a constitutional amendment that would require a national referendum to declare war unless a U.S. territory was directly attacked. Depression-era Americans wanted to stay out of war at almost any price. Even as international troubles flared across the Atlantic and in the Pacific, in the heartland of America the sentiment for an isolationist foreign policy remained resiliently strong. Only an unforeseen and shocking attack on the United States would change this deep-rooted passion to stay out of the world's problems.

CHAPTER 11

THE DAY OF INFAMY

December 7, 1941

Pearl Harbor and the Transformation of the Modern World

Roosevelt Delivers Message to Congress

(Photoprint by International News, 1941. Prints and Photographs Division, Library of Congress, LC-USZ62–78575. http://hdl.loc.gov/loc.pnp/cph.3b25662)

TIME LINE

1933–41 The Good Neighbor policy improves relations between the United States and Latin America

1938 Adolf Hitler and Neville Chamberlain agree to the Munich Pact

1939 Germany invades Poland; World War II begins

1940 Franklin Roosevelt defeats Wendell Willkie to win an unprecedented third term as president

1941 The United States extends lend-lease aid to Britain and the Soviet Union

Japan attacks the United States at Pearl Harbor; the United States enters World War II

1944 On D-day, the Allies strike at Germany; France is liberated

Roosevelt defeats Thomas Dewey; Harry Truman is elected vice president

1945 Roosevelt dies; Truman becomes president

V-E, UN, Potsdam, *Enola Gay,* and V-J become household words as World War II ends

1946 U.S. inflation rates exceed 30 percent

1947 The Truman Doctrine announces the beginning of the Cold War

The Marshall Plan seeks to rebuild western Europe

1948 Truman defeats Dewey to win reelection

1949 NATO is created to contain communism in Europe

1950 The Korean conflict begins

Senator Joseph McCarthy charges that communists have infiltrated the U.S. State Department

1952 Dwight Eisenhower defeats Adlai Stevenson to win the presidency

1953 The Korean conflict ends

1954 *Brown v. Board of Education* overturns the "separate but equal" doctrine

1956 In the Suez crisis, Eisenhower forces the withdrawal of Britain, France, and Israel from Egypt

Eisenhower wins a second victory over Stevenson

1957 The Soviets launch *Sputnik* into orbit

1960 The Cold War takes center stage in the Kennedy-Nixon debates

I t was much like any other Sunday. In New York City, concertgoers filled Carnegie Hall for an afternoon concert by the Philharmonic Orchestra. The program began with a mild show of patriotism. The orchestra played "The Star Spangled Banner" and most attendees hummed along to the familiar tune or ignored it completely, waiting for Artur Rodzinski to lead his musicians in the main event—including the Shostakovich Symphony No. 1 and the Brahms Piano Concerto No. 2 with Arthur Rubinstein at the piano.

Those attending the concert were typical Americans. They preferred diversion over concern about the raging disturbances in Europe and the Far East. After all, America stood isolated, protected by vast oceans east and west, like an island in the middle of a placid stream. Few realized that the storm emerging in the East soon would devastate the American sense of tranquility.

From the late 1930s to the early 1940s, most Americans watched the progress of the conflicts in Europe and the Far East with detached concern. They were not interested in joining the fight. Wilson's "war to end all wars" had not ended war, and Americans were skeptical about participating in another European conflict. Even the Nazi invasion of Poland in 1939 and Japan's takeover of northern French Indochina in 1940 failed to significantly change America's isolationist mind-set. Polls in the early 1940s showed that 80 percent of Americans opposed any American involvement in the war. Only a minority believed that American pacifism would encourage more aggression. These Americans were not ignorant of their history nor apathetic about current events. To the contrary, these peace activists protested aggressively in American streets, giving passionate support to well-known politicians and celebrities like Congressman Hamilton Fish, journalist John T. Flynn, industrialist Henry Ford, senators Gerald Nye, Arthur Vandenberg, and Burton Wheeler, and aviator Charles Lindbergh. These powerful men spoke out against any American participation in the conflict. In fact, the America First Committee, the most prominent antiwar organization in the country, boasted of 800,000 members. When Congress debated neutering the neutrality acts, an America First poster encouraged its members to remain vigilant:

The Fight Against Foreign War Has Just Begun!
The vote on neutrality revision was the
closest on any war legislation yet.
There is still time to keep out—IF you do your part by joining
AMERICA FIRST.

The End of Isolationism

As troubles escalated between Japan and China in the Far East and as the Nazi machine began to roll across Europe, however, more and more Americans began to question the isolationist hard line. As early as October 1937, President Franklin Roosevelt attempted to nudge the public out of its isolationist posture when he compared Japan's expansion into China with the spread of a disease. "When an epidemic of physical disease starts to spread," he warned, "the community approves and joins in a quarantine of the patients in order to protect the health of the community against the spread of disease. . . . There must be positive endeavors to preserve peace."

Over the next two years, world conditions deteriorated rapidly. In 1938, Germany under Adolf Hitler annexed Austria, and after a meeting in Munich with Britain's prime minister, Neville Chamberlain, Germany received Britain's blessing to annex portions of Czechoslovakia, so long as it promised to guarantee civil rights to the Czech minorities and not to demand any more territories. Hitler, however, kept this promise less than half a year. In spring 1939, Hitler annexed the rest of Czechoslovakia while his Axis partner, Benito Mussolini of Italy, invaded Albania.

Following these developments, Roosevelt again urged the public to awake from its isolationist slumber. In a radio address to the nation, he stated,

> It is easy for you and me to shrug our shoulders and say that conflicts taking place thousands of miles from the continental United States, and, indeed, the whole American hemisphere, do not seriously affect the Americas—and that all the United States has to do is to ignore them and go about our own business. Passionately though we may desire detachment, we are forced to realize that every word that comes through the air, every ship that sails the sea, every battle that is fought does affect the American future. . . . This nation will remain a neutral nation, but I cannot ask that every American remain neutral in thought as well. Even a neutral has a right to take account of facts. Even a neutral cannot be asked to close his mind or his conscience.

Slowly, even former isolationists softened their rhetoric. After Hitler invaded Poland in September 1939, Congress revised the neutrality acts to allow nations at war to purchase American arms on a cash-and-carry basis. Then, in 1940, when Denmark, Norway, the Netherlands, Belgium, and France fell to the Nazi onslaught, Roosevelt asked Congress for the nation's first peacetime draft. Equally important, following his victory over Republican Wendell Willkie in the election of 1940, the nation's only third-term president urged Congress to offer assistance to Britain with a lend-lease program that provided ships, aircraft, arms, and other support. By the end of this program in 1946, the United States would funnel over $50 billion ($400 billion in today's currency) to Allied nations in lend-lease aid.

Learning lessons from the political mistakes of President Wilson, Roosevelt formed a coalition government by adding two Republican interventionists to his cabinet: Secretary of War Henry Stimson and Secretary of the Navy Frank

Knox. Like Wilson, however, Roosevelt defended intervention by enunciating to the nation a vision for a better world, a future world that would grant to all peoples the four great freedoms—freedom of speech and expression, freedom of worship, freedom from want, and freedom from fear. By early 1941, convoys of American ships were carrying arms to Britain with the U.S. Navy providing protection.

In response, America First continued to passionately advocate neutrality. In a highly publicized speech in New York City on April 23, 1941, aviator-hero Charles Lindbergh stated,

> Over a hundred million people in this nation are opposed to entering this war. If the principles of democracy mean anything at all, that is reason enough for us to stay out. If we are forced into a war against the wishes of an overwhelming majority of our people, we will have proved democracy such a failure at home that there will be little use to fight for it abroad.

Such words, however, could not arrest America's drift toward war. In June 1941, Germany invaded the Soviet Union. Friends of Britain could only tremble at what would happen if the huge resources of the Soviet Union fell into Hitler's hands. Two months later Roosevelt agreed to a secret rendezvous with Britain's new prime minister, Winston Churchill. Telling the nation that he was going on a fishing trip, Roosevelt boarded his presidential yacht, but out at sea he was transferred to the battleship *Augusta* and taken to secluded Argentia Bay in Newfoundland. There he met privately with Churchill, who begged the president to extend lend-lease aid to the Soviet Union. Roosevelt agreed to solicit Congress for this aid. Before departing, the two leaders signed the Atlantic Charter, a brief statement of shared postwar goals: no territorial gains, self-determination, freedom from want and fear, freedom of the seas, and national disarmament. Later, in September 1941, after a German attack on the U.S. destroyer *Greer,* Roosevelt ordered the navy to shoot on sight any German submarine. The Germans reciprocated. On October 30, the German navy sank the USS *Reuben James,* taking the lives of a hundred sailors in the first American warship sunk in the war.

To complicate matters, by the fall of 1940, Germany, Italy, and Japan signed the Tripartite Pact, forming the Berlin-Rome-Tokyo military Axis. This pact stated that an attack by any other power (except the USSR) against one of the three Axis nations would be considered an attack against all. This partnership encouraged Japan to flex its military muscles and gain dominance over French and Dutch interests in the Pacific. After Japan signed a neutrality treaty with the Soviet Union in 1941, the only countries that stood between Japan and a complete Japanese domination of the Pacific were Great Britain and the United States. Suddenly, the U.S. territories of Hawaii, the Philippines, Samoa, Guam, and Wake stood in the way of Japanese supremacy of the region.

Japanese interest in taking control of the Pacific, including American territory, had been evident since the late 1930s. In 1938, a U.S. War Department survey reported that if the Japanese attacked the Pacific Fleet it would be done without warning and "there can be little doubt that the Hawaiian Islands will be the initial scene of action." In January 1941, Navy Secretary Knox wrote, "If war eventuates with Japan, it is believed easily possible that hostilities would be initiated by a surprise attack upon the Fleet or the Naval Base at Pearl Harbor."

These comments, however, were buried among thousands of pages of foreign policy documents and received little attention. The Pentagon gave little credence to the threat of a surprise attack since the Army Signal Corps had cracked the complex Japanese "purple code" and Army intelligence had intercepted and translated a number of Japanese transmissions (nicknamed Magic) between Tokyo and emissaries in Washington. Although these messages indicated growing tensions between the United States and Japan as well as Japan's interest in Southeast Asia, they never mentioned any specific attack on Pearl Harbor. Ironically, America's success in breaking this code may have backfired since most of the U.S. government decision makers believed that the messages did not indicate a specific and immediate Japanese threat.

Thus, on Saturday, December 6, 1941, unaware of any imminent danger, U.S. sailors in Hawaii celebrated in the holiday spirit. Multicolored Christmas lights decorated Fort Street in Honolulu and store windows brimmed with toys and cheerful holiday displays. Twenty-four thousand fans attended a football game between the University of Hawaii and Willamette. The Rainbows clobbered the Willamette Bearcats by a score of 20–6. That evening navy officers and wives attended a black-tie dance at the Fort Debussy Officer's Club on Waikiki beach. Sailors on leave walked the streets of Honolulu and some attended a local battle of the bands. The band from the USS *Pennsylvania* prevailed. The balmy, easygoing evening ended quietly and in peace.

The next morning at 7:55, boatswains piped whistles on the small ships in the harbor, buglers sounded colors on the larger ships, and American flags were hoisted at the stern of each vessel. During the ceremony, the noise of airplanes could be heard across the sky. In complete surprise, the first wave of 183 Japanese torpedo planes made its run from the northwest to the big ships lying in neat rows in the harbor. Most sailors initially thought the activity was another drill. But the grim truth quickly became evident. Wave after wave of Japanese planes swept across the battleships in the harbor. A bomb hit the *Raleigh* and it listed to port. Sailors jumped to their turrets to fire on the Japanese planes, but there were too many. The target ship *Utah* took several torpedoes. Another torpedo exploded between the minelayer *Oglala* and the cruiser *Helena*, damaging both. The *Arizona* took hits from eight bombs and torpedoes. At 8:10 one of the bombs exploded in *Arizona*'s forward magazine, causing the ship to burst into a ball of fire.

It sank so quickly that many crewmen were unable to escape being trapped in the hull of the sinking ship. Three torpedoes cut holes in the side of the *Oklahoma.* As it sank, its port bilge struck the harbor bottom and it rolled almost completely over. Its crew scrambled onto the nearby *Maryland* just before two bombs pounded into its deck. The *West Virginia,* the *Tennessee,* the *California,* and the *Pennsylvania* took numerous hits, along with many other smaller ships.

On the land, U.S. airplanes, which were lined up wing to wing along the runways at Kaneohe and Ewa, were destroyed before they could take off. Several hundred men were killed in their barracks as bombers scored direct hits.

When the Japanese fighters finally disappeared from the sky about 10:00 AM, the American forces were decimated. Of the ninety ships in harbor, twenty-one were sunk or damaged. A total of 188 aircraft were destroyed and 159 damaged. American dead numbered 2,403, including sixty-eight civilians. A total of 1,178 military personnel and civilians were wounded.

Numerous stories record the bravery of the American sailors during the attack. One memorable hero of the day was Doris ("Dorie") Miller, an African-American from Waco, Texas, serving aboard the *West Virginia* as the ship's cook. When he heard the alarm for general quarters, he rushed up to the deck and helped several wounded sailors to safety, including the ship's captain. He then manned a .50-caliber Browning antiaircraft gun (which he had never been trained to use), and as his ship roared in flames and confusion surrounded him, he fired at the oncoming Japanese aircraft until he heard the call to abandon ship. He describes the moment: "It wasn't hard. I just pulled the trigger and she worked fine. I had watched the others with these guns. I guess I fired her for about fifteen minutes. I think I got one of those Jap planes. They were diving pretty close to us."*

On that same Sunday at the New York Polo Grounds, a record-breaking 55,051 spectators watched the last regular game of the National Football League season as the New York Giants suited up against their crosstown rivals, the Brooklyn Dodgers. (Yes, there was a football team named the Brooklyn Dodgers.) Around 2:00 PM a public address announcement paging Colonel William J. Donovan to the phone interrupted the buoyant game-day atmosphere. A few minutes later an ominous announcement instructed all navy men in the audience to report to their posts immediately. Those listening to the game on WOR radio at 2:26 heard the game announcer describe a Ward Cuff kickoff return to his twenty-seven-yard line. Following that play,

---

*Admiral Chester W. Nimitz personally presented Doris Miller with the Navy Cross in May 1942. Miller died in action in 1943, and in 1973 the USS *Miller,* a *Knox*-class frigate, was commissioned in his honor.

another voice broke in with an announcement that crackled over the airwaves: the Japanese had attacked Pearl Harbor.

At Carnegie Hall, announcer Warren Sweeny stepped out onstage and informed the audience about the attack. The relaxed mood of the concertgoers changed immediately. The orchestra played "The Star Spangled Banner" and this time the concertgoers stood up and sang the words to the national anthem with intensified fervor that most had never experienced before.

Across the United States, people from all walks of life marked the moment they heard about the attack on Pearl Harbor. Immediately, they realized that a historical and nation-defining event had occurred. Vocal isolationists changed their minds immediately. They called for Americans to stand united against Japan. Newspapers called for quick and decisive action. In living rooms, cafés, stores, train depots, and workplaces, radios tuned to the news, and everyone waited for the reaction from the White House. The *Wall Street Journal* reported, "The things that business and finance discussed last week seem now to have no relation to tomorrow nor to the many days to come after tomorrow. . . . There is no division among us in regard to that one purpose for which we accept the war that has been forced upon us." Senator Gerald Nye, a prominent member of the pacifist America First Committee, reflected on the new mood of the nation:

> It is not time to quibble over what might have been done or how we got where we are. We know only that the enemy chose to make war against us. To give our Commander in Chief unqualified and unprejudiced backing in his prosecution of the war is an obligation which I shall gladly fulfill. Differences over matters of foreign policy up to this hour are abandoned and unity shall be accorded in every particular.

Less than twenty-four hours after the raid, President Roosevelt arrived solemn-faced at the south entrance to the Capitol. Senators and congressmen filed into the House chamber to hear the president's message, Democrats and Republicans arm in arm in a show of unanimity. Members of the Supreme Court arrived along with military leaders, including General George C. Marshall and Admiral Harold R. Stark. First lady Eleanor Roosevelt and former first lady Edith Wilson also attended. After a brief introduction from Speaker Samuel Rayburn, President Roosevelt stood at the podium, opened a black loose-leaf notebook, and spoke.

> Yesterday, December 7, 1941—a date which will live in infamy—the United States of America was suddenly and deliberately attacked by the naval and air forces of the Empire of Japan. . . . The attack yesterday on the Hawaiian Islands has caused severe damage to American naval and

military forces. Very many American lives have been lost. . . . I ask that Congress declare that since the unprovoked attack by Japan on Sunday December 7, a state of war has existed between the United States and the Japanese Empire.

Radio carried President Roosevelt's speech across America, and in the six minutes it took him to deliver it, Americans became keenly aware that the debris of disillusionment that had slowed America's involvement in world affairs since the aftermath of the first Great War had been swept away by the rising tide of World War II. The Japanese invasion of Pearl Harbor "woke the sleeping giant,"* silenced influential pacifists, and instantly shifted American thought from that of a neutral country to one fully committed to defeating the Axis powers.

Dr. New Deal Gives Way to Dr. Win the War

After war with Japan erupted, Germany and Italy declared war on the United States under the terms of the Tripartite Pact. Without debate, the United States reciprocated. In the U.S. declarations of war against Japan, Germany, and Italy, only one dissenting vote was cast—that of Republican pacifist Jeannette Rankin, who also had voted against the U.S. entry into World War I.

In the months that immediately followed U.S. entry into World War II, the Allied outlook for victory looked bleak. In Europe, the Axis powers controlled virtually the entire continent from Norway to Greece. They had conquered Ukraine and were threatening to take the oil fields in the Caucasus. In Africa, they occupied Libya and pushed the British into Egypt, threatening the Suez Canal. In Asia, after hitting Pearl Harbor, the Japanese conquered Malaysia and the rich oil fields of the Dutch East Indies, forced an American surrender at Corregidor, and pushed the British back in Burma and New Guinea. Two years would pass before the Allies would halt Axis expansion into Europe and Asia. Stopping the Axis expansion was an important first step, but before peace could be contemplated, the Allies still had to liberate the conquered territories and defeat the Axis powers on their home soils.

A huge advantage for the Allies was their ability to stand as a largely united front against the Axis powers. Unlike Germany and Japan, who each fought

---

*The source of this phrase was not an American, but rather Japanese admiral Isoroku Yamamoto. After the attack on Pearl Harbor, Yamamoto said, "I fear all we have done is to awaken a sleeping giant and filled him with a terrible resolve."

a separate war without efforts at cooperation, as early as January 1942 the United States and twenty-five other Allied powers signed the United Nations Declaration, pledging to embrace the principles in the Atlantic Charter and to fight together until the Axis powers were defeated. This solidarity was in part a dividend of Roosevelt's "Good Neighbor" policy, launched in the early 1930s to restore trust between the United States and other nations. To break the "big stick" image that had been associated with U.S. foreign policy since the times of Theodore Roosevelt, Franklin Roosevelt permitted the United States at the 1933 Pan American Conference to repudiate the Roosevelt Corollary to the Monroe Doctrine by acknowledging that "no state has the right to intervene in the internal affairs of another." Shortly thereafter, he agreed to abrogate the Platt Amendment that was so hated by Cuba, to modify the Hay-Buneau-Varilla Treaty in ways that gave Panama more commercial rights over the Canal Zone, and to withdraw the U.S. troops that had occupied Haiti since 1915. Good Neighbor actions also took place farther from home. Early in his first administration Roosevelt granted recognition to the Soviet Union (1933), signed the Tydings-McDuffie Act (1934), which promised to grant independence to the Philippines within ten years, and used his discretionary presidential powers to reduce tariffs with twenty-one nations. The decade he spent mending fences deposited goodwill in the bank of trust that America would be able to draw upon during the crisis of World War II.

Of course, the strain of war produced some tensions between the Allied partners. The Allied agreement to defeat Hitler first, for instance, antagonized the Chinese, who preferred an anti-Japan initial strategy. Also, the Soviets were displeased that the United States and Britain delayed launching a second front against Germany from the west that would relieve the Soviet armies on the eastern front. Roosevelt promised the Soviets he would open a second front as soon as possible, and was prepared to do so after the Allied victories in North Africa. At a summit meeting in Casablanca early in 1943, however, Churchill urged Roosevelt to delay the direct attack on Germany until Italy was decapitated. Roosevelt agreed. Churchill then informed Stalin that there were two ways to kill a crocodile—hit it in the snout or kick it in the under-belly. By focusing next on the defeat of Italy, Churchill said the Allies would be assisting the Soviets by kicking the Axis beast in the belly. Stalin reacted coolly to this news, believing that the Western democracies were purposefully delaying the invasion of Germany in order to bleed the Soviets dry. The wartime rift between Stalin and the West would never fully heal.

Finally, after the successful Italian campaign of 1943–1944, the Allies were ready for the long awaited second front. On D-day, June 6, 1944, the Allies hit a sixty-mile shoreline along the coast of Normandy with a force of 176,000 troops landed by 4,000 invasion craft and supported by 600 warships and 11,000 planes. This invasion, under the united command of General Dwight Eisenhower, was the largest amphibious operation in human history. Fighting was intense and the number of casualties immense, but within a month the Allies had landed a million soldiers and more than 500,000 tons of military supplies on the western front. By the end of the summer, France, Belgium, and Luxembourg were liberated, Bulgaria had surrendered, and Allied forces had entered Germany. In December 1944, a last-ditch German counteroffensive known as the Battle of the Bulge temporarily slowed the Allied progress, but by early 1945, victory in Europe could be seen as a glimmer of light flickering at the end of a long tunnel.

The previous November Roosevelt had defeated Republican Thomas Dewey in the election of 1944. Although it was the closest of Roosevelt's four presidential victories, the aging incumbent, looking older than his sixty-three years, still worked his magic, carrying nearly 54 percent of the popular vote and winning thirty-six of the forty-eight states. An important footnote to this election was the elevation of Harry Truman to the vice presidency. At the Democratic convention, conservative Democrats had maneuvered to replace the ultraprogressive vice president, Henry Wallace, with the more conservative Senator Truman of Missouri. While largely unnoted at the time, this decision would prove to be of epoch-changing importance.

As the Allied war in Europe progressed toward its victorious ending, Roosevelt traveled to Yalta in the Crimea to meet in summit with Churchill and Stalin. At Yalta, the president secured from Stalin two key promises: to join the war against Japan within ninety days after victory in Europe and to support an upcoming conference in San Francisco to create a charter for a new world organization, the United Nations (UN). In return, the United States and Britain agreed to accept the Lublin Polish government (installed by the Soviets after the Red Army liberated Poland) as the de facto government of Poland until "free elections" could take place after the war. In time, many Americans would criticize this concession, saying that the Yalta agreement essentially secured Poland's future as a communist state. Roosevelt's defenders would counter that this concession simply recognized the fact that the Red Army occupied Poland and had no intention of leaving voluntarily.

After returning from Yalta, Roosevelt appeared before a joint session of Congress on March 1, 1945. In this address, Roosevelt opened with an apology: "I hope that you will pardon me for the unusual posture of sitting down. It makes it a lot easier for me not having to carry about ten pounds of steel around the bottom on my legs." These were unusual words to come from a man who had spent the last twenty-four years trying to hide his physical handicap. They were also a telltale sign of what was to come. The president's health was deteriorating. Hoping to regain his strength, Roosevelt retreated to his Little White House in Warm Springs, Georgia, to recuperate as he had done on numerous former occasions. On Thursday, April 12, the president sat for a portrait that was commissioned by his lifelong friend, Lucy Mercer. About 1 PM, as the butler was serving lunch, the president gripped his head with his left hand and said, "I have a terrible headache." These would be his final words. At 3:35 PM, his physician, who had accompanied him to Warm Springs, pronounced his death.

Two hours later, Vice President Truman, summoned to the White House, was told by Eleanor Roosevelt that the president was dead. Truman asked if there was anything he could do for her. Knowing the tremendous responsibility of the office, the first lady replied, "Is there anything we can do for you?" At 7:09 that evening, Truman stood before the assembled cabinet and his wife and daughter to take the presidential oath, administered by Chief Justice Harlan Stone. After swearing the oath, Truman turned to reporters and said in his high-pitched, midwestern twang, "Boys, if you ever pray, pray for me now."

The Buck Stops Here: The Presidency of Harry S. Truman

One can only speculate about what flashed across Truman's mind during the next several days as he witnessed the great outpouring of sympathy for the fallen American hero. An editorial in the *New York Times* captured the sentiment of millions:

> Men will thank God on their knees a hundred years from now that Franklin D. Roosevelt was in the White House. It was his hand, more than that of any other single man that built the great coalition of the United Nations. It was his leadership which inspired free men in every part of the world to fight with greater hope and courage. Gone is the fresh and spontaneous interest which this man took, as naturally as he breathed air, in the trouble and the hardships and the disappointments and the hopes of little men and humble people.

Similar reactions were expressed around the world. When Churchill learned of Roosevelt's death, he said he felt as if he had been "struck a physical blow," and he wept as he delivered the news to the House of Commons. Even Stalin was saddened, and he allowed Roosevelt's picture and story to appear on the front pages of Soviet newspapers, a space normally reserved for national stories. To Allied soldiers and civilians at home and abroad, life without Roosevelt seemed almost inconceivable. The unanswered question on the minds of millions was whether the diminutive former Kansas clothes salesman without a college degree and with only eighty-two days of vice presidential experience would be able to adequately fill the void left by the giant who had occupied the Oval Office for more than twelve years.

Ready or not, it was Truman's hour. Fortunately, since the issues confronting the world gave him little time to grow into the job, he was a quick study.

Just two weeks into the office, Truman addressed by telephone the delegates from nearly fifty nations that had gathered at San Francisco to draft the Charter of the United Nations. When their work was done, the charter provided for six major organs: (1) the General Assembly of all member nations, each with a single vote, (2) the Security Council of eleven members, of which five seats would be permanently held by the Big Five (United States, Britain, Soviet Union, France, and China), (3) the Economic and Social Council to deal with issues of human welfare and freedoms, (4) an International Court of Justice to deal with legal disputes, (5) the Trusteeship Council to administer trust territories, and (6) the Secretariat to perform the routine administration work. The late President Wilson's dream was finally a reality.

Even as the UN was being birthed, the Allied world celebrated as the Axis powers in Europe collapsed with a whimper. On April 28, Mussolini was captured and killed by Italian partisans as he tried to flee into Switzerland. Several days later the provisional German government announced Hitler's death, an alleged suicide. On May 2, Berlin fell and the German troops in Italy surrendered. Then on May 8, Victory in Europe (V-E) Day, Germany's unconditional surrender was formally ratified.

The war, however, was not over. As the United States geared up for a massive assault against Japan, an invasion that was expected to take another 100,000 American lives, Truman traveled to Potsdam, a suburb of Berlin, for his first summit with the leaders of Britain and the USSR. The cast at the Potsdam summit (July 17–August 2) differed significantly from that at the Yalta Conference just five months earlier. Truman now represented the United States, and Clement R. Attlee, elected prime minister during the conference, replaced Churchill as Britain's representative. Of the Big Three at Yalta, only Stalin of the USSR remained. Critical decisions about the structure of postwar Europe were hashed out at Potsdam, although signs of discord between Stalin and the West also appeared. The Allied leaders agreed that Germany would be temporarily divided, with each nation taking reparations largely from its own occupation zone. This solution would make possible the future division of Germany. While at Potsdam, the Allies also sent an ultimatum to Japan, demanding an immediate, unconditional surrender. Otherwise, according to this Potsdam Declaration, Japan "would lay herself open to complete and utter destruction."

This threat was no bluff. On July 16 in the desert near Los Alamos, New Mexico, American scientists, some of whom, ironically, had fled from the Axis dictatorships, had demonstrated the massive power that could be released by breaking an atom. Work on the creation of an atomic weapon had been launched with President Roosevelt's approval in early 1940; the Manhattan Project remained so secret that even Truman was not informed of it until he assumed the office of the presidency. Five years and $2 billion dollars ($25 billion in today's currency) later, Truman now had the weapon of mass destruction in his hands, and the only question that remained was whether he would use it. An advisory Interim Committee created by Truman and chaired by Secretary of War Henry Stimson recommended to the president that the bomb be used without warning as soon as it was available. However, a number of Manhattan Project scientists urged Truman not to use the weapon on Japan, arguing that the naval blockade coupled with conventional weapons would soon force Japan into surrendering. Still others advised a third option: before using the bomb on a live target, America should first demonstrate to Japan and to the world the potency of the new weapon on an uninhabited island. After hearing all the arguments, Truman made his decision. To save American lives and to end the war quickly, if Japan did not respond to the surrender ultimatum, the bomb would be used, depending on weather conditions, on one of four selected cities previously untouched by the war.

On August 6, a lone American bomber, the *Enola Gay,* released a single atomic bomb above the military base city of Hiroshima. Moments later, 4.4 square miles of the city were incinerated. More than 100,000 people would die, and tens of thousands of others would be wounded. Two days later, precisely ninety days after V-E Day, the Soviets, as promised, declared war on Japan and began speeding their armies into Manchuria and Korea. The more territory the Red Army could control at the time of the Japanese surrender, the more bargaining power Stalin would have in determining the ultimate division of Japan's holdings. Before getting word of the success of the Manhattan Project, the United States had wanted Soviet help against Japan, but now this help was viewed as more a liability than an asset. From Truman's perspective, the war needed to be ended immediately. On August 9, a second bomb was dropped on the naval base city of Nagasaki, taking another 80,000 lives. The following day, Tokyo sued for peace on one condition: Hirohito, the "Son of Heaven" believed to be the descendant of the sun goddess Amaterasu, would be allowed to maintain his religious title as emperor. Despite the unconditional surrender policy, on August 14, Victory over Japan (V-J) Day, the Allies accepted the conditional offer. Three weeks later, on September 2, the formal surrender ceremonies were held aboard the battleship *Missouri* in Tokyo Bay. After the papers had been signed, General Douglas MacArthur set the tone for the new postwar atomic age with the prophetic warning: "We have had our last chance. If we do not devise some greater and more equitable system, Armageddon will be at our door."

World War II was a total war. Sixty-one nations representing 1.7 billion people spent $1 trillion dollars and mobilized 110 million soldiers to wage a war that claimed 55 million lives, including 30 million civilians. Proportionately, the United States contributed more in dollars than in blood, spending about $341 billion ($3.4 trillion in today's currency), which was more than any other nation, and sacrificing 400,000 American lives, less than 1 percent of the total human loss. The Soviet Union, in comparison, lost over 20 million lives in the war effort. The costs of the war were great, but so were its immediate benefits and long-term consequences. At home, the war ended the Great Depression, restored full employment, brought millions of women and minorities into the labor force, and raised family incomes by 25 percent. The mobilization efforts and wartime taxes also expanded the scope and authority of the federal government and the executive branch and redistributed wealth from America's upper to its middle classes. Internationally, the war demonstrated the will of the world to unite against bully nations that resorted even to ethnic genocide in order to achieve their expansionist agendas. The war shattered the illusion that the United States could stand aloof from world affairs without suffering devastating consequences, and it also brought the United States into the UN. For better or worse, postwar America would become involved in all parts of an altered world that would be dominated by only two surviving superpowers, the United States and the USSR.

Cold War Politics

Life in the atomic age would not be easy. The year 1946 was difficult for many Americans, particularly for President Truman. Nearly 5 million American workers, most of whom had pledged not to strike for the duration of the war, walked off their jobs, demanding higher wages. Meanwhile, inflation soared over 30 percent in a single year as rationing and the wartime price controls were lifted. In eastern Europe, a paranoid Stalin, unable to rid his mind of the two devastating invasions into Russia during the last generation, insisted on creating a sphere of friendly communist regimes to protect his borders. One by one, the coalition governments in Poland, Hungary, Romania, and Bulgaria became communist satellites as Stalin erected what Churchill would call an "iron curtain" across eastern Europe. American voters assessed the sad state of current affairs by electing in 1946 solid Republican majorities in both the House and the Senate.

By 1947, whatever goodwill that had existed between the United States and the Soviet Union during the war had been depleted, and the two nations entered into a state of mutual hostility and distrust that became known as the Cold War. Truman's principal foreign policy objective for the remainder of his presidency would be to "contain" the expansion of communism around the world. To achieve this goal, Truman advocated

- the Truman Doctrine (1947), which sent $400 million ($3.3 billion in today's currency) in aid to Turkey and Greece to fight communist insurgents
- the Marshall Plan (1947), which ultimately funneled $13 billion ($107 billion in today's currency) to rebuild western Europe
- an airlift of supplies to Berlin (1948) to prevent this island within Soviet-controlled East Germany from falling into communist hands

- the creation of the North Atlantic Treaty Organization (NATO) (1949), which integrated the defenses of signatory nations and declared that an attack against one nation would be construed as an attack against all
- UN Security Council resolution (1950) that would send troops from multiple nations into Korea "to restore international peace and security in the area"

Truman's get-tough-with-the-Soviets containment policy was not supported by everyone, not even all Democrats. In the election of 1948, Truman supported containment in foreign affairs and a progressive agenda that included significant civil rights reform in domestic affairs. Believing that Truman's confrontational tone with Stalin would lead to World War III, former vice president Henry Wallace broke from the Democratic Party to run for president as the Progressive Party candidate. Also challenging Truman in the election was South Carolina governor Strom Thurmond, a former Democrat who demonstrated his hostility to the party's civil rights agenda by running for the office himself as a Dixiecrat. With Truman being simultaneously attacked from the right and the left by former Democrats, most Americans assumed that the Republican Thomas Dewey would win easily. The nation was stunned, however, when the final votes came in showing Truman the victor. Democrats across the nation also ran strong as the president's party regained a narrow control of both houses of Congress.

Notwithstanding the Democratic victory, little of Truman's progressive program, known as the Fair Deal, ever became law. Even four score and seven years after Lincoln reminded the nation that it was "conceived in liberty and dedicated to the proposition that all men are created equal," the legislative efforts to secure these liberties for American minorities died by filibuster on the Senate floor. Truman achieved some reforms, like integrating the military by executive order, but by and large the civil rights movement was unable to gain much traction during the Truman years because Americans were more concerned with issues of security than liberty.

On President Lincoln's birthday in 1950, just a few weeks after a former State Department official, Alger Hiss, was convicted for perjury in denying that he had passed government secrets to a communist agent, Republican senator Joseph McCarthy told the world that he had a list of 205 names that were "made known to the secretary of state as being members of the communist party and who nevertheless are still working and shaping policy in the State Department." These charges never would be substantiated, but for the next four years McCarthy, always more feared than respected, led a witch hunt against alleged communist infiltrators. McCarthyism fueled domestic and racial intolerance and destroyed the careers of many innocent people, but it also convinced the American public that Truman's containment policies had not eliminated the communist threat at home or abroad.

The military stalemate in Korea also did not help the president's popularity. During the early months of the Korean conflict, UN forces pushed the North Koreans back to the thirty-eighth parallel, the preinvasion boundary that separated the communist north from the anticommunist south. Encouraged by this early, relatively easy success against the North Koreans, the UN decided to use the occasion to unify Korea. The prospects for a quick UN victory evaporated, however, when China, which had become a communist state in 1949, began to send troops to aid its North Korean neighbors. Some Americans, like General Douglas MacArthur, wanted to expand the war into China, using tactical nuclear weapons in the process. General Omar Bradley, the chair of the Joint Chiefs of Staff, argued that such an action was risky and would involve the United States in "a wrong war at the wrong place and against a wrong enemy." Following Bradley's advice, Truman refused to take the war into China and ultimately fired MacArthur for publicly criticizing his decisions. The sacking of MacArthur and the stalemate of UN actions in Korea drained Truman's popularity. Thus, in 1952, the wearied president, frustrated by his inability to get his Fair Deal initiatives through Congress, by two years of disappointing military stalemate in Korea, and by opinion polls showing only 26 percent public support, announced that he would not seek reelection.

Liking Ike in the Happy Days of Death Valley

In March 1952, *Death Valley Days* appeared for the first time on the television airwaves. This thirty-minute program would be watched weekly for the next twenty-three years. Stanley Andrews, the "old Ranger," hosted the program for eleven years, until he was replaced by another celebrity, Ronald Reagan. The show told heroic stories of American adventurers in the Old West who conquered their world through pluck, sweat, ingenuity, and good old-fashioned horse sense. It was a nostalgic look at the past, but it also was an inspirational metaphor for contemporary Americans pursuing their dreams during the treacherous good-versus-evil days of the Cold War.

Thus, in the presidential election of 1952 and again in 1956, it was the good old-fashioned horse-sense Republican Dwight ("Ike") Eisenhower who easily defeated the oratorical Illinois Democrat Adlai Stevenson for the presidency. For most Americans of the 1950s, the beloved and respected hero of World War II was just the doctor the nation needed to cure its ills. Within several months after taking office, Eisenhower secured an armistice in Korea, which ended the fighting but left North and South Korea still divided at the prewar boundary. Americans accepted the armistice, but unlike V-E or V-J, there was little dancing in the streets. For most, the price of the conflict was excessively high for its modest outcomes. Among the sixteen UN nations that fought the war (South Korea was not a UN nation), the United States contributed the most, both in dollars, $54 billion ($370 billion in today's currency), and in blood, 157,000 casualties, including nearly 34,000 deaths. On the positive side, the Korean conflict did contain communism in Asia and, by strengthening NATO, perhaps contained it in Europe as well. The war also exhibited America's willingness to assume its role as leader of the noncommunist world and demonstrated the ability of the UN to teach aggressor nations that there are consequences to reckless activities. Unlike the former League of Nations, the UN, led by America's power and prestige, refused to roll over and play dead when troublesome times erupted.

After Korea, the Eisenhower administration viewed the air force, not the army or navy, as the best foundation for the defense of the free world. With the development in 1954 of hydrogen bombs that were hundreds of times more powerful than the A-bombs used in World War II, Eisenhower and his advisers believed that the United States could deter aggressors by resting the nation's defense on the threat of massive retaliation against any country that disrupted the peace. Since the Soviets also developed atom (1949), thermonuclear (1954), and hydrogen bombs (1955), the citizens of the Cold War world had to learn to live with the constant threat of a nuclear holocaust. In hindsight, the bomb shelters and civil defense drills of the time evoke smiles of bemusement, but the humor of these activities was lost on the youth of the Cold War generation.

As frightening at it was, living under the threat of nuclear holocaust did carry peace dividends. In 1956, shortly before the U.S. presidential election, Britain, France, and Israel invaded Egypt to prevent Egyptian president Gamal Abdel Nasser from nationalizing and controlling the Suez Canal. To restore peace, Eisenhower acted promptly, first by threatening to suspend U.S. aid to Israel and second by joining the Soviet Union in demanding a cease-fire in the region. After the UN General Assembly voted 64–5 for the cease-fire, Britain, France, and Israel agreed to withdraw, and soon their solders were replaced by UN troops to police the Egyptian frontier. Eisenhower's refusal to overreact effectively instilled the peace by insisting that aggressive actions, even if committed by America's friends, would not be tolerated. In an age in which the world seemed to be only a short fuse away from destruction, even Allies would not be allowed to play with matches. Eisenhower's coolness in this crisis added to his popularity and helped him win reelection by landslide margins. Later, the president announced the Eisenhower Doctrine, which stated that the United States would offer economic aid to anticommunist governments in the Middle East and, if necessary, send American troops to protect Middle East states from communist aggression.

Aside from the intense traumas associated with McCarthyism, the Cold War, and the nuclear arms race, America in the mid-1950s was a relatively quiet place symbolized by white picket fences, motherhood, and apple pie. Most college girls at the time told pollsters they wanted babies, not careers, although they also wanted the phone number of a nearby babysitter. Young men, meanwhile, wanted to find a good job in the suburbs, and live *The Life of Riley*, the title of a popular television sitcom about an airplane riveter who lives comfortably, though not lavishly, in a Los Angeles suburb. The portrayal of this likable yet bungling blue-collar husband and father, always baffled by the latest household consumer gadgets and always getting into trouble when he interferes with household affairs, reinforced the idealistic promises of the good suburban life that were open to hardworking Americans.

Of course, progressive critics at the time insisted that the good life was more fantasy than reality and pushed from the left for civil rights legislation, federal aid to education, free vaccinations for all children, and a government-assisted health program for the elderly. Meanwhile, conservative critics from the right advocated a return to the normalcy of the pre–New Deal days. None of the crusades for change, however, gained much support either from President Eisenhower or from Congress, which before 1959 was evenly split between Republicans and Democrats. Other than the passage of the National Highway Act of 1956 that promised to spend $25 billion ($175 billion in today's currency) to build 41,000 miles of interstate highways—a boon for both business and national security—few major legislative initiatives were launched during the Eisenhower years.

Rather than an innovator or a crusader, Eisenhower is best described as a caretaker president who was content to take care of the programs that he inherited and who resisted pressures, from both the left and the right, to enact dramatic changes. A moderate in an age of moderation, President Eisenhower tried to follow his own advice: "In all those things which deal with people, be liberal, be human. In all those things which deal with people's money, or their economy, or their form of government, be conservative." Democrat Adlai Stevenson responded, "I assume what it means is that you will strongly recommend the building of a great many schools to accommodate the needs of our children, but not provide the money." Another critic of Eisenhower's reluctance to spend federal monies on defense quipped that he hoped future historians would not write that "in the second decade after World War II freedom throughout the world died of a balanced budget." Based upon the results of two elections, however, apparently most Americans of the fifties preferred the ambiguities of Eisenhower's conservative liberalism to any other option.

Ironically, the driving force for change during these years was neither the president nor Congress, but the Supreme Court. In its 1954 *Brown v. Board of Education* decision, the Earl Warren Court stimulated the embryonic civil rights movement by declaring that racially segregating public schools was unconstitutional. Millions of southern conservatives viewed the decision as unwarranted social legislation enacted by an antisouthern Court determined to infringe on the rights of the states. Southern school districts controlled by white politicians used a variety of means to resist the Court's decision, and another fifteen years would pass before many southern public schools would be desegregated. *Brown v. Board of Education*, however, was a historic decision. It did not immediately end legal discrimination, but after it, the days of segregationist Jim Crow laws in the land of the free would be limited.

From Sputnik *to Camelot*

Although true equality had not yet been achieved, by the late 1950s more and more Americans enjoyed a life of material comfort. In 1956, for the first time in history, one half of the American labor force worked in white-collar occupations. During the summer of 1957, 90 million Americans, over half of the population, traveled on out-of-town vacations, spending $2.5 billion in the process. For those who chose not to pay in cash, credit cards such as the Diner's Club became fashionable. One in three women regularly visited beauty shops to have their hair tinted the color of their desire, while men groomed their automobiles, which were growing longer, wider, cushier, shinier, with wider fins and more gadgets each year. Televisions and hi-fi sets filled American living rooms, even as washing machines and dryers were packed into the utility closets of modernized households. To help Americans cope with the stress of life, churches ran ad campaigns: "For a spiritual lift in a busy day, Dial-a-Prayer. Circle 6-4200." For many Americans, the good life was a life of ease that offered ample time for fun, fellowship, faith, and family.

On Saturday morning, October 5, 1957, Americans woke up to disturbing news. At the breakfast table they read a report quoted from the Soviet news agency:

> The first artificial earth satellite in the world has now been created. . . . [and] successfully launched in the U.S.S.R. . . . Artificial earth satellites will pave the way for space travel and it seems that the present generation will witness how the freed and conscious labor of the people of the new socialist society turns even the most daring of man's dreams into reality.

The satellite that the Soviets called *Sputnik*, meaning an object traveling with a traveler (i.e., the earth), was twenty-two inches in diameter and weighed about 185 pounds. The news stunned Americans. One month later, an even more shocking headline appeared. The Soviets announced the launch of *Sputnik II*, a 1,120-pound satellite carrying a live dog, with instruments strapped to its chest, inside an orbiting air-conditioned compartment.

At first the Eisenhower administration sought to downplay these events, saying that the United States was in no race with the Soviets since it had intentionally separated its military-missile and space-missile programs. Soon, however, U.S. scientists argued not only that the separation policy was a mistake, but also that America's progress had been slowed by interservice rivalries and the insistence of the administration to hold down costs. America's current program, they said, was designed only to launch a 21.5-pound satellite, less than one-fiftieth the weight of *Sputnik II*. The success of the sputniks, at the very least, called into question America's claim to technical supremacy over the Soviets.

Alarmed and humiliated, the administration scampered to save face. Within a week after *Sputnik II*, Eisenhower appointed James R. Killian Jr., the president of Massachusetts Institute of Technology, as special assistant to the president for science and technology and ordered that the space satellite program, previously under the charge of the navy, be joined with the army's efforts to develop long-range ballistic missiles. Rushing to demonstrate U.S. ballistic technology, the Defense Department announced that it would launch a satellite on December 4. Tens of thousands of people jammed into Cape Canaveral, Florida, on that day to watch the lift, but the countdown was stopped due to mechanical failure. The foreign press had a field day, calling the American satellite "Flopnik," "Stay-putnik," and "Kaputnik." Even Americans wisecracked, saying it should be called "Civil Servant" since "it won't work and you can't fire it." Two days later the satellite was launched, but seconds into flight it exploded. This time Nikita Khrushchev of the Soviet Union poked fun at the American failures, saying the Soviet sputniks were "lonely" waiting for "American satellites to join them in space."

America's initial space failures, however, launched Congress into action. Soon, U.S. satellites were orbiting the earth, even as Congress doubled the funds for missile development, created the National Aeronautics and Space Administration (NASA), and passed the National Defense Education Act, which provided loans to college students and funds for the development of instructional materials in the sciences, mathematics, and foreign languages. The Soviets may have gotten off to a quick start, but the space race would be a marathon that the Yanks were determined to win.

In the midterm elections of 1958, voters expressed their anxiety over the apparent or real loss of America's technological superiority over the Soviets by throwing out the incumbents and electing the largest Democratic majorities in Congress since Democrats had used Franklin Roosevelt's coattails to sweep them into power in the 1930s. This Democratic victory presaged a more complete change in political power to come.

In 1960, the Democrats nominated John F. Kennedy, the young, vigorous senator from Massachusetts, who shrewdly exploited the national mood of frustration that followed *Sputnik*. Promising, if elected, to pursue long-overdue reforms in civil rights, education, and health care, Kennedy also pledged to lead America to a Cold War victory over the Soviet Union. To do this, he said, America must develop highly effective armed forces with state-of-the-art technologies that would be flexible enough to wage whatever type of war was needed, be it a counterinsurgency war, a conventional war, or a nuclear war.

The Republicans also nominated a renowned anticommunist in Vice President Richard Nixon. During the campaign, for the first time in history, the presidential candidates squared off in a series of televised debates. Kennedy's youthful energy played well on the air, convincing just enough voters to give the Irish Catholic a chance to lead the nation into a "new frontier." When the final votes were in, Kennedy eked out a paper-thin victory, winning the popular vote by only one-fifth of one percent. With the election of this handsome Cold Warrior, nearly three decades younger than the grandfatherly Eisenhower, an ambitious, affluent, yet anxious America turned a corner to enter the age of Camelot.

CHAPTER 12

A NATION MOURNS

November 22, 1963

The Assassination of John F. Kennedy and
the End of American Innocence

John F. Kennedy Motorcade, Dallas, Texas, November 22, 1963

(Photo by Victor Hugo King, 1963. Prints and Photographs Division, Library of Congress, LC-USZ62–134844. 9-29-2006. http://hdl.loc.gov/loc.pnp/cph.3c34844)

TIME LINE

1954	Vietnamese nationalists defeat the French at Dien Bien Phu
1959	Fidel Castro takes power in Cuba
1961	John Kennedy is inaugurated as president
	The United States land anti-Castro Cubans at the Bay of Pigs
	CORE sends freedom riders on buses in the South
1962	The Cuban missile crisis
1963	Martin Luther King Jr. delivers his "I Have a Dream" speech
	John Kennedy is assassinated; Lyndon Johnson becomes president
1964	Congress enacts the Civil Rights Act; the Office of Economic Opportunity is created
	The Gulf of Tonkin Resolution is passed
	Johnson wins a landslide victory over Barry Goldwater
1965	The Medicare and Medicaid programs are established
	Congress enacts the Voting Rights Act; race riots erupt in Watts
1967	Antiwar songs and rallies become widespread
1968	Following the Tet Offensive and the New Hampshire primary, Johnson decides not to seek reelection
	Martin Luther King Jr. and Robert Kennedy are assassinated
	Richard Nixon is elected president
1969	Neil Armstrong walks on the moon
1970	United States invades Cambodia; National Guardsmen kill four students at Kent State
1972	The Watergate break-in; Nixon wins a landslide victory over George McGovern
1773	The Paris Accords result in the withdrawal of U.S. troops from Vietnam
	Senate hearings on Watergate reveal the existence of White House tapes
	Vice President Spiro Agnew resigns
1974	Nixon resigns; Gerald Ford becomes president
1975	North Vietnamese troops take Saigon

When John F. Kennedy took office in 1961, the country overflowed with optimism and expectations for a bright future. After all, despite slow economic growth and rising unemployment during the latter years of the Eisenhower administration, America by world standards was a land of affluence. Sixty percent of American families owned (or paid mortgages on) homesteads, 75 percent owned automobiles, and 87 percent owned TVs. With 6 percent of the world's population, Americans owned half of everything made on the planet. America also had largely recovered from the inferiority complex it briefly experienced following the *Sputnik* launching and once again felt, if not secure, at least confident. True, the nation no longer held a monopoly on atomic technology as it did in 1945, but, it still was the first among equals in the development and delivery of nuclear weaponry. If the Soviets had more powerful missile boosters, this largely was because their cruder and heavier warheads, owing to inferior technology, demanded greater lift than the American counterparts. Moreover, the United States, with its high-flying U-2 spy planes with cameras on board sensitive enough to read license plate numbers on the streets below, could keep a close eye on the intercontinental ballistic missiles (ICBMs) that the Soviets were producing. Both superpowers had enough weapons to destroy the world several times over, but the United States at least could take comfort in knowing that it was not outgunned.

After winning the election, Kennedy came to symbolize the can-do spirit that energized America in the early 1960s. Elected at age forty-two, younger than any man in history, Jack Kennedy, with his elegant and beautiful thirty-one-year-old bride, Jackie, replaced the oldest man ever previously to occupy the White House. Kennedy's family and staff, which included the boyish, thirty-five-year-old attorney general Robert Kennedy, played touch football, not golf. The glamorous style of Jack and Jackie caused such a stir that reporters began to use the Greek word *charisma* to describe the growing Kennedy mystique. Good looks, poise, charm, self-assurance, energy, and intelligence characterized both the president and the first lady. Kennedy's cabinet appointments, labeled by author David Halberstam as the "best and the brightest," also looked sexy when contrasted with the staid businessmen of the Eisenhower administration.

"The world is changing," proclaimed Kennedy in his acceptance speech. "We stand on the edge of a New Frontier . . . of unknown opportunities and perils . . . the New Frontier of which I speak is not a set of promises—it is a set of challenges." At his inauguration, he returned to these same themes of opportunity, optimism, and sacrifice:

> Let the word go forth from this time and place, to friend and foe alike, that the torch has been passed to a new generation of Americans— born in this century, tempered by war, disciplined by a hard and bitter peace, proud of our ancient heritage—and unwilling to witness or

permit the slow undoing of those human rights to which this nation has always been committed. . . . In the long history of the world, only a few generations have been granted the role of defending freedom in its hour of maximum danger. . . . The energy, the faith, the devotion which we bring to this endeavor will light our country and all who serve it—and the glow from that fire can truly light the world. And so, my fellow Americans: ask not what your country can do for you—ask what you can do for your country.

The Legend of Camelot

Just one month after Kennedy's election, a new musical, *Camelot,* opened on Broadway and would run to full houses for 873 performances. Starring Richard Burton as King Arthur, Robert Goulet as Lancelot, and Julie Andrews as Queen Guinevere, the popular show portrayed the legend of King Arthur and his knights of the Round Table in the mythic land of Camelot, where chivalry, truth, honor, and sacrifice reigned. The theme song of the musical, written by Kennedy's Harvard classmate, Alan Lerner, became the unofficial song of the new administration. "Camelot," as the lyrics described, was the ideal place for "happy-ever-aftering," a perfect symbol for an administration that asked the people to deny themselves for the good of their country and to renew their dedication to the cherished principles of the land.

Of course, the Camelot legend elicited visions of utopia, not reality. With his razor-thin victory, the young president had no mandate beyond whatever he could persuade Congress to support. Leading Congress into the New Frontier would be as difficult for Kennedy as leading the Hebrews into Canaan had been for Moses. In the Senate, he often could get his way, but in the House, the power brokers were not the 160 northern Democrats or the 174 Republicans, but the 101 southern Democrats who more often than not made alliances with conservative Republicans to block or dilute any legislation that was tainted with progressive reform. As a result, much of Kennedy's New Frontier came in pieces, often in partial installments.

Sometimes, unusual coalitions stalled the president's initiatives. Shortly after taking office, for instance, Kennedy boldly asked Congress for $5.6 billion ($38 billion in today's currency) in federal aid to education that would build public schools, raise teachers' salaries, and provide scholarships for needy college students. When Roman Catholic bishops demanded that the bill include aid to parochial schools as well, the first Roman Catholic president refused on constitutional grounds. Enough Roman Catholic congressmen joined their conservative colleagues in the House to block the measure. Similarly, Kennedy's plan to provide medical care for the elderly through the Social Security system (Medicare) also was rejected following the intense lobbying of the American Medical Association. His plan to cut corporate and personal taxes in order to encourage greater investment and consumption also never was enacted during his lifetime, this time owing to the foot-dragging of liberals who grumbled that such economic policies sounded more suited for a "third Eisenhower administration."

Kennedy achieved some victories, however, sometimes via legislation and other times through executive orders. Through legislative actions, he increased Social Security benefits and raised the minimum wage to $1.25 per hour ($8.30 per hour in today's currency); secured a housing act that authorized nearly $5 billion ($33 billion in today's currency) in urban renewal projects; financed a space program, ultimately costing $25 billion ($165 billion in today's currency), that would take a man to the moon by the end of the decade; boosted the defense budget by 20 percent in order to provide for the development of Special Forces units like the Green Berets; provided $400 million ($2.7 billion in today's currency) in federal grants to assist "distressed areas" of economic stagnation and high unemployment; and launched the Alliance for Progress economic development program for Latin America that tied aid to social reform. Kennedy also established the Peace Corps by executive order. Under this program, thousands of mostly young men and women traveled to underdeveloped countries to provide technical and educational assistance in health care and agriculture. On a tiny budget, the Peace Corps showcased American idealism and ingenuity, helping America to win over impoverished peoples around the world.

For Camelot to be Camelot, justice had to be universally applied. During the presidential election campaign, Kennedy promised to strive toward this ideal, pledging to use federal power to assure equal opportunities for all races in housing, employment, schools, and public facilities. He also pledged to move toward the elimination of literacy tests and poll taxes that were being used to disenfranchise millions of potential American voters. As president, however, fearing the wrath of the southern Democrats, Kennedy moved slowly in the promotion of civil rights. Rather than initially sending a reform package to Congress, he instead directed his brother, Attorney General Robert Kennedy, to use the powers of the Justice Department to expand efforts to register disenfranchised citizens. Under Robert Kennedy's leadership, in two years the Justice Department increased the number of voting rights suits by 500 percent.

Many civil rights activists, however, were not satisfied with this slow, indirect approach to change. In the summer of 1961, the Congress of Racial Equality (CORE) announced plans to test a recent Supreme Court decision (*Boynton v. Virginia*) that prohibited racial segregation in bus terminals, train stations, and airports. After selecting and training volunteers, CORE sent seven black and six white "freedom riders" on a bus trip across the Deep South, ignoring at each stop the "whites only" signs that were commonly displayed near lunch counters and restrooms. In Alabama, the freedom riders were assaulted. This did not stop the crusade, since new freedom riders volunteered to replace the injured. Although embarrassed by the international attention given to these civil injustices, the Kennedy administration sent federal marshals to the South to protect the freedom riders and later convinced the Interstate Commerce Commission to ban segregation in interstate terminals. During the next two years, Kennedy also sent federal troops to ensure the integration of the University of Mississippi and the University of Alabama. With or without congressional action, momentum for civil rights reform continued to build.

In the spring of 1963 television cameras captured Birmingham, Alabama, police armed with cattle prods and water hoses unleashing snarling attack dogs against nonviolent civil rights demonstrators. Such images on the nightly news outraged Americans and pushed Kennedy to arrange a settlement. Birmingham would desegregate its downtown stores and upgrade the status of black workers, and in return, the demonstrators would call off the protest. On June 11, Kennedy went on national television to announce that the United States was facing a "moral crisis." America could not promote freedom abroad, he said, if it practiced discrimination at home. Eight days later, roughly one and a half years into his administration, Kennedy sent to Congress a comprehensive civil rights program.

A coalition of civil rights leaders called the "Big Six" met at the Roosevelt Hotel in New York on July 2 to plan a march on Washington in support of the bill. The meeting included Roy Wilkins of the National Association for the Advancement of Colored People (NAACP), James Farmer of CORE, John Lewis of the Student Nonviolent Coordinating Committee (SNCC), Whitney Young Jr. of the Urban League, and Baptist minister Martin Luther King Jr. of the Southern Christian Leadership Conference (SCLC). On August 28, nearly a quarter of a million Americans gathered before the Lincoln Memorial in Washington, DC. The huge crowds sang "We Shall Overcome," chanted "Freedom Now," and listened to King express his vision of a coming day:

> I have a dream that one day this nation will rise up and live out the true meaning of its creed: We hold these truths to be self-evident that all men are created equal. . . . I have a dream that my four little children will one day live in a nation where they will not be judged by the color of their skin but by the content of their character. . . . This is our hope. . . . With this faith we will be able to transform the jangling discords of our nation into a beautiful symphony of brotherhood. With this faith we will be able to work together, to pray together, to struggle together, to go to jail together, to stand up for freedom together, knowing that we will be free one day. And this will be the day, this will be the day when all of God's children will be able to sing with new meaning, "My country, 'tis of thee, sweet land of liberty, of thee I sing."

Despite the moving words of King and the growing passion of millions in favor of lifting the barriers of racial discrimination, southern obstructionists like Senate Judiciary Committee chair James Eastland of Mississippi kept the civil rights bill bottled up in Congress until adjournment. It would be left to the next Congress to decide whether America would reject its segregationist ways and reaffirm through federal legislation its creed that all citizens are created equal.

Foreign Concerns: Cuba and Vietnam

The president's preoccupation with foreign affairs also slowed the march into the New Frontier. During the 1960s America continued to wage war, but the battle lines for this war no longer pitted tank against tank as in World War II. This war was the subtle, covert, spy-against-spy Cold War in which Western democracies struggled against a relentless and confident communist movement throughout the world. Russian premier Nikita Khrushchev exacerbated American worries in 1956 when he told Western ambassadors in Moscow, "History is on our side. We will bury you." With each side fearing the other's intent and capability, an intelligence network characterized by intrigue mushroomed within each nation. To counter the likelihood of communist influence, U.S. intelligence at the highest levels developed secret plans for eliminating former friends and foes that were thought to threaten the future of world democracies. In the communist bloc, Soviet leaders similarly initiated plans to eliminate democratic leaders around the world in an attempt to inject communism into any vulnerable country.

In particular, the growing communist influence only ninety miles from the United States consumed much of Kennedy's energy as soon as he took office. In 1959, the revolutionary Fidel Castro had overthrown the pro-American, but corrupt dictatorship of Fulgencio Batista in Cuba. The Castro revolution initially had solid public support, especially from the poor, largely landless peasants who resented both Batista and the American corporations that controlled 40 percent of Cuba's sugar fields, 80 percent of its utilities, 90 percent of its mines and cattle ranches, and nearly all of its oil. Castro exploited this anti-Yankee sentiment in order to seize control and then dominate the country much as his predecessor had. The Eisenhower administration, rightly or wrongly, increasingly identified the new regime with the Communist Party and thus distanced itself from the island to the south.

The more the United States attempted to isolate Castro, the closer Castro moved toward the Soviet Union. Soon 75 percent of the island's trade was with countries behind the iron curtain. After Castro recognized communist China (which friends of the United States did not do) and expropriated American businesses in Cuba, the United States blocked the importation of Cuban sugar (June 1960), imposed an embargo on nonfood and nonmedical exports to Cuba (October 1960), and finally, shortly before Eisenhower left the Oval Office, formally severed diplomatic ties with Cuba (January 1961). Historian William Appleman Williams labels this inadvertent push of Cuba into the Soviet orbit the great "tragedy of American foreign diplomacy."

Still unknown to the world was a Central Intelligence Agency (CIA) plan to topple the Castro regime. According to the plan, the United States would recruit, train, arm, and assist anti-Castro exiles in an invasion of Cuba. After the invaders secured a foothold on the island and made contact with rebel guerrillas in the mountains, the people of Cuba, the CIA hoped, would rise up and overthrow the Castro regime. The Eisenhower administration already had twice pulled off similar escapades, in Iran in 1953 and in Guatamala in 1954, and therefore had reason to feel confident in this risky venture. U.S. intervention could easily be justified internationally if Castro would carry through with his threats to seize America's naval base at Guantánamo on the island. Without this aggression, however, a U.S. invasion would be more difficult to explain to the Latin American nations of the Western Hemisphere.

Kennedy found out about the plan to overthrow Castro's government before he took office. Despite his personal reservations and the strong opposition of J. William Fulbright, the chair of the Senate Foreign Relations Committee, Kennedy gave his presidential approval. However, before the invasion was launched in April 1961, Kennedy scaled back U.S. support. He agreed, for instance, to allow B-26 fighter bombers to attack Cuban airfields, blaming the U.S. air assault on defecting Cuban air force pilots, and to use the navy to land a brigade of 1,500 CIA-trained, anti-Castro Cubans ashore at the Bay of Pigs. Refusing to commit American troops, however, Kennedy failed to provide vital air and naval support after delivering the invaders to the island. What would have transpired with such support is unknowable, but it is clear that without this support the plan failed miserably. Within forty-eight hours, the Cuban army killed or captured the helpless invaders who waded ashore at the Bay of Pigs.

Nothing fails like failure. The fiasco alienated Castro even further from the United States and sent him into a deeper alliance with the Soviets. He now had the excuse he needed to legitimately ask for defensive protection against possible future U.S. invasions. Furthermore, the debacle humiliated the new administration and further damaged the moral and military credibility of the United States. Journalist Cyrus Sulzberger summed up the situation best: "We looked like fools to our friends, rascals to our enemies, and incompetents to the rest." Ironically, after Kennedy accepted full responsibility for the failed mission, his approval ratings soared to the highest levels of his presidency, evoking from the remorseful president the comment, "It's just like Eisenhower. The worse I do the more popular I get."

Owing to Kennedy's caution with regard to the use of military force against Cuba, the Soviets perceived a weakness in American resolve. In June 1961,

Kennedy met Khrushchev in Vienna, and the Soviet premier used the occasion to bully the young president, threatening to disavow previous agreements by allowing East Germany to close road and rail access into West Berlin. By isolating West Berlin, the USSR hoped to stop the defection of communist technocrats into this free city inside East Germany.

Refusing to be intimidated, Kennedy announced that NATO forces would defend West Berlin at all costs. During the summer of 1961, Kennedy called the National Reserve to active duty and increased American military strength by 25 percent. At this time many Americans, with the President's encouragement, began building fallout shelters in their backyards. American citizens were taught to "duck and cover" if they saw a bright flash of light. Signs displaying the Civil Defense "CD" inside a triangle were common on buildings designated as nuclear shelters. The not-so-subtle message in these actions was to suggest that a well-prepared citizenry could survive an atomic war. The crisis eased in August when the Soviet-led East Germans chose a less aggressive way to stop the leakage of talent into West Berlin by erecting a wall of barbed wire and concrete around the western portions of East Berlin. This Berlin Wall became a symbol of the growing separation and antagonism between communist and democratic philosophies, between coercion and freedom.

Several weeks after the construction of the Berlin Wall, the USSR broke the three-year American-Soviet moratorium on the testing of nuclear bombs by launching a series of tests that soon would lead to the detonation of a fifty-eight-megaton weapon—a bomb 3,000 times more powerful than the ones dropped on Japan during World War II. Kennedy responded by reinitiating American underground testing and by escalating the construction of U.S. nuclear weapons. The Soviets followed suit and a full-blown arms race ensued, with both sides vowing not to be caught in a "missile gap." Meanwhile, the CIA responded by increasing covert missions within Cuba to try to overthrow Castro or assassinate him. Not to be left out, Congress passed legislation that authorized the use of force "to curb Cuban aggression and subversion in Latin America." To protect his new friend in Cuba and act as a deterrent against an American invasion, Khrushchev secretly installed missiles in Cuba that had the capability to strike the United States with nuclear weapons.

On October 16, 1962, when high-flying U-2 spy planes discovered the installation of Soviet nuclear missile sites in Cuba, Kennedy promptly assembled the Executive Committee of the National Security Council, known as ExCom, to provide him with response options. Working around the clock, the ExCom advisers presented the president with two major options: bomb the sites or blockade the island to prevent more Soviet hardware from arriving and insist upon the dismantling of the missiles. Former secretary of state Dean Acheson, Generals Maxwell Taylor and Curtis LeMay, and other military brass argued vigorously for the strike, while Undersecretary of State

George Ball, Attorney General Robert Kennedy, and Secretary of Defense Robert McNamara were equally passionate in recommending a blockade. At that time U.S. intelligence believed that no Soviet missiles in Cuba were as yet operational. Only in 1992, after the unraveling of the USSR, did historians learn that forty-two intermediate-range missiles and nine short-range nuclear missiles for use against invading forces had already been installed during these treacherous days. The danger in October 1962 was even greater than the advisers at the time dared to think. After listening to all the arguments, the president made his decision. The United States would blockade Cuba and demand the removal of the Soviet missiles.

On October 22, Kennedy in a televised address told the American people about the Soviet threat: "Within the past week, unmistakable evidence has established the fact that a series of offensive missile sites is now in preparation on that imprisoned island. The purpose of these bases can be none other than to provide a nuclear strike capability against the Western Hemisphere." He then announced his decision to use the navy to prevent the landing of Soviet ships in Cuba. The speech electrified and terrified the nation. That night millions of Americans crammed into Safeway supermarkets (one of the few food chains at the time with twenty-four-hour service) and convenience stores to purchase bottled water, Spam, and other survival and food items. Over the ensuing days, an anxious world watched and waited. Then the Soviets blinked. Khrushchev offered to remove the missiles in return for a U.S. pledge not to attack Cuba. One day later, the Soviets shot down a U.S. spy plane flying over Cuba, killing the pilot. That very day they also sent a second note that insisted that the United States remove missile sites in Turkey as a precondition for the Soviet removal of the Cuban missiles. Kennedy, at the suggestion of his brother, decided to accept the conditions of the first note without officially responding to the second. Unofficially, however, Robert Kennedy was told to inform a Soviet official in Washington that several months earlier an order had already been given to remove the obsolete and redundant missiles in Turkey. The crisis was ended. Months later, the U.S. missiles in Turkey were quietly dismantled. In the history of life on this planet, humanity has never been as close to obliteration as it was during these intense October days.

On the other side of the world, in Indochina, another Cold War incident erupted. Vietnam, once a French colony, had been taken by Japan during World War II, but returned to the French following the war. In 1954, Vietnamese nationalists struggling for their independence won a major victory against the French at Dien Bien Phu, forcing the French to withdraw from the region. According to the armistice, the region temporarily was to be divided at the seventeenth parallel, with President Ho Chi Minh in control of the northern, communist region and the Western-backed regime of President Ngo Dinh Diem in control in the south. Plans for an election in 1956 to unify the region also were discussed, but the United States, fearing that a democratic vote would install a communist government, refused to support the elections. Vietnam remained divided at the seventeenth parallel.

To contain the spread of communism in the area, the United States turned to its trusted friend Diem. During the Eisenhower administration, the United States sent millions of dollars and 900 military advisers to assist Diem in withstanding the communist menace in his land. When Kennedy assumed office, the United States poured additional funds and military advisers into South Vietnam.

Although Diem was an ardent anticommunist, a Roman Catholic, and an avowed friend of the United States, he was also a corrupt, repressive autocrat hated by millions in his predominantly Buddhist country. In May 1963, when Diem's troops fired into a crowd of Buddhists celebrating the Buddha's birthday, Diem's popularity plummeted and Buddhist-led, anti-Diem riots broke out in Saigon. Diem retaliated by destroying Buddhist pagodas. To protest, Buddhist monks burned themselves to death in front of photographers on sidewalks of Saigon. Soon American political insiders came to see Diem as a liability rather than an asset. Consequently, in early November 1963, with the blessing of the United States, a military coup toppled the South Vietnamese regime and assassinated Diem and his brother. This would not be the last Cold War–inspired assassination.

Dallas, Texas: November 22, 1963

After a thousand days in office, Kennedy had not accomplished all that he had hoped to do. This self-proclaimed knight of Camelot recognized that his future, and the future of his vision for America and the world, rested upon the outcome of the upcoming 1964 elections. If he and the Democrats were to be successful, the wounds caused by the conservative-liberal split in his party had to be healed. In an effort to unite the party, Kennedy planned a trip to Texas, the home of Vice President Lyndon Johnson and a critical battleground state in their reelection bid.

November 22, 1963, was a clear, sunny day in north Texas. Without the threat of rain, the president and his wife, Jackie, did not need the bubbletop on the presidential limousine and chose to ride through downtown Dallas in full view of the thousands of admirers who lined the streets to greet them. Kennedy and his wife sat in the back seat behind the conservative, Democratic governor of Texas, John Connally. The president waved and flashed his winsome smile at the enthusiastic crowd, and Jackie set the fashion statement of the day with her pink suit and pillbox hat. Bouquets of roses sat on the seat between the president and his wife—gifts from well-wishers at the Dallas airport at Love Field.

At 12:29 PM President Kennedy's motorcade approached a place known as the "triple underpass" near the Texas School Book Depository. The sound of gunfire erupted, and a bullet hit the president in the back of the neck. He slumped and a second shot hit Governor Connally in the back. A third shot rang out and hit Kennedy in the head. Jackie Kennedy almost stood up in the car to grab him. The crowd heard her cry out, "Oh no!" With the president slumped over in his wife's lap, the startled crowd watched as the motorcade sped off toward Dallas's Parkland Hospital. The physicians at the hospital met the limousine at the emergency entrance and rushed Kennedy into a treatment room, but it was obvious to all of them that there was no hope. One of them described how he ran to the president's side only to be appalled at the extent of the wounds: "There was nothing to work with. He was gone."

Questions and theories still flourish regarding who took part in this tragic murder. The official Warren Commission that investigated the assassination claimed that one man, Lee Harvey Oswald, was solely responsible for the shooting. As a child, Oswald lived with his mother at times in New York City, Fort Worth, and in a seedy section of the New Orleans French Quarter called Exchange Alley. In 1956 he left high school to join the U.S. Marines but was dishonorably discharged in 1959 after assaulting a superior officer. Openly committed to Marxist ideology, he defected to Russia in 1959 and married Marina Prusakova Nichilayeva in Minsk. They returned to the United States in 1962 and Oswald held a number of menial jobs in the Fort Worth and Dallas area. After his return to the United States, Oswald had dealings with the Communist Party, USA, and with the Fair Play for Cuba Committee. In early November 1963, Oswald traveled to Mexico City, where he claimed in a letter to the Soviet Embassy in Washington to have conferred with "comrade Kostine in the Embassy of the Soviet Union in Mexico City, Mexico." He also attempted to get a visa to visit Cuba. It is conceivable that Oswald, a mentally troubled fanatic for the communist cause, alone took opportunistic advantage of his position along Kennedy's parade route to kill the president.

Other theories speculate that Castro was involved in the assassination. Others suggest that it was anti-Castro Cubans, not pro-Castro ones, who co-operated in an assassination conspiracy. Still others speculate that organized crime was involved. No matter how the riddle of the assassination is solved, the murder of John Kennedy remains a tragic example of the intrigue and intensity emblematic of the Cold War era.

The sudden death of the young husband and father plunged the nation into mourning. As Jackie Kennedy remarked, "There'll be great presidents again . . . but there'll never be another Camelot." Americans still sang the Broadway song composed by Kennedy's friend Alan Lerner, but now it was the final stanza that captured the sullen national mood that followed Kennedy's death:

> *Don't let it be forgot*
> *That once there was a spot*
> *For one brief, shining moment that was known as Camelot.*

The Political Consequences of Kennedy's Death

The moment radio and television announced the death of the president, the political landscape of the nation shifted. The impact of this etched-in-the-mind turning point in American history served as a haunting reminder of the heart-stopping mental nausea following the attack on Pearl Harbor. In the same way the surprise attack in Hawaii silenced the isolationists and united the nation in a war crusade, the shock of the assassination silenced Kennedy's outspoken critics and gave impetus to the promised reforms of the New Frontier. As large as he was in life, the Kennedy mystique grew even larger in death. Years later, historians would write about the "darker side of Camelot," including the president's extramarital affairs, but these stories were unknown or irrelevant to the great majority of Americans in the 1960s. In the aftermath of the assassination, Kennedy was viewed by most Americans as a noble knight who was willing to sacrifice himself for noble causes.

Lyndon Johnson also deserves much credit for what took place in Congress during the months that followed Kennedy's death. An experienced and shrewd southern Democrat himself, Johnson told the grieving nation that "the ideas and ideals which [Kennedy] so nobly represented must and will be translated into effective action." He promptly went to work, asking Congress to reduce personal income taxes by $10 billion ($66 billion in today's currency) and to approve an uncompromising civil rights bill. The latter bill would prohibit discrimination based on race, color, religion, sex, or national origin in employment and public places and create an Equal Employment Opportunity Commission (EEOC) to ensure the enforcement of the law. The tax law came quickly and was signed by Johnson early in 1964. Securing civil rights legislation took more work. Joining with the NAACP, the AFL-CIO, the National Council of Churches, and the American Jewish Congress, President Johnson launched an intensive lobbying campaign in Congress. The six-foot four-inch Texan used his towering size and the power of the presidential office to cajole, flatter, and, if necessary, threaten key members of Congress. His persistence paid off. In July, Johnson signed the Civil Rights Act of 1964, the most comprehensive civil rights package passed since Reconstruction.

Johnson also adopted Kennedy's antipoverty program as his own. In his 1964 State of the Union address, Johnson told the nation, "This administration, today, here and now, declares unconditional war on poverty in America." By the end of the year, a new Office of Economic Opportunity (OEO) was providing oversight to a broad range of antipoverty programs, from Head Start, which provided educational opportunities for preschool children, to the Job Corps, which provided high school dropouts with vocational training. Johnson's war on poverty, coupled with a booming economy, raised 10 million Americans out of poverty within three years.

Even as Johnson brought unity to the Democratic Party, divisions between conservatives and liberals split the Republican Party in the 1964 election campaign. Arizona senator Barry Goldwater championed the Republican right while New York governor Nelson Rockefeller led the Republican left. Each leader carried large negatives. Goldwater's promise to make Social Security voluntary and to give NATO commanders the right to use nuclear weapons made him appear irresponsible and extreme, while Rockefeller's recent divorce and remarriage, an action unacceptable to many voters at that time, severely crippled his popularity. Both candidates, in fact, were defeated by a write-in candidate, Henry Cabot Lodge Jr., in the New Hampshire primary. Ultimately, Goldwater won the nomination, but only after he overcame a last-minute Stop Goldwater movement led by Republican liberals. His delegates at the nominating convention drafted an unashamedly conservative platform that pledged a "limited, frugal and efficient" government in domestic affairs and a tough foreign policy pledging no "capitulation" to communism. In accepting the nomination, Goldwater refused to extend an olive branch to his liberal foes: "Any who join us in all sincerity, we welcome. Those who do not care for our cause we do not expect to enter our ranks in any case." Then he concluded: "I would remind you that extremism in the defense of liberty is no vice. And let me remind you also that moderation in the pursuit of justice is no virtue."

During the campaign, Republican loyalists said of Goldwater, "In Your Heart You Know He's Right." This slogan served as an easy target for Democrats and moderate Republicans, who countered with "Yes, the extreme right" or "In Your Guts You Know He's Nuts." When Americans went to the polls in 1964, Johnson carried over 61 percent of the popular vote, the largest landslide victory since the popular vote had been counted. Equally important, the Democrats won huge majorities in Congress, controlling the House 295–140 and the Senate 68–32. Republicans also lost over 500 state legislative seats across the country. The election of 1964 clearly signaled America's affirmation of progressive reform.

Johnson wasted no time in fulfilling the mandate given to him. His vision of a "Great Society" promised equal opportunities and an improved quality of life for everyone. This program advocated the continuation of antipoverty and civil rights legislation, plus greater federal attention to controlling water and air pollution, rebuilding American cities, and promoting education at all levels.

Over the ensuing months, Johnson signed dozens of Great Society bills, providing massive funds for economic development in impoverished regions and for the building of low-rent public housing units. He signed the Medical Care Act, which created federally funded health insurance for the elderly (Medicare) and state subsidies for medical care for the poor (Medicaid), and a variety of education bills that provided billions of federal dollars for textbooks, special education, and college loans for poor students. The Great Society program also struggled to reverse historic patterns of racial discrimination with the Immigration Act of 1965, which eliminated the national origins quotas and bans on Asians that had been in effect since the 1920s, and the Voting Rights Act, which suspended literacy tests and empowered federal examiners to register qualified voters in the South. Johnson promoted artistic and cultural development by signing the National Endowment for the Arts and Humanities Act and the Public Broadcasting Act, which established a nonprofit corporation to support educational and cultural programming. He protected consumers with the Truth-in-Packaging Act, which required sellers to provide accurate labeling on foods, drugs, cosmetics, and household supplies. Johnson also created new cabinet-level departments—the Department of Housing and Urban Development, headed by Robert Weaver, the first African-American to serve in a cabinet position, and the Department of Transportation. In a wide range of domestic areas, Johnson's Great Society program expanded the role of the federal government in American life suddenly and dramatically.

The swift changes of the mid-sixties were indelible. Before the new immigration laws of 1965, for instance, 90 percent of the immigrants to the United States came from Europe; after 1965, only 10 percent came from Europe, while the majority came from Korea, Taiwan, India, the Philippines, Cuba, the Dominican Republic, and Mexico. Similarly, within a few years after the ratification of the Twenty-fourth Amendment, which eliminated the poll tax, and the passage of the Voting Rights Act, the numbers of African-Americans registered to vote increased by about 100 percent in Georgia and Louisiana, 200 percent in South Carolina, 300 percent in Alabama, and over 1,000 percent in Mississippi. This belated enfranchisement of millions of African-American voters forever altered the political landscape of the South.

Moreover, within five years after Johnson launched the antipoverty programs of the OEO, poverty rates in America were cut almost in half, dropping from over 22 percent to under 13 percent. Since the enactment of these OEO programs—eleven of which still remain active in the twenty-first century—American poverty rates have remained remarkably stable. Despite many other changes in American society in the last thirty-five years, the percentage of Americans living in poverty has never fluctuated more than three points above or below the 13 percent poverty levels of 1969. For good, for bad, or for both good and bad, the reforms that immediately followed the assassination of President Kennedy fundamentally altered the flow of the American past. By the middle years of the 1960s, the federal government was a largely welcomed, but sometimes irritating, intrusive, and expensive force in the lives of all Americans.

The Whiplash of Backlash:
America in Troubled Times

In physics, every action has an equal and opposite reaction. Often, the same can be said of politics. Johnson had little time to enjoy the good feeling that normally follows political success. In fact, even before all the pieces of the Great Society program had been woven together, the social fabric of the nation began to unravel.

One source of social unrest was the frustration of American blacks with the slow progress toward achieving racial equality. As early as 1963, black author James Baldwin in *The Fire Next Time* warned of a growing rage among African-Americans who felt increasingly alienated from mainstream American society. Despite the gains that resulted from the first significant civil rights legislation in almost a century, in overcrowded and impoverished black communities across America unemployment was high, schools were inferior, and police brutality was feared. In the summer of 1965, the fires that Baldwin predicted were ignited in Watts, a black neighborhood in Los Angeles that was protected by a police force of 200 whites and five nonwhites. The spark that set the community ablaze was only a minor incident—the arrest of a young African-American for drunken driving by a white highway patrol officer. What followed, however, was anything but minor. Rioting, looting, and arson spread throughout the neighborhood, and before the National Guard was able to subdue the violence, thirty-four people were dead, more than a thousand were wounded, and $40 million in property (about $260 million in today's currency) had been destroyed.

Watts came to symbolize the rage of black Americans in these troubled times. During the hot summers of the late 1960s, local incidents ignited race riots in many cities across the nation. In 1966, the streets of Chicago, New York, and Cleveland burned with racial unrest as fire bomb attacks, sniper shootings, and violent clashes between police and white, Puerto Rican, and black gangs were televised nationally on the evening news. The next year the racial violence turned even uglier. In July 1967, riots in Newark, New Jersey, left twenty-six dead and one thousand injured; one week later, riots in Detroit took another forty lives and destroyed some $150 million ($910 million in today's currency) in property.

Even as the smell of ashes from the arson fires lingered in the air, black activist Stokely Carmichael, former chair of the Student Nonviolent Coordinating Committee (SNCC), rejected nonviolent methods and called for a black revolution in America. "We have no alternative," Carmichael said, "but to use aggressive armed violence in order to own the land, houses, and stores inside our communities, and to control the politics of those communities." That very week black militant Adam Clayton Powell echoed the same sentiments, stating that the riots in Detroit and other cities were "a necessary phase of the black revolution." For many activists in the late 1960s, the desegregationist objectives of the NAACP and the Urban League appeared both wimpy and naive. For these militants, black separatism replaced integration as the objective, and "Black Power" through armed strength replaced passive, nonviolent disobedience as the preferred method to obtain these desired ends.

Many activists still embraced the integrationist goals and nonviolent methods of Martin Luther King Jr., but by the late sixties, other, more radical options appealed to millions of American blacks whose expectations were rising more rapidly than social progress. Many, like Malcolm X, became interested in the Nation of Islam (also known as the Black Muslims), an organization founded in 1931 that combined tenets of the Islamic tradition with the call for racial separatism. Others joined the Black Panthers, an organization founded by Bobby Seale and Huey Newton in 1966 that urged blacks to carry rifles to defend themselves against the "racist-capitalist police state." Even as black nationalism mounted, Hispanic activists like Reies Lopez Tijerina promoted the rise of "Brown Power" and demanded that the United States return to Hispanic peoples the land they had lost to the Anglo-Americans in the 1848 Treaty of Guadalupe Hidalgo. Meanwhile, the American Indian Movement (AIM) dramatized the need for Native Americans to seek reparations for past injustices. The Black Power, Brown Power, and Red Power movements challenged the basic assumptions of the civil rights movement by stating unequivocally that not everyone wanted to assimilate into the same homogeneous society. The movement spread beyond race, with other minority groups seeking equal treatment. Atheists, for example, fought for and obtained rulings from the Supreme Court banning prayer, Bible courses, and other religious activities in schools and other public institutions.

The unrelenting and ineffective war in Vietnam added fuel to the fires of discontent. American military advisers had been supporting the South Vietnamese regime since the days of Eisenhower, but after Vietcong (South Vietnamese communist) mortar fire killed eight Americans in early 1965, President Johnson approved the launching of Operation Rolling Thunder, the code name for bombing raids on targets in North Vietnam. In 1965, Johnson also sent 180,000 more American soldiers into the jungles of southeast Asia. This was only the first major installment of Johnson's escalation efforts. By the end of 1968, more than 500,000 American soldiers were waging war against the difficult-to-find and difficult-to-identify communist insurgents.

The war did not go as planned. Under the leadership of General William Westmoreland, the United States intended to fight a limited war using conventional (nonnuclear) weapons against military targets, hoping to kill enough insurgents to persuade the North Vietnamese and the Vietcong to give up.

Between 1965 and 1969, the U.S. bombing raids and search-and-destroy missions killed over 400,000 enemy combatants—about the same number of Americans who lost their lives between 1941 and 1945 in World War II. America's problem, however, was that these deaths did not arrest the resolve of the communist insurgents.

Moreover, for every ten enemy soldiers eliminated, the United States also lost one man. Over time, as the American body count mounted, Americans, particularly American youth, began to question both the morality and the winnability of the war effort. Groups such as Students for a Democratic Society (SDS) organized massive antiwar rallies to protest America's involvement in the war. By 1967, antiwar songs by artists such as Bob Dylan, Creedence Clearwater Revival, and Peter, Paul and Mary had become staples of the emerging youth counterculture. A popular Dylan song included the lyrics:

> *How many times must a man look up*
> *Before he can see the sky?*
> *Yes, 'n' how many ears must one man have*
> *Before he can hear people cry?*
> *Yes, 'n' how many deaths will it take till he knows*
> *That too many people have died?*
> *The answer, my friend, is blowin' in the wind,*
> *The answer is blowin' in the wind.*

Even the son of Secretary of Defense Robert McNamara took to the streets to protest America's war in Vietnam. The war was splitting America along generational, if not ethnic, lines.

A decisive turning point in the war occurred in early 1968 when the communists launched the Tet offensive, so named because it was begun on the lunar New Year holiday of Tet. A coordinated attack of 70,000 communist troops assaulted American and South Vietnamese positions across South Vietnam. On national television, Americans watched General William Westmoreland duck for cover as communist insurgents shelled Saigon, the capital of South Vietnam. Ultimately, the American forces were able to repel the offensive and kill more than 5,000 enemy combatants. Although a tactical victory for the United States, the Tet offensive was a strategic defeat because it made Americans distrust the credibility of General Westmoreland's optimistic claims that the enemy was demoralized. After the Tet offensive, when Westmoreland requested 200,000 more troops, the advisers to the president, including the new secretary of defense, Clark Clifford, told Johnson that the war was unwinnable. Meanwhile, growing numbers of Americans became convinced that sending troops to fight in Vietnam had been a mistake.

The Election of 1968 and the
Return of Richard Nixon

In March 1968, following a surprisingly weak showing in the Democratic New Hampshire primary, President Johnson—the incumbent who had carried over 61 percent of the popular vote four years earlier—announced that he would not seek reelection. The race for the Democratic nomination became a three-way scramble between peace Democrats Eugene McCarthy and Robert Kennedy, and Johnson's choice, the prowar vice president, Hubert Humphrey. During the ensuing months, tragedy struck the nation twice. In April, a deranged white racist, James Earl Ray, assassinated civil rights leader Martin Luther King Jr. Then on June 5, on the evening after winning the California Democratic primary, Robert Kennedy was assassinated by a troubled Palestinian, Sirhan Sirhan. The death of the late president's brother ultimately secured the nomination for Humphrey, but it did not heal the bitter divisions between the hawks and the doves within the Democratic Party.

Humphrey's chances were further undermined when the former Democratic governor of Alabama, George Wallace, entered the race as a third-party candidate. Wallace, whose motto while governor was "Segregation now . . . segregation tomorrow . . . segregation forever," advocated a law-and-order platform that promised to use troops if necessary to deliver the nation from the disruptions caused by radicals, peaceniks, black militants, hippies, integrationists, and "pointy-headed professors." His diatribes against black leaders and their liberal white allies appealed both to southerners and to blue-collar workers in the North, voting groups once a part of the Democratic New Deal coalition.

Meanwhile, the Republicans turned in 1968 to Richard Nixon, the former vice president who narrowly lost the presidency in 1960 and the governorship of California in 1962. Appealing to "the forgotten Americans, the non-shouters, the non-demonstrators," Nixon criticized the intrusiveness and costs of the Great Society programs and promised, if elected, to deliver a secret plan to end the war in Vietnam with honor. Although a moderate Republican, Nixon boosted his credentials among conservatives in his party by selecting as his running mate the tough-talking, law-and-order Maryland governor, Spiro Agnew.

Nixon's early, comfortable lead in the polls dwindled in the last weeks of the campaign, but on Election Day, American voters by razor-thin margins elected Nixon to the presidency. Democrats, however, maintained slight majorities in both the House and the Senate. The split decision signified the shifting, unstable mood of the nation. While Nixon received just over 43 percent of the popular vote, his triumph signaled that the old New Deal coalition that had promoted progressivism at home and activism abroad was no longer intact. Humphrey carried just 38 percent of the white vote and less than half of the labor vote, an ominous sign that the once dominant Democratic Party was well past its prime. What coalition would form to create a new ruling majority was still unknown, but time would show that the 57 percent who voted for Nixon or Wallace would dominate American politics for the next generation. Divided before the election, America would remain divided after the ascendancy of President Nixon.

The Nixon years were a time of contradiction, paranoia, and sadness. Of course, there were moments of gladness and celebration. On July 21, 1969, for instance, television audiences estimated at 600 million—one-fifth of the earth's population—watched anxiously and then cheered when *Apollo 11*'s captain, Neil Armstrong, stepped on the moon's surface, stating triumphantly, "One small step for man, one giant leap for mankind." Even this great technological marvel, however, was berated by social critics who questioned the morality of appropriating such massive funds toward a project that was less committed to getting to the moon than to getting there before the Soviets.

Besides the moon walk, news headlines in 1969 covered student protests against the Vietnam War, the Charles Manson family's brutal massacre of actress Sharon Tate, the arrest on murder charges of Black Panther leader Bobby Seale, and the Woodstock Music Festival. The latter event, advertised as "Three Days of Peace and Music," attracted 400,000 fun-loving rock fans grooving to the music of Jefferson Airplane, the Grateful Dead, the Who, Janis Joplin, Jimi Hendrix, and the other pop artists who attended the extravaganza. Not all the young people at Woodstock were long-haired, pot-smoking, LSD-dropping hedonists, but the extracurricular activities tolerated at the festival were a direct challenge to the moral values held sacrosanct by many mainstream Americans.

The year 1969 cast doubt on America's moral integrity. Reports surfaced of atrocities that had occurred twenty months earlier in the Vietnamese hamlet of My Lai. In this March 1968 incident, emotionally troubled American soldiers dismembered bodies, gang-raped women and girls, tortured captives, murdered women, children, and old men, and then burned the village. The horrors of the incident caused many people to wonder if such wartime atrocities were aberrations or commonplace happenings. Indeed, the decade that opened with the patriotic call to "ask what you can do for your country" and the challenge to place a man on the moon ended with rising protests against war (both hot and cold), the space race, traditional expressions of morality, and the overt intrusion of government into the affairs of citizens. Even as pockets of America were becoming more tolerant of intolerance, growing numbers of vocal young Americans were stating their preference to make love in the fields of Woodstock rather than war in the jungles of Vietnam. For this generation, the age of Camelot had become the age of Aquarius.

Governing during such divided times would be difficult for anyone, and it proved to be particularly difficult for President Nixon. Arguably among the most intelligent of the nation's presidents, Nixon also was aloof, secretive, suspicious, and vindictive. Fellow Republican Barry Goldwater called him "the most complete loner I've ever known." At Nixon's instructions, the White House staff was structured to isolate the president from Congress, the media, and even his own cabinet. Nixon empowered his subordinates H.R. Haldeman, his chief of staff, and John Ehrlichman, special adviser on domestic affairs, with wide authority to act on his behalf in domestic matters. In foreign affairs, he trusted most his national security adviser, Henry Kissinger, a master of realpolitik who, like Nixon, thought that policies must be based on pragmatic national interests rather than on ethical goals. With his team of loyal associates, Nixon accomplished many goals, both domestically and internationally. Unfortunately, his perplexing distrust of others, even those within his own party, coupled with his personal ambitions, insecurities, and Machiavellian instincts, drove him to take risks that ultimately would threaten the nation and bring down his presidency.

The complex and contradictory components of Nixon's nature were reflected in the diversity of initiatives pursued by his administration. As the first newly elected president since 1849 whose party did not control either the House or the Senate, Nixon worked with the Democrats to extend a number of the liberal agendas initiated in the New Deal, Fair Deal, and Great Society programs. For instance, he supported legislation that raised Social Security benefits and increased subsidized housing for low-income Americans. He also signed legislation that protected endangered species, regulated consumer product safety, limited pesticide use, and established clean air standards. To enforce these laws, he created the Environmental Protection Agency (EPA) and the Occupational Safety and Health Administration (OSHA). To stimulate economic growth and to curb inflation, Nixon tried a variety of tactics, including traditional approaches, like cutting government spending and encouraging the Federal Reserve Board to raise interest rates, and unorthodox methods, such as submitting an unbalanced federal budget that produced the largest budget deficit since World War II and imposing a ninety-day freeze on wages, prices, and rents. Although none of the latter initiatives cured the chronic economic disease of the 1970s known as stagflation (i.e., slow or stagnant economic growth coupled with rising prices), Nixon's efforts demonstrated his nondoctrinaire approach to solving economic difficulties.

While the above initiatives appealed to moderates, Nixon also knew how to lean to the political right. To appease southerners and blue-collar northern conservatives, Nixon opposed the extension of the Voting Rights Act of 1965, urged the courts to delay the orders to desegregate Mississippi schools, asked Congress to enact a moratorium against the use of busing to achieve school desegregation, appointed strict constructionist federal judges opposed to "meddling" in social issues, and took strong law-and-order stands against radicals, criminals, and drug users.

Nixon also ordered clandestine operations against his political foes which, if known, would have made even law-and-order conservatives blush. For instance, Nixon used campaign funds to create a spy network to find dirt on liberal journalists and Democrats; drew up an "enemies list" and then ordered the IRS to audit their tax returns, the Small Business Administration to deny them loans, and the CIA and the FBI to wiretap their phones; and created a secret task force (the "plumbers" unit) headed by former CIA and FBI operatives and gave it the assignment of monitoring and finding information that could be used to discredit whatever individuals the president deemed dangerous to the nation. Punishment for these illegal activities would wait until a later day.

It was foreign, not domestic, affairs, however, that interested Nixon the most. Having promised a plan to end the war with honor, in 1969 Nixon announced a Vietnamization policy in which he pledged to gradually replace U.S. troops with South Vietnamese ones. Periodically, Nixon withdrew American forces from Vietnam, slowly reducing the number of U.S. military personnel from 543,400 in April 1969 to 334,660 by the end of 1970 to just 24,200 by early 1973.

Even while withdrawing foot soldiers from Vietnam, in an attempt to secure "peace with honor" Nixon also escalated the bombing of North Vietnam, mined its harbors, and secretly approved air attacks in the neighboring countries of Cambodia and Laos. In April 1970, without the approval of Congress, Nixon ordered American soldiers to seize large caches of arms in Cambodia. The U.S. invasion of Cambodia provoked massive student protests on college campus. During one of these protests at Kent State University, National Guardsmen called to protect the school from violence panicked and fired into a crowd of 200 students, killing four and wounding nine. Days later a similar incident was repeated at Jackson State University, where state troopers killed two students and wounded twelve others. Outraged by these tragedies, the Senate repealed the 1964 Gulf of Tonkin Resolution, which authorized the war in Vietnam, and adopted a resolution (never passed by the House) that prohibited spending funds for military operations in Cambodia. A political tug-of-war between Congress and the executive branch would continue throughout the remainder of Nixon's presidency.

America's involvement in Vietnam ended with a negotiated truce with North Vietnam in January 1973. According to the terms of the Paris Peace Accords, the United States would withdraw its remaining forces and North Vietnam would return all U.S. prisoners of war. Meanwhile, South Vietnam carried on the fight without U.S. military assistance for two more years. In April 1975, however, North Vietnamese troops overran Saigon and unified the nation under the communist Democratic Republic of Vietnam. This great civil war, which devastated the land and claimed 2 million Vietnamese casualties, was finally over. Ultimately, America's longest war cost the United States

58,000 lives, $150 billion ($850 billion in today's currency), and a substantial loss in military and moral prestige. Moreover, the ghosts of the failures in Vietnam would haunt the nation for decades to come.

Aside from deescalating the war in Vietnam, Nixon achieved some outstanding foreign policy successes. Before Nixon, U.S. presidents from Truman onward had refused to recognize the People's Republic of China, allow its admission into the UN, or permit friends of the United States to trade with this most populated communist country on the planet. Realizing the advantages of exploiting the natural rivalries between the USSR and China, however, Nixon toned down his once hostile rhetoric toward the communist giant (referring to it as the People's Republic rather than as Red China) and sent first a U.S. ping-pong team (April 1971) and later Kissinger (February 1972) on friendship missions to China. Later in 1972, Nixon and his wife, Pat, visited the land of the Great Wall, setting in motion a normalization process that would culminate under President Jimmy Carter in America's recognition of this communist regime. America's warming relationship with the Chinese pressured the Soviets also to accept détente (the relaxation of tensions) with the United States. After visiting China, Nixon went to Moscow to sign a billion-dollar grain deal with the Soviets and to begin Strategic Arms Limitation Talks (SALT)—negotiations that ultimately produced a treaty that limited both superpowers to 200 antiballistic missiles (ABM) and two ABM systems.

Withdrawing forces from Vietnam and achieving détente with the communist superpowers, however, did not produce a peaceful world. Kissinger's "shuttle diplomacy" in the Middle East failed to prevent Egypt and Syria from invading Israel in October 1973. With rushed military aid from the United States, Israel repelled the assault, but in retaliation against U.S. interference, the oil-producing Arab nations stopped shipments of oil to the United States and its allies. Ultimately, Kissinger negotiated a cease-fire, persuading the Arabs to end the embargo in return for Israel returning some territory that it had taken from Arab states in 1967. The five-month oil embargo, however, produced acute fuel shortages, increased the price of petroleum, exasperated inflation rates, and dramatized America's heavy dependence on foreign oil. America's economy in 1974 was sicker than it had been at any time since the Great Depression.

Elsewhere around the world, Nixon supplied arms to the shah of Iran, backed the white-supremacist apartheid government of South Africa, assisted antidemocratic regimes in Argentina, Brazil, Nigeria, South Korea, and Angola, and secretly funded a coup that brought down a democratically elected president in Chile. These actions, each undertaken in the name of realpolitik, underscored Nixon's determination to base military and economic aid on a nation's opposition to American enemies, not on the legitimacy or the nature of its government. Despite these effects, the United States during the early 1970s continued to lose ground as a superpower.

Watergate and the Fall of a President

In the election of 1972, the silent majority spoke with a roar. Nixon easily defeated the liberal Democrat George McGovern in one of the most lopsided victories in election history. The margin of the victory simply added irony to the events that transpired during the campaign, events that not only tarnished Nixon's reputation, but destroyed his presidency.

A small incident triggered the national crisis. On the evening of July 17, 1972, five men wearing surgical gloves and carrying telephone bugging devices were arrested for breaking into the headquarters of the Democratic National Committee, located in the plush Watergate complex in Washington, DC. The five men later were convicted of conspiracy and burglary. Nixon disclaimed any knowledge of the plan, and the Watergate incident had little impact on the election of 1972. Two *Washington Post* reporters, Bob Woodward and Carl Bernstein, however, refused to let the story die. The more they investigated, the more they suspected that the bungled break-in was but one example of chilling abuses of power that flowed from the White House. Following clues furnished by an unnamed informant known only as Deep Throat, Woodward and Bernstein published front-page stories asserting connections between the break-in and other alleged illegal actions of Nixon's Committee to Re-elect the President (CREEP).

After the Senate established a special committee to investigate the allegations, Nixon allowed his new attorney general, Elliott Richardson, to appoint a special Watergate prosecutor with broad investigative and subpoena powers. The Senate hearings, televised during the summer of 1973, revealed that Nixon illegally had ordered government agencies to harass foes on the president's enemies list. The hearings also exposed the president's attempt to impede the government's investigations into the Watergate incident. Nixon, of course, denied these accusations. Then a bombshell exploded at the hearings when a former Nixon aide testified that secret tape recordings of conversations in the Oval House were extant. When the special prosecutor, Archibald Cox, demanded to hear these tapes, Nixon told Attorney General Richardson to fire Cox. Richardson refused and promptly was fired. Richardson's deputy, William Ruchelshaus, also refused and was also fired. Finally, the third in command at the Justice Department, Robert Bork, fired Cox. The dismissal of Richardson, Ruchelshaus, and Cox, known as the Saturday Night Massacre, turned many against the president.

Even as the noose tightened around the president's neck, Vice President Agnew was charged with income tax evasion and accepting illegal bribes. Pleading no contest to the charges, Agnew resigned from the vice presidency and received a mild, three-year suspended sentence for his offenses. Later, Nixon selected House minority leader, Gerald Ford, a popular congressman known for his integrity, to replace Agnew as vice president.

Meanwhile, the legal battle over control of the controversial tapes contin-ued. After months of wrangling, the Supreme Court ordered Nixon to release the tapes to the new special prosecutor, Leon Jaworski. Finally, Nixon was trapped. He could not deny the words on the tapes that documented not only his vulgar language, but also his ordering of illegal wiretaps on political foes and his involvement in the cover-up of the Watergate break-in. When it became evident that the president did not have the support in Congress to withstand impeachment and conviction, Nixon announced that he would resign from the presidency. On August 9, 1974, Gerald Ford, a politician who had never run for office outside his home district in Michigan, was sworn in as the president of the United States.

Looking backward on the events of their youth, the baby boomers who came of age rocking to the music of Elvis Presley and the Beatles realized that the America of their childhood had changed radically into a more cynical and complex world. The titles of the songs of their favorite musicians seemed to echo both the story of their lives and the greening of their nation. As young teens they swooned to Presley's romantic classics "Love Me Tender" (1956) and "Don't Be Cruel" (1956) and later grooved to the upbeat, early Beatles hits like "She Loves You" (1964) and "I Want to Hold Your Hand" (1964). A few years later they turned on to the Beatles' subtle reference to LSD in "Lucy in the Sky with Diamonds" (1967) and the band's not-so-subtle reference to the sexual revolution in "Why Don't We Do It in the Road?" (1968). In confusing times, America's youth were stilled and inspired by the softer protests of Simon and Garfunkel's "The Sounds of Silence" (1964) and "Bridge Over Troubled Waters" (1970) and were moved and distressed by the faster, scorching sounds of Led Zeppelin's "Communication Break-down" (1969) and "When the Levee Breaks" (1971). As they watched folk rock evolve into hard rock and back again into country rock, they somberly reflected on the changes they had witnessed by singing Dion's "Abraham, Martin and John" (1968) and Don McLean's "American Pie" (1972). Lyrics from Dion's song reflected the turbulent decade:

Has anybody here seen my old friend Martin?
Can you tell me where he's gone?
He freed a lot of people,
But it seems the good die young,
But I just looked around and he's gone.

Memories of assassinations, Vietnam, oil shortages, Watergate, seculariza-tion of morality, the ever-present stagflated economy, the tragic death by drug overdose of rock-and-roll "King" Elvis Presley (1977) and, later, the senseless murder of the Beatles' John Lennon (1980) tarnished American idealism, dampened expectations for the future, and reminded baby boomers of the lost innocence of their youth. To the thirty-something Americans of the late seventies, the ages of Camelot and Aquarius were but memories of a distant past.

While Americans tried to forget the unraveling of Vietnam, another foreign government that had long been held together by American foreign policy teetered on the verge of a collapse that would bring about another turning point in American history.

CHAPTER 13

AMERICA TAKEN HOSTAGE

November 4, 1979

The Iranian Hostage Crisis and the Restructuring of the World Order

America Taken Hostage. January 1, 1979

(Photo by MPI/Getty Images)

TIME LINE

1974   OPEC hikes oil prices; stagflation disrupts the U.S. economy

1976   Jimmy Carter defeats Gerald Ford to win the presidency

1978   Carter brokers the Camp David Accords between Egypt and Israel

1979   The Iran hostage crisis begins

1980   The Soviets invade Afghanistan; the United States boycotts the Moscow Olympics

Ronald Reagan defeats Carter to win the presidency

1981   Personal income taxes are reduced

1984   Reagan wins a landslide victory over Walter Mondale

1987   Congress holds hearings on the Iran-contra scandal

1988   George Bush defeats Michael Dukakis to win the presidency

1989   Germans tear down the Berlin Wall

1990   Iraq invades Kuwait

1991   Operation Desert Storm liberates Kuwait

1992   Race riots break out in Los Angeles

Bill Clinton defeats George Bush and Ross Perot to win the presidency

1993   Congress passes NAFTA

1994   Promoting their Contract with America, Republicans win control of Congress

1996   Clinton defeats Robert Dole and Ross Perot to win a second term

1998   The House impeaches Clinton following the Monica Lewinsky affair

1999   The Senate acquits Clinton; Clinton's approval ratings soar to 70 percent

Taking in more income than it spends, the United States begins to reduce the national debt

In November 1979, on a misty morning in Tehran, the capital of Iran, an angry crowd of several hundred Iranian students gathered one block east of the American embassy. Waving placards scrawled with curses, the students shouted slogans of hatred against President Jimmy Carter for allowing the exiled shah of Iran into the United States for cancer treatment. To these angry protesters, President

Carter's action was not a gesture of humanitarian concern for a dying man, but a nefarious ploy to protect the despised shah against justice. Most Americans on that morning knew little and cared even less about the circumstances in Iran that produced such pent-up anger against the shah and those who befriended him. As a result of this event, however, Americans would take notice of the turmoil in Iran and learn that geographical distance did not isolate them from the consequences of violence sanctioned in the name of religion.

Like pieces of a mysterious jigsaw puzzle, clandestine and overt events within America and throughout the world came together at the right time and in the right place to instigate this history-changing event. Only in retrospect do the disparate pieces fit together to predict the issue that would define the new millennium.

The Watergate scandal left a legacy of mistrust that soured relations not only between U.S. citizens and their political parties, but also between the branches of American government. After jail terms for implication in the scandal were handed down to a Nixon cabinet member and twenty-five presidential aides, Congress became less trusting of the executive office and more protective of its own constitutional powers. Even before Nixon left office, Congress over-rode his veto on the War Powers Act (1973), which limited the authority of the president to make war without the approval of Congress. Around the time of Nixon's resignation, Congress reacted further to perceived abuses in the Nixon White House by passing a campaign reform bill that set limits on the amount of money that could be contributed and spent in political campaigns and a budget reform bill that limited the power of the president to impound (refuse to spend) funds appropriated by Congress. The Watergate fiasco did not immediately send a message about the strength of American democracy to the rest of the world. Instead, it continued a pattern of disintegration in the perceived strength and trustworthiness of America, which had already been weakened by the Bay of Pigs incident.

Relations between the executive and legislative branches improved somewhat after Nixon's resignation since most members of Congress—Republicans and Democrats alike—viewed his successor, Gerald Ford, as an affable and honorable man of integrity. Still, all was not well. Ford's honeymoon ended when he issued a "full, free and absolute pardon" for any crimes Nixon "committed or may have committed" while in office—a blanket pardon that infuriated Democrats, who insisted that the former president should be treated like any other private citizen. The fact that Congress waffled for four months before it confirmed Ford's nomination of Nelson Rockefeller as vice president demonstrated Ford's difficulty in working with the Democratic-controlled Congress.

Energy and the Stagflated Economy

Finding a solution to the tricky economic problem of the 1970s, stagflation (inflation + stagnation), preoccupied the Ford administration as it had the later years of the Nixon administration. Everyone knew the culprit: the decision by the Arab members of the Organization of Petroleum Exporting Countries (OPEC) to retaliate against America's expression of support for Israel in the 1973 October War. The cutback in oil production and the petroleum embargo to the United States had triggered a swift escalation of oil prices. These soaring oil prices caused inflation and contributed to slow economic growth. Within three months of the embargo, the price of oil in the United States quadrupled.

The OPEC decision instigated, but did not entirely cause the soaring price of oil. America's dependency upon foreign oil, particularly Middle Eastern oil, had been long in coming. After World War II, the United States reigned as the world's largest oil producer, but by the mid-1960s, Middle Eastern oil output exceeded that of North America. Moreover, Congress placed a quota on oil imports during the Eisenhower administration, a move designed less to prevent foreign dependency than to protect the domestic price of oil from foreign competition. The quota assured good times for American oil companies, but resulted in a rapid depletion of America's domestic reserves. By the late sixties, the volume of known reserves in America was in ominous decline. By the early seventies, declines in domestic production levels followed. Even as business executives complained that government price controls discouraged oil companies from exploring for new reserves, Americans, addicted to energy habits acquired in eras of cheap oil, continued to consume oil at rapid rates. For a while, the purchase of additional import-exempt "residual oils" used largely by utility companies to generate electricity delayed the energy shortage, but by 1973, the demand for oil in America was running far ahead of its supply. America's declining oil reserves and growing dependence on foreign oil presented an opportunity to OPEC nations to improve their economic interests. That non-Arab as well as Arab members of OPEC hiked their prices in 1974 suggests that their motive was economic strategy rather than the anti-Israel rhetoric expressed after the October War. While it is true that OPEC nations and the major U.S. oil companies slowed production and raised prices to take advantage of America's lust for oil, much of the blame for the crisis rested with the insatiable habits of American consumers, who lavishly spent 35 percent of the world's energy on just 6 percent of the world's population.

Stagflation had a staggering impact on American life in the seventies. In Detroit, sales of gas-guzzling American-made automobiles plummeted, and a quarter of a million automobile workers lost their jobs. In the Midwest, American firms shut down the historic steel mills, idling tens of thousands of additional laborers. Soon both annual inflation rates and unemployment hit double-digit figures. Each president, beginning with Nixon and continuing through Ford and Carter, tried a variety of methods to stimulate economic growth without flaming inflation. Nixon attempted wage and price controls to slow inflation and attempted to deal with the energy crisis by reducing highway speed limits to fifty-five miles per hour, reestablishing daylight saving time, easing environmental regulations on coal mining, and authorizing the building of an 800-mile trans-Alaska pipeline to connect northern oil reserves with the lower forty-eight states. Ford tried to curb inflation by pushing for a balanced federal budget, vetoing dozens of high-priced federal bills, and asking citizens to embrace his "Whip Inflation Now" (WIN) campaign by voluntarily agreeing not to raise prices. Later, Carter attempted to solve the economic mess thorough a mixture of pump-priming methods, including tax cuts and the creation of public works and employment programs, and an energy policy that forced public conservation of natural resources and that encouraged tax breaks for oil exploration and for the development of alternative (solar, nuclear, and coal) sources of energy. All of these activities had some effect, but none produced all the desired outcomes. Meanwhile, during the 1970s the cost of a loaf of bread, along with countless other items, increased fourfold and the inflation-adjusted real wages of American workers fell by more than 5 percent.

Jimmy Carter: Humble, Humanitarian, and Hard to Know

With the Republican Party tarnished by the Watergate scandal, in the election of 1976 the incumbent, President Ford, narrowly lost his reelection bid to the Democratic challenger, Jimmy Carter, a political newcomer and relatively unknown former one-term governor of Georgia. Before entering politics, Carter graduated in the top tenth of his class from the U.S. Naval Academy, served as an officer in the nuclear submarine program, and, after his father's death, returned to his hometown in Plains, Georgia, to oversee the family's peanut farm. A soft-spoken, slow-speaking, "born-again Christian," Carter spent most Sundays during his adult life teaching Bible classes in the Southern Baptist churches he regularly attended. From Plains, this former naval officer and businessman-farmer launched a political career that ultimately took him from the Plains school board to the Georgia statehouse to the White House.

A different kind of politician with few ties to the power brokers inside the Washington beltway, Carter appeared, even to his foes, as a man of integrity and high principles. However, as a white southerner who affectionately hung Martin Luther King's portrait in his office, as a military officer who disliked accepting military solutions to international crises, and as a Southern Baptist whose moral views, particularly on issues regarding women's rights, differed widely from the great majority of those within his own denomination, Carter proved difficult to anticipate and hard to understand. For many, his strong convictions were riddled with contradictions, but to others, his honesty, deep religious faith, patriotism, and desire for reform were just the medicines the nation needed—the ideal antidotes for the ailments that beset America during the corrupted Watergate era.

After swearing the presidential oath, Carter's first words to the American people were gracious statements about Gerald Ford: "For myself and for our Nation, I want to thank my predecessor for all he has done to heal our land." Then, more like a pastor than a president, he quoted a text from the prophet Micah—"What doth the Lord require of thee, but to do justly, and to love mercy, and to walk humbly with thy God"—and followed it with a homily that reminded the nation of its origins as "the first society openly to define itself in terms of both spirituality and of human liberty." This "unique self-definition," he insisted, imposed certain moral obligations on the nation. "Our commitment to human rights," he said, "must be absolute, our laws fair, our natural beauty preserved; the powerful must not persecute the weak, and human dignity must be enhanced." He closed his first address by expressing the hope that when his administration had ended, people would say

> that we had remembered the words of Micah and renewed our search for humility, mercy, and justice; that we had torn down the barriers that separated those of different race and region and religion, . . . that we had ensured respect for the law, and equal treatment under the law, for the weak and the powerful, for the rich and the poor; and that we had enabled our people to be proud of their own Government once again.

Carter's inaugural address would not be the last time that he would preach to Americans about the need to live selfless lives, to be good stewards of the nation's natural resources, to view diversity as a strength, not a weakness, to gain the world's respect through moral example rather than physical intimidation, to sacrifice economic self-interest for communal goals, and to make the expansion of human rights abroad the fundamental tenet of America's foreign diplomacy. Over time, Americans grew weary of being scolded by their president for simply being human. Even if humility, mercy, and justice were godly virtues, this did not mean that all Americans supported Carter for pardoning the "draft dodgers" of the Vietnam era or promoting a treaty that allowed the gradual transfer to Panama of control over the Panama Canal. Even if most citizens agreed with Carter that "America did not invent human rights" but "human rights invented America," this did not mean that they all agreed with Carter that the United States should refuse to support anticommunist dictators simply because of their poor human rights records. Similarly, even if the president lectured that using car pools, taking public transportation, obeying the speed limit, and turning down the thermostat to save energy were acts of patriotism, this did not mean that Americans relished the inconveniences of these sacrifices or enjoyed feeling hot in the summers and cold in the winters.

Carter achieved some successes, but often even his victories were short-lived or partial. For example, he brought more minorities into government, appointing women, Hispanics, and African-Americans in record numbers as federal judges, ambassadors, and high-ranking policy makers, but he failed to persuade the states to ratify the equal rights amendment, a constitutional amendment that would have prohibited discrimination based on sex. He created a Department of Energy and signed a major energy act, but only a watered-down version of the comprehensive energy package he originally requested became law. He deregulated the transportation industry, thus resulting in more competition and lower airfares, lifted price controls on natural gas, which had been regulated since the New Deal, and secured the creation of the controversial Department of Education. He also raised the minimum wage in stages from $2.30 to $3.35 per hour (equivalent to over $8 per hour in today's currency), but these benefits to low-income Americans also compounded the national problem of soaring inflation.

In foreign affairs, Carter's policies also received mixed reviews. Building upon the initiatives of Nixon and Ford, Carter established diplomatic relations with China and, after a bitter senatorial debate, secured the ratification of a canal treaty with Panama that had been supported by all American presidents since Lyndon Johnson. These achievements, however, came at the price of alienating conservatives, many of whom had supported Carter in 1976.

Carter's greatest diplomatic accomplishment came when he brokered the historic Camp David Accords between Egypt and Israel. This 1978 "framework for peace" led to Israel's withdrawal from the rich oil fields and airfields of the Sinai Peninsula, Egypt's recognition of Israel's right to exist, the establishment of diplomatic ties between these perennial enemies, and a tacit agreement to continue negotiations toward resolving issues involving autonomy for Palestinians living in lands occupied by Israel. Although hailed by most of the world, the Camp David Accords were rejected by Islamic fundamentalists, who vilified President Carter and, years later, would assassinate Anwar Sadat, the Egyptian leader who signed the agreement. Nevertheless, most Americans at the time felt that the conflict between Israel and the Arab world was finally near a solution.

The Crisis of Confidence of 1979

Unfortunately, the historic Camp David Accords among world leaders failed to arrest the populist crisis brewing in the Middle East. Back in the early 1950s, elected Iranian authorities had nationalized the oil companies in the region, and in response, the United States had used the CIA to instigate a coup to place Shah Mohammad Reza Pahlavi in power. For the next quarter of a century, the United States and the shah befriended each other, although Iran's Shiite population never forgot the memory of the coup that created this partnership. Early in 1979 the unexpected overthrow of the shah by revolutionary supporters of Iran's exiled Shiite Muslim spiritual leader, Ayatollah Ruholla Khomeini, upset the balance of power in the region. After the shah fled the country, Khomeini returned to Iran triumphantly to help establish a state governed by fundamentalist Islamic rule. Eager to restore Islamic values to the region, the ayatollah stirred up a religious fervor among the people by preaching contempt toward the shah and his Western allies, and by sanctioning riots, demonstrations, and spontaneous executions as ways to purge the land from the "satanic evils" that had infiltrated the nation during the decades of the shah's rule.

Curious Americans read about these developments in newspapers, but the events taking place in Iran paled in importance to other more pressing concerns that consumed their attention. In 1979, when the OPEC nations again hiked prices, doubling the price of oil, gasoline shortages and powerful inflationary pressures returned with a vengeance. To combat inflation, interest rates were raised to record levels, but even the tight monetary policy could not still the escalating inflation. By late spring the telltale signs of recession—factory layoffs, drops in automobile sales and housing starts, and declining labor productivity—were surfacing. Moreover, a pump failure at a nuclear power plant on Three Mile Island, near Harrisburg, Pennsylvania, forced an evacuation of citizens in the region that triggered both fear and distrust of President Carter's plan to ease the energy crunch by relying more on nuclear power. As gasoline prices broke the dollar-a-gallon barrier, summer tourism fell, further evidence of the deteriorating economic conditions.

In July, Carter invited more than a hundred political and economic leaders to the presidential retreat at Camp David to counsel him on the domestic crisis inflamed by the revolution in Iran. Following the marathon brainstorming session, Carter went to the airwaves to tell the American people how he proposed to respond. In a thirty-two-minute address heard by 60 million Americans, Carter presented a number of energy-specific proposals, but more memorably, he announced that the nation was facing a "crisis in confidence" that was "more serious than energy or inflation." "The erosion of our confidence in the future," Carter sermonized, "is threatening to destroy the social and political fabric of America."

Following in the American jeremiad tradition—a warning of impending doom—Carter first confessed his and the nation's inadequacies and then followed with a call for the nation to rededicate itself to its original goals. Like a fiery preacher upset at his congregation, Carter bemoaned the nation's materialism: "In a nation that was proud of hard work, strong families, close-knit communities, and our faith in God, too many of us now tend to worship self-indulgence and consumption. Human identity is no longer defined by what one does, but by what one owns." He followed this litany of shortcomings with a promise of hope for the future:

> We are strong. We can regain our unity. We . . . are the same Americans who just ten years ago put a man on the Moon. We are the generation that dedicated our society to the pursuit of human rights and equality. And we are the generation that will win the war on the energy problem and in that process rebuild the unity and confidence of America.

This "malaise speech," as it came to be called, alienated Americans who were weary of being admonished by their president, but it did spur Congress to move forward with Carter's energy proposals, which included a controversial "windfall profits" tax on oil companies.

However, America's energy and international problems worsened when Carter, without great forethought, granted the exiled shah a visa to come to the United States for cancer treatment. In Iran, Khomeini reacted by condemning the United States as the "Great Satan" and encouraging demonstrations against the action. As a result, on October 23, thirty thousand Iranians marched past the U.S. embassy in Tehran to demand the return of the shah for trial. A few days later, a group of students, all members of the Society of Islamic Students, met at the Tehran Poly-technical College to devise a plan to seize the American embassy and stage a sit-in for several days. They enlisted several hundred fellow students and assembled on the morning of November 4, 1979, about a block away from the embassy compound.

On this Sunday morning, the embassy employees did not expect trouble from the students marching down Taleghani Street. The employees had seen protests before. But this time they were wrong. The student protesters had a plan. At the front of the crowd, a wave of nonthreatening women students led the march. They approached the gates of the embassy without interference from the Iranian police, who watched with interest but made no move to stop or control them. At a preset instant the women at the front of the crowd parted. Several agile students lunged ahead and climbed up and over the embassy gates. Within seconds they unlocked the gates and threw them open to the crowd. The startled Iranian police backed away as the students stormed forward into the embassy compound.

As the students rushed inside the grounds of the embassy, several U.S. Marine guards took up positions to protect the buildings. At least one fired a tear gas canister. This action provoked the students even further. With orders not to fire or use any more tear gas, the marines retreated into the compound. With only a few handguns in their possession, the students spread out into the embassy ground, taking over predefined areas until they had captured every building. Within minutes following the breach of the gates, more than fifty stunned American staff members and marines were blindfolded, with their hands tied behind their backs, and led into a holding area. A marine later reported that while one student told him not to worry, another held a knife to his throat.

A Nation Held Hostage:
The Aftermath of the Student Takeover

With no opposition or direction from the confused Iranian government, the student protest turned from a sit-in to an occupation. Khomeini declared that any Iranian who negotiated with any U.S. government official would be treated as a traitor. The secular Iranian government officials were too afraid of being charged with treason to intervene. President Carter could find no authority with whom to negotiate.

For over a year the hostages remained in the hands of the Iranian students. Although many captors treated the hostages with some dignity, others detested the Americans. They kept all news and information away from the captives. One student told a hostage that his mother had died. He learned months later that she was still alive.

Diplomacy with Iran went nowhere and pleas to the students to respect international law and human rights were ignored. The Iranian government not only refused to intervene, it even refused to talk to anyone associated with the U.S. government. President Carter's wife, Roslyn, remembered her own frustration when she recounted a conversation with the president:

> No one can know how much pressure there was on Jimmy to do something. I would go out and campaign and come back and say, "Why don't you do something?" And he said, "What would you want me to do?" I said, "Mine the harbors." He said, "Okay, suppose I mine the harbors, and they decide to take one hostage out every day and kill him. What am I going to do then?"

With no real government operating in Iran, President Carter's administration found it difficult to negotiate a release. Plan after plan failed. As Americans tired of the delay, Carter found his popularity fading. Americans wanted action. Finally, Carter ordered a military rescue of the hostages, but it failed, resulting in the deaths of several soldiers.

The standoff lasted 444 days. This "hostage crisis," as it was commonly called, caught America off guard, consumed the American airwaves, and influenced a presidential election. It exposed many Americans to the politics of the Middle East for the first time. Today's ABC *Nightline* news commentary show is the direct descendant of a series of news specials with journalist Ted Koppel titled *The Iran Crisis: America Held Hostage*. Every night the program reminded the nation how much time had passed since the hostage takeover by posting on the television screen the pertinent tag, Day 10 . . . Day 159 . . . Day 285 . . . Day 378 . . . and on and on. No matter what other news was reported, every day Americans were reminded of the events of November 4, 1979. The nation could not, would not forget the American citizens held hostage in Iran. Because of the intensity of the news coverage of this incident, Americans who had previously shown little interest in Middle Eastern politics and Islamic fundamentalists came to realize that the policies of these faraway people could influence the future of the United States and the future of their everyday lives. The actions of angry students on the other side of the world swept away the popularity of a U.S. president and set in motion a flow of history that changed American lives and politics for decades to come.

Standing Tall: Ronald Reagan and the Rise of the New Right

Neither America's embarrassment in Iran nor President Carter's calls for energy conservation played well on Main Street. In the summer of 1980, the former movie star and politically conservative California governor Ronald Reagan won the Republican presidential nomination and selected his more moderate Republican challenger, George H.W. Bush, as his running mate. The election campaign pitted a somber incumbent besieged by stagnant wages, soaring inflation, and troubles abroad against an untried, celebrity politician with a sunny disposition. Although Carter's approval ratings were lower than any president's since Herbert Hoover, polls indicated that the race was tight, largely because the electorate was unsure about the competence of Reagan, the oldest man ever to run for the presidency, and the questionable wisdom of a Republican Party platform that favored a constitutional amendment to protect the right to life for unborn children, the repeal of environmental protection legislation and gun control legislation, and the elimination of the recently created Department of Education and the Department of Energy. In the one televised debate, however, Reagan's folksy demeanor reassured voters that he was competent and trustworthy. Moreover, Reagan's closing request for voters to ask themselves one simple question—"Are you better off today than you were four years ago?"—sounded reasonable to American voters.

In the final days of the campaign, large numbers of undecided voters fell into Republican hands. On Election Day, Reagan carried 51 percent of the popular vote while Carter, independent candidate John Anderson, and a host of minor party candidates carried the rest. In addition, for the first time since 1952, the Republican Party won control of the Senate. The once dominant Democratic Party crumbled into disarray. Among Franklin Roosevelt's old New Deal coalition, only African-Americans remained securely in the Democratic fold. Preferring change to status quo, American voters in 1980 favored the candidate who promised a future of abundance, not austerity; increased production, not conservation; and an unwavering commitment to building America's might, not giving lip service to human rights abroad.

As prearranged by Iranian and U.S. authorities, at the very minute that Reagan was sworn in as president the Iranians released the fifty-two Americans held hostage for 444 days. Carter could take solace that no American hostage died on his watch, but the nation paid a heavy price for their freedom. With the hostage problem resolved, Reagan could go to work addressing the other pressing concerns facing the nation.

Reagan's proposed solution to the nation's economic ills sounded painless enough. He promised a dramatic tax cut that would stimulate the economy by leaving taxpayers with more money to spend and businesses with more money to invest. As new businesses appeared and old ones grew, Reagan asserted, jobs would be created and additional tax revenues would pour into the treasury—funds that would enable the government to balance its budget and thereby reduce inflationary pressures. Not even all Republicans were confident that the plan would work. Before accepting the invitation to be Reagan's vice presidential running mate, George Bush had called this unorthodox plan "voodoo economics." This "supply-side" theory for economic growth, however, appealed to conservatives who disliked high taxes and big government. As Reagan said in his inaugural address, "Our government is too big and it spends too much." For the president and his conservative friends, big government was the cause, not the solution, of the nation's economic problems.

Balancing the budget through tax cuts was made more difficult since President Reagan also felt that America's military had weakened during the 1970s and needed to be revitalized. Consequently, even as he secured legislation that reduced income taxes by 25 percent, he also pushed Congress to increase defense spending by 75 percent. To dent the rising deficit, Reagan pressed Congress to cut $136 billion ($300 billion in today's currency) in federal spending in some 200 social and cultural programs, including programs that subsidized school lunches for low-income children, student loans, job training programs, and urban mass transit. The cut could have been deeper. After an unsuccessful attempt to reduce Social Security benefits in 1981, the president agreed to exempt safety-net programs such as Social Security and Medicare from cutbacks. Reagan also attacked the power of "big government" by continuing the deregulation efforts begun under Carter. Reagan, for instance, deregulated the banking and savings-and-loan industry, reduced federal authority over the telecommunication industry, and weakened the Antitrust Division of the Justice Department and the Security and Exchange Commission. He also opened federal wilderness areas and forest lands to developers and weakened or abolished hundreds of federal regulations regarding environmental protection, workplace safety, and consumer protection. Even with these reductions in the federal government, however, the size of the federal budget continued to grow during the 1980s, although at a slower pace than at any time since the Eisenhower presidency.

These actions produced dramatic results, some good and some bad. During the early years of Reagan's administration, the worst recession since the 1930s gripped the nation, raising unemployment rates to almost 11 percent. The tax cuts, coupled with dramatic increases in defense spending, also created a federal deficit that ballooned the national debt. Within eight years, the debt of the United States, which had been acquired over two centuries, doubled. On the upside, however, the tight-money, high-interest policies of Paul Volcker and Alan Greenspan, Carter's and Reagan's appointees to head the Federal Reserve Board, coupled with a worldwide decrease in the cost of energy, ultimately brought inflation under control. With inflation subdued, the stagnated economy, fed by massive defense spending and tax relief, finally began to rebound. In mid-1983, unemployment declined and stocks rose, igniting a period of economic growth that would continue for nearly a decade. When good times returned, America consumers shifted their spending patterns into high gear, purchasing personal computers, microwave ovens, fax machines, compact disc players, cordless telephones, and a variety of other newfangled gadgets that hit the market.

The pop culture of the period reflected America's newly acquired interest in luxurious living. Television shows such as *Dallas* and *Dynasty*, the sagas of wealthy, wheeling-dealing families, and *Lifestyles of the Rich and Famous* soared in popularity, even as pop singer Madonna's hit "Material Girl" celebrated the good life sought by America's youth. Gone was the social activism of the 1960s. Gone also was the learn-to-live-with-less ethic of the 1970s. In their places emerged a "yuppie" (young urban professionals) culture that promoted the right to work hard and the right to enjoy without guilt the benefits of that work. The avid pursuit of wealth, luxury, and pleasure no longer carried the negative connotations it had a generation earlier. Business values resonated in the opulent eighties to a degree not seen since the roaring twenties.

The booming economy came just in time for the next presidential election. Like most majority parties during midterm elections, the Republicans during the recession of 1982 lost seats in Congress. With the return of prosperity, however, in 1984 the Republicans were well positioned for a victory of landslide proportions. The Democrats nominated former vice president Walter Mondale, who made history by selecting Geraldine Ferraro as his running mate, the first female vice presidential nominee of a major political party. The Mondale-Ferraro ticket, however, could not derail the Republicans' uplifting campaign that featured the themes "Morning in America" and "Life is better, America is back." President Reagan received almost 59 percent of the popular vote, losing only the District of Columbia and Mondale's home state of Minnesota. The president, however, had short coattails. While the Republicans held control of the Senate, even with Reagan's landslide victory they failed to win a majority in the House of Representatives.

Second-Term Troubles and Successes

No U.S. president has had smooth sailing during his second term in office, and the second term jinx hit the popular Reagan as it did all his predecessors. Reagan's greatest difficulty stemmed from a scandal dubbed the Iran-contra affair. During his first term, the president announced that the United States would make distinctions between "totalitarian" regimes hostile to America and "authoritarian" governments friendly to American security interests. This Reagan Doctrine particularly influenced America's relations with nations in the Western Hemisphere. In El Salvador, for example, Reagan supported a repressive, anticommunist regime because its strength prevented leftist revolutionaries from gaining ascendancy in the area. Similarly, in Nicaragua Reagan halted U.S. aid to the leftist Sandinista regime and used the CIA to train, arm, and supply anti-Sandinista "contra" rebels who hoped to topple the regime. Rejecting this military assistance to the contras, Congress in 1982 passed the Boland Amendment, which specifically banned U.S. efforts to destroy the Sandinista regime.

Early in his second administration, however, developments in the Middle East gave the president, or at least members of his administration, an opportunity to circumvent the will of Congress. In 1985, the Reagan administration negotiated a deal that sent antitank and antiaircraft missiles to Iran in exchange for Iran's promise to use its influence to secure the release of American hostages that had been captured by Shiite militants in Lebanon. The profits obtained in the exchange, which according to the plan would remain unknown to Congress and the public, would be funneled to the contras in Nicaragua. Unfortunately for the administration, a disgruntled Iranian political faction leaked news of the activity in October 1986, causing a scandal that ultimately would send six members of the Reagan administration to prison. Insisting that he did not remember approving the arms-for-hostages exchange, Reagan appointed former Republican senator John Tower to head a commission to investigate the matter. After conducting the investigation, the Tower Commission chastised the president for an inept "management style," but concluded that Reagan himself "did not seem to be aware" of the illegal activities. With less than two years remaining in Reagan's second term, Congress chose not to bring impeachment charges against him. The scandal temporarily hurt the president and tarnished his legacy, but it did not destroy his popularity. Reagan's approval ratings remained high throughout his presidency.

One reason the public was willing to forgive Reagan's shortcomings was his determined effort to win the Cold War. When Reagan took residence in the White House, U.S. relations with the Soviet Union were strained, partly because of President Carter's decision to protest the 1980 Soviet invasion of Afghanistan by stopping grain exports to the USSR and boycotting the 1980 Moscow Olympic Games. Although Reagan reestablished grain trade with the Soviets, he had no desire to return to days of détente with America's archenemy. Reagan summed up his attitude toward the Soviet Union in a 1983 speech to the National Association of Evangelicals, a convention of Protestant Christians. "If history teaches us anything," Reagan warned, "it teaches that simple-minded appeasement or wishful thinking about our adversaries is folly"; America must not ignore "the aggressive impulses of an evil empire" or remove itself "from the struggle between right and wrong and good and evil." To Reagan and many Americans, the Cold War was not simply a struggle between two superpowers; it was a contest between the forces of good and evil.

To resist this "evil empire," Reagan reignited an arms race with the Soviets. In addition to enhancing America's nuclear arsenal, Reagan proposed launching the Strategic Defense Initiative (SDI), commonly known as "Star Wars" after a popular movie of the period. This plan involved appropriating funds to develop a system of laser weapons based in space that could shoot down enemy missiles before they could reach targets in the United States. Although expensive and scientifically problematic, the development of Star Wars technology challenged the premise of massive mutual retaliation that had kept the superpowers from using nuclear warheads throughout the Cold War. The Soviet Union's immediate response to Reagan's initiative was to accelerate its weapons buildup. The arms race of the 1980s, however, was also a race toward bankruptcy. Fortunately, the Soviets approached this finish line ahead of the United States. By 1986, after Mikhail Gorbachev came to power in Moscow, the financially crippled Soviets announced a desire to reduce the deployment of missiles and restructure Soviet society along more Western lines, a policy known as perestroika. By the end of Reagan's presidency, the United States and the USSR agreed to remove and destroy 2,500 nuclear missiles from Europe. When the Soviet Union also pulled its troops from Afghanistan, having failed in its war against the determined Islamic rebels, relations between the two superpowers became closer than at any time since the beginnings of the Cold War.

Reagan began his second administration with the inaugural charge, "Let history say of us, these were golden years—when the American Revolution was reborn, when freedom gained new life and America reached for her best." During his presidency, a revolution of a sort did take place in America, but whether the Reagan revolution expanded freedom is a question that has prompted a variety of partisan answers. Friends of the conservative president applauded the economic growth that the nation experienced during the 1980s and attributed the liberalizing tendencies afoot in the Soviet Union to the hard-line policies of the Cold Warrior president. Critics, however, pointed to the growing numbers of homeless Americans, to the widening gap between rich and poor and white and black Americans, and to the political and economic scandals that riddled both Wall Street and Washington. Asserting that the majority of the new jobs created during the decade were menial, low-paying positions, Reagan's opponents also charged that the wealthy minority received the greatest benefits from the alleged economic boom-times, gaining ground at the expense of a shrinking middle class and a future generation of taxpayers who would be saddled with repaying the national debt produced by the massive deficit spending of the Reagan years. As often is the case, the truth lies somewhere between these partisan statements. The charismatic Reagan bought together a conservative coalition of corporate leaders, suburbanites, and evangelical Christians that was able to accelerate the downsizing of government services and the upsizing of military spending, trends that were emerging during the later years of the Carter presidency. Moreover, America after Reagan was more confident about itself and its future. Yet, despite the rhetoric against the size of government, the Reagan revolution left intact most of Roosevelt's New Deal programs, Johnson's Great Society programs, and even Carter's newly created Department of Energy and Department of Education. The Reagan years diverted the flow of history, but did not reverse it.

George Bush and the Ebb of Republican Ascendancy

Although never loved by conservatives as much as Reagan, Vice President George Bush won the Republican nomination in 1988 and selected as his running mate Dan Quayle, an Indiana senator with strong conservative credentials. In accepting the nomination, Bush called for a "kinder, gentler America" and promised "no new taxes" under any circumstances. In the general election, the Bush-Quayle team faced the Democratic ticket of Massachusetts governor Michael Dukakis and his vice presidential running mate, Senator Lloyd Bentsen of Texas. The Republicans won with a 54 percent majority of the popular vote, a comfortable victory, although five points under the size of Reagan's landslide victory of 1984.

Three major happenings consumed the Bush presidency, two developments abroad and one at home. First, Bush had the privilege of serving as president as the Cold War came to a happy ending. Since the Truman Doctrine was announced in 1946, nine American presidents had been vigilant in fighting communism. Under Bush, all these efforts paid off. After Gorbachev liberalized Soviet society and refused to send troops to prop up unpopular Marxist regimes in Europe, the eastern block began to crumble. In November 1989, East German border guards watched passively as West Berliners tore down the Berlin Wall, the Cold War symbol of the East-West divide. Soon Germany reunited as a democratic government, and the former Soviet puppets of Estonia, Latvia, and Lithuania and, later, the separate republics within the Soviet Union declared their independence. Although communist regimes held ground in China, North Korea, Vietnam, and Cuba, the seemingly endless Cold War with the Soviets that had dominated America's political life for more than four decades was over.

As Americans cheered what was happening in Europe, they looked with concern at developments in the explosive Middle East. During the 1980s, a savage war had raged between two vastly different Middle Eastern states with large Islamic Shiite majorities: Iran, a theocracy controlled by radical Shiites sympathetic to the fundamentalist teachings of the Ayatollah Khomeini, and Iraq, a largely secular state controlled by dictator Saddam Hussein. Although 56 percent of Iraq's population was Shiite, Hussein himself was a Sunni Muslim who feared that Iran's new revolutionary leadership could threaten Iraq's delicate Sunni-Shiite balance. In 1980, the ambitious Hussein, who also hoped to consolidate his prestige among Arab states, invaded Iran. The grisly eight-year war that followed left one million dead, but settled little. During the war, the United States officially remained neutral, although it assisted both sides. Secretly, the United States sold the infamous arms-for-hostages weapons to Iran, while publicly the United States reestablished diplomatic relations with Iraq (which had been broken since 1967), removed Iraq from its list of nations that supported terrorism, sold Boeing jets to Iraq, extended it $400 million in credit, and established a Washington-to-Baghdad link to provide Iraq with faster intelligence from U.S. satellites. After the war, the United States continued to pursue a conciliatory policy toward Iraq, allowing Hussein to purchase heavy machinery and to develop the technology needed to produce weapons of mass destruction.

Saddam Hussein tragically misinterpreted the extent of U.S. friendship toward him. Angered at the neighboring nation of Kuwait for pumping more oil than the OPEC quotas allowed, thus lowering the world price of oil, Hussein asserted that this tiny, oil-rich nation to his south was an ancient Iraqi province. In August 1990, Hussein sent Iraqi troops into Kuwait and seized its oil fields. In response to the invasion, President Bush moved quickly and decisively. Bush rallied both Congress and the United Nations to support a clearly defined military objective: Iraq must withdraw from Kuwait or a UN coalition of nations would force it to withdraw. The UN promptly imposed economic sanctions against Iraq and gave the aggressor six months to withdraw. When the deadline passed without Iraqi withdrawal, on January 16, 1991, Operation Desert Storm, a war that pitted thirty-four UN nations against Hussein's regime, began.

Every day for six weeks, Americans watched CNN's live coverage of the air war that pounded Iraqi troops and supply lines. To Americans seated comfortably in their living rooms, the war seemed like a glorified action-packed video game. By late February, the ground phase of the war began as 200,000 coalition troops under General Norman Schwarzkopf swept into Kuwait. Within three days, the Iraqi army crumbled. During the brief war, 148 Americans and more than 100,000 Iraqis lost their lives. With the Iraqi army in ruins and Kuwait's ruling family safely returned to power, the combatants declared a cease-fire. Under the declaration, the badly bruised Hussein reluctantly admitted teams of UN weapon inspectors into his country, although he would survive in power by using his loyal army to brutally suppress Shiite uprisings against his regime in the south and Kurdish rebellions in the north.

A largely unnoticed and unpredicted problem resulted as a consequence of Desert Storm. During and after the war, Saudi Arabia allowed U.S. troops to occupy Saudi territory. This presence of Western soldiers near Islamic holy sites infuriated many Muslims, who felt it violated Quranic law. Among those opposed to America's occupation of the region was Saudi millionaire Osama bin Laden. This radical, who once cooperated with the CIA to repel the Soviets from Afghanistan, now used his wealth and position to build al Queda, a clandestine organization dedicated to eliminating all Western influences in the Middle East. A decade later, Osama bin Laden would become the most vilified person in America since Adolf Hitler.

Despite the success of the war to liberate Kuwait, in time escalating domestic troubles cut into President Bush's popularity. Early in his administration, Bush secured the passage of the Clean Air Act (1989) and the Americans with Disabilities Act (1990), significant environmental and social measures that were applauded by moderates, but dismayed conservatives reluctant to expand the size and regulatory powers of the federal government. Later in his presidency, Bush's popularity began to sink along with the U.S. economy. Many of the economic ills that plagued Bush actually were not his doing. Rather, just as Bush inherited the short-term benefits of the popular Reagan revolution, he also inherited some of its long-term negative consequences. For example, Reagan's deregulation of the savings-and-loan industry had allowed fund managers to invest in risky ventures, many of which failed in the speculative markets of the 1980s. Since the government insured these lost deposits, the federal government faced an enormous bailout bill approaching $500 billion. This unexpected expense raised even higher the massive deficits that resulted from the tax cuts and increased military spending of the Reagan years. The national debt, which in 1981 was still under $1 trillion, quadrupled to an astronomical $4 trillion in just over a decade.

To compound this problem, in July 1990 the seven-year expansion of the economy ended and the nation plunged into a recession. As housing starts and auto and retail sales fell and unemployment rates rose, millions of additional Americans fell into poverty. The inner cities of America were particularly hard-hit. In 1992, riots broke out in a black ghetto in Los Angeles that left forty-four dead and a billion dollars in property destroyed. Racial tensions rose and unpleasant memories of the turbulent 1960s resurfaced. As one journalist remarked, if 1984 was "morning in America," the early 1990s were "the morning after."

Bush responded to the mounting problems of soaring debt, slow growth, high unemployment, low wages, and growing poverty by making a necessary but unpopular deal with Capitol Hill. In late 1990, Congress passed and Bush signed a deficit reduction plan that included both tax increases and spending cuts. Many conservatives in his party refused to support this legislation and never forgave Bush for breaking his "no new taxes" promise. The same president who earlier enjoyed 90 percent approval ratings suddenly found himself in hot political water.

Bill Clinton and the Politics of the Nasty Nineties

Despite Bush's foreign policy successes, by 1992 American voters were anxious, frustrated, and even angered at the direction that the United States was taking. Capitalizing on the economic difficulties of the early 1990s were two emerging political stars, Democrat governor Bill Clinton of Arkansas and Texas billionaire businessman Ross Perot. Intelligent, articulate, and ambitious, Clinton won the Democratic nomination and selected Senator Al Gore of Tennessee as his running mate. Having two southerners running on the same ticket defied political wisdom, but given the angry mood of the nation against politics as usual, political unorthodoxy at this time was an asset, not a liability. Equally unorthodox in style and background was the feisty, tough-talking independent candidate, Perot, who insisted that America needed a CEO with business sense to clean up the mess made by professional politicians. For their part, the Republicans renominated Bush, although during the primary season he was challenged by the cable television commentator Patrick Buchanan, who questioned Bush's conservative credentials and sounded the pressing need to liberate America from the control of liberals, feminists, immigrants, and homosexuals. By the November election, the besieged president, heading a bruised and divided party, had to confront simultaneously a hungry and energetic Democratic Party and a powerful billionaire who appealed to many disenchanted Republicans.

The election of 1992 resulted in the worst debacle for an incumbent in eighty years. Clinton won the election by carrying 43 percent of the popular vote. Bush carried only 37 percent of the popular vote, the worst showing for an incumbent since Taft's defeat in 1912. Perot, in contrast, with 19 percent of the vote, made the best showing for a third-party candidate in American history. The only good news for Republicans was that Clinton had no coattails. Although the Democrats maintained a narrow control of Congress, they lost seats in both the House and the Senate.

A minority elected president with little if any national mandate, Clinton never enjoyed the honeymoon period traditionally allotted to new presidents. The nineties were not times for niceties, particularly when a controversial politician like Clinton was involved. He immediately infuriated conservatives with his call for gun control legislation and his "Don't ask, don't tell" policy that allowed homosexuals to serve in the military as long as they hid their sexual orientation. Liberals also were miffed with his crusades to reduce the deficit, to reform the welfare system, and to eliminate tariff protection legislation. A centrist "New Democrat" with a sharp mind and big ego, Clinton enjoyed being the center of attention and seemed even to revel in the controversies that followed him at every turn.

During his first term, Clinton achieved many, but not all, of his major domestic objectives. For instance, he overcame the lobbying efforts of the powerful National Rifle Association by signing the Brady bill, which required a waiting period before the sale of handguns. He also persuaded enough reluctant members of both parties to pass two major trade agreements, the North American Free Trade Agreement (NAFTA), which eliminated tariff barriers that stifled trade between Canada, Mexico, and the United States, and the General Agreement on Tariffs and Trade (GATT), which reduced tariffs worldwide and established the World Trade Organization to mediate commercial disputes among 117 nations. In addition, Clinton secured the narrow passage of a controversial deficit reduction plan that included both federal spending cuts and significant tax increases, and he signed an anticrime bill that banned assault weapons and provided funds for building more prisons and placing more police officers on the streets. His greatest first-term disappointment was his failure to get an ambitious health care package through Congress. This plan, which was prepared by a blue-ribbon commission headed by the president's wife, Hillary Rodham Clinton, offered medical coverage to all U.S. citizens, but came with a price tag most members of Congress were unprepared to accept.

Despite or perhaps because of these accomplishments, Clinton had to constantly dodge the slings and arrows of foes who despised him, his wife, and his political agenda. Right-leaning talk show hosts accused the president of murdering his friend Vincent Foster, of illegalities regarding some real estate deals he made in the 1980s, of turning the government over to a cadre of radical feminists and homosexuals, and of engaging in extramarital affairs. The latter charge carried with it the merit of being true.

With character issues swirling around the president's head, Republican congressman Newt Gingrich of Georgia seized the opportunity to move in for the political kill. Supported by a coalition of Christian evangelicals, gun owners, and conservative think tanks, Gingrich gathered 300 Republican candidates on the steps of the Capitol to sign a "Contract with America," promising to work toward lower taxes, congressional term limits, a balanced budget amendment, and a host of other popular reforms. Gingrich's Contract with America movement paid immediate political dividends both for himself and for his party. In the midterm 1994 elections, Republicans gained control of both houses of Congress for the first time since 1954, and Gingrich became the Speaker of the House. Republicans stunned by their loss of the White House in 1992 eagerly looked forward to the opportunity to regain it in the next presidential election.

If Clinton was anything, however, he was a survivor. Shortly before the 1996 election season, Clinton delivered a promised bipartisan welfare reform bill that limited welfare benefits to two years of continuous benefits and made work a condition for public assistance. Although the bill disappointed liberals such as Massachusetts senator Edward Kennedy, its passage enhanced Clinton's reputation as a centrist New Democrat who rejected the tired tax-and-spend policies of his Democratic predecessors. Riding the waves of his political successes and a booming economy, in the ensuing election Clinton easily defeated his two challengers, Republican senator Robert Dole and the once intriguing but now tiresome independent candidate, Ross Perot.

The Twin Legacies of President Clinton

Like his first four years, Clinton's second term was an emotional roller coaster ride. On the upside, Clinton achieved fame playing David taking on the Goliath of the tobacco industry. Using the powers of the attorney general's office, Clinton forced the tobacco companies to reimburse the states $200 billion for tobacco-related medical costs and to end advertisements aimed at teenage populations. He also signed key legislation that not only offered tax relief, but also provided a timetable for a balanced budget within five years. Rapid economic growth during the late 1990s allowed Clinton to beat the targeted deadline by three years. In 1999, when for the first time in three decades the government took in more revenue than it expended, Clinton used the surplus to reduce the national debt and to strengthen the future solvency of the Social Security system.

Meanwhile, during his presidency the Dow Jones average increased 8,000 points in eight years, poverty rates declined to their lowest levels in decades, unemployment dipped to about 4 percent, inflation was lowered to insignificant levels, property crime rates and violent crime rates fell, and educational attainment statistics of America's youth improved. By the numbers, America during the Clinton years was better off than any time in its history.

These victories, however, were offset by one of the most sordid and embarrassing moments in the nation's history. During Clinton's first term, an independent counsel, Kenneth Starr, was appointed to investigate alleged improprieties Bill and Hillary Clinton may have committed when Clinton was the governor of Arkansas. Public investigations into what a president or his family may have done before coming to the White House would have been considered unseemly in previous eras, but in the charged, nasty nineties, presidents were fair game in any season.

In time, the Starr probe expanded to include a wide range of possible wrongdoings, but after four years of investigations, no major indictments against the Clintons were presented. However, in early 1998, President Clinton was subpoenaed to give testimony in a sexual harassment suit filed against him by Paula Jones, who charged that Clinton had solicited sexual favors from her when he was governor of Arkansas. Seeking to establish a pattern of harassment, Jones's lawyers asked Clinton about his sexual relationship with a White House intern named Monica Lewinsky. Clinton denied having a sexual relationship with Lewinsky. Unbeknownst to Clinton, however, a friend of Lewinsky, Linda Tripp, secretly (and illegally) had taped her telephone conversations with Lewinsky. In these conversations, Lewinsky boasted of sexual encounters she had had with the president. Although a judge ultimately dismissed Jones's suit, Tripp gave the tapes of Lewinsky's conversations to Starr, who then extended his probe to determine if Clinton had committed perjury in his testimony in the Jones case.

Initially, Lewinsky refused to cooperate with the Starr investigation, but in August 1998, after being given the choice of prison for failing to cooperate or the promise of immunity for providing testimony, Lewinsky appeared before Starr's grand jury to acknowledge her relationship with the president. Under oath, Clinton then testified that he had committed "conduct that was wrong" with Lewinsky, but insisted that his earlier testimony was "legally accurate" since he had never had sexual intercourse with her.

The sex scandal created more media coverage that any other event in 1998. Historians know that extramarital affairs among people of power—presidents, members of congress, generals, cabinet members—are not uncommon, but this scandal was unique. Never before had the public been so bombarded with graphic descriptions of a president's intimate sexual activities or the contours of the private parts of his anatomy. Moreover, in the politically savage, post-Watergate era of special prosecutors, Clinton faced more than simply public humiliation. In September, Starr presented a 4,800-word report to the House Judiciary Committee that detailed the sordid affair and concluded that there were "credible" grounds for impeachment. For three months, first the Judiciary Committee and later the House debated whether the president had committed "high crimes and misdemeanors" worthy of impeachment. Ultimately, in a fiercely partisan vote, the House approved two articles of impeachment, charging Clinton with perjury in his grand jury testimony and with obstruction of justice in his attempts to conceal the truth. For the first time since the 1860s, a sitting president was formally impeached.

Before the Senate could hold the impeachment trial, American voters in the midterm elections of 1998 expressed their anger, but their dissatisfaction was directed less at the president accused of misconduct than at the zealous partisans who made the accusations. Contrary to Republican hopes, the Democrats not only held their Senate seats, but also picked up five seats in the House. The stunning debacle for the Republicans at the polls forced the resignation of House Speaker Newt Gingrich, who not only gave up his leadership position but resigned his House seat. Ironically, within a few weeks, Gingrich's assumed successor as House Speaker also resigned from Congress after a journalist published a report of his adulterous relationships. The partisans of 1998 learned the hard way the wisdom of Jesus's injunction, "Let he who is without sin cast the first stone."

In early 1999, the Senate conducted the impeachment trial. During the trial, Clinton's approval ratings soared to nearly 70 percent. Although Americans disapproved of the president's moral lapses, many were even angrier at the supporting characters in the lurid saga—Independent Counsel Kenneth Starr; Henry Hyde, the Republican chair of the House Judiciary Committee; and Linda Tripp, Lewinsky's faithless friend. When the Senate acquitted the president of the charges, the public finally got the resolution it wanted: Clinton would stay and the long impeachment ordeal would go away. Following the verdict, the president again expressed his remorse and urged the nation to move on.

As the new millennium approached, America, notwithstanding all its flaws, was a confident and prosperous land. The United States not only had ended the hostage crisis and won the Cold War, but it also seemed to have conquered the problem of its massive debt. Times were good. Proud of their past and optimistic for their future, Americans believed that both liberty and security were within their reach. Although the promise of "liberty and equality for all" was still more of an aspiration than a reality, Americans once again were confident that their best times were yet ahead.

CHAPTER 14

TERRORISTS STUN AMERICA

September 11, 2001

Negotiating Security and Liberty in the Twenty-first Century

Attack on The World Trade Center. 2001

(Photo by Douglas Longenecker, The September 11 Digital Archive, August 25, 2005. http://911digitalarchive.org/images/details/2792).

TIME LINE

1948   The United States recognizes the State of Israel

1973   Arab-Israeli conflict results in an oil embargo against the West

1979   Iranian hostage crisis begins

1983   Islamic Jihad terrorists attack the U.S. embassy in Beirut

1985   The Palestinian Liberation Front hijacks the Italian cruise ship *Achille Lauro*

1988   Libyan terrorists bomb a Pan American passenger jet over Lockerbie, Scotland

1991   Operation Desert Storm liberates Kuwait

1993   Al Queda terrorists bomb the basement of the New York World Trade Center

1996   Osama Bin Laden establishes a terrorist training camp in Afghanistan

1998   Al Queda bombs U.S. embassies in Kenya and Tanzania

2000   Bin Laden's network attacks the USS *Cole*

   George W. Bush defeats Al Gore in a disputed presidential election

2001   Al Queda terrorists attack the World Trade Center and the Pentagon

   President Bush's approval ratings soar to 90 percent

   U.S. and British forces topple the Taliban government of Afghanistan

2003   Believing Saddam Hussein holds weapons of mass destruction, the United States and Britain overthrow Hussein's government in Iraq

2004   No weapons of mass destruction are found in Iraq

   Bush defeats John Kerry to win reelection

   An undersea earthquake in the Indian Ocean triggers a series of devastating tsunamis

2005   Hurricane Katrina causes massive destruction in Louisiana, Mississippi, and Alabama; the government is faulted for an insufficient response to the tragedy

   Bush appoints John Roberts and Samuel Alito to the Supreme Court

2006   Hot topics include immigration reform, the effectiveness of the war in Iraq, and nuclear crises with North Korea and Iran

On the morning of September 11, 2001, an appalling drama played out on the radios of commuters and on the televisions of unbelieving audiences at home and work. At first, reports suggested that at 8:46 AM a wayward private plane had hit a building in downtown New York. Black smoke billowed from a hole in the North Tower of the World Trade Center. Emergency workers and the media scrambled to the location. At 9:02 another plane slammed into the South Tower of the World Trade Center. Reports confirmed that the planes were passenger jets. At 9:43 a third passenger jet crashed into the Pentagon. Shortly after 10:00 news stations flashed a report about a passenger jet crashing in Pennsylvania.

When the first alarms sounded, New York firefighters rushed to the North Tower and set up a command post in the lobby. They climbed the stairs to find and rescue the thousands of stunned people in the burning tower. On the top floors, trapped workers called for help on their cell phones. Blinding smoke blocked passageways. Fuel and fire poured down the elevator shafts. The 110-story towers shook as the fire weakened the buildings' superstructure. People jumped or fell from broken windows ninety floors up. At 9:59, with a sudden roar, the South Tower collapsed, crushing and incinerating all who remained inside. At 10:28 the North Tower collapsed. A grisly total of 2,617 people perished. Among that number were 343 firefighters who lost their lives trying to save others. A total of 685 employees of Cantor Fitzgerald, an investment banking company, were lost. Marsh & McLennan, an insurance brokerage firm, lost 295 employees. Employees of dozens of other companies and hundreds of people aboard the airplanes all vanished into the tons of rubble dust.

Millions of people across the world witnessed the collapse of the World Trade Center towers and the scene of destruction at the Pentagon. The horrific scenes televised on that day were suddenly and permanently etched into the minds of millions of Americans. Web pages and blogs appeared overnight where people from all over the world shared feelings and reactions. One student in Chicago known only as Kristin recalled:

> I was waking up to attend school on September 11th to my mom telling me that "a plane hit the trade towers." I will never forget the fear and urgency in her voice. I turned on CNN just in time to see the second plane hit and then I knew it was no accident. . . . When I reached my university, there were a lot of parking spots open . . . I turned around and went back home. That night, I went with a friend of mine to donate blood at a local organization. I remember sitting there with several people (the line of donors was amazing) and everyone sat in silence to hear the President address the nation.
>
> . . . I remember crying when I saw the individuals pleading on

television to find their loved ones and attending memorial services and candlelight vigils. September 11th is an event that I will never forget.*

Stunned by the attack, people from every U.S. city and town responded by raising flags, putting up banners saying "God Bless America," and standing arm in arm in nonpartisan shows of support. Politicians from both parties pledged to bring the perpetrators to justice. The world soon learned that Muslim extremists took credit for the attack. Why they staged a strike against nonmilitary working men and women remained a mystery to most Americans.

Tracing the Sources of Hate

In 1969, Martin Luther King Jr. challenged the people of the United States with the statement, "We must learn to live together as brothers or perish together as fools." Although his comment referred directly to the American racial struggle, the words rang out with a universal truth. As unpredictable and unprecedented as the September 11 attack appeared, it is only one of many incidents in the world's long history of ethnic, cultural, and religious clashes.

Even the "ethnic cleansing" during World War II did not stem the hatred among the world's peoples. Responding to the Holocaust, which took the lives of six million Jews, and to the survivors' desire for a homeland, in 1947 the United Nations divided Palestine into Jewish and Arab areas, and the next year the State of Israel was established. Immediately, the surrounding Arab countries declared war on the new country based on centuries-old religious and ethnic differences. Israel survived constant war with its Arab neighbors while the United States and others tried to negotiate an equitable peace. The Arab-Israeli conflict resulted in Arab retaliation against the West in 1973. The oil embargo led to a gasoline shortage, long lines at the pumps throughout the United States and Europe, and an economic crisis. Negotiations ended the embargo at the governmental level, but some fundamentalist Muslims of the Middle East saw the episode as an example of how they could fight against the "Satanic" Western enemy.

In addition to U.S. support of Israel, the proliferation of American and Western ideas (such as the equality of women, freedom of religion, and individual rights) threatened the cultural and moral ideals of many Muslims. Television, compact discs, the Internet, and American marketing prowess inundated Islamic countries with all things American. No ambassador revealed more about America than Hollywood celluloid, and it was not always a pretty

---

*Kristin, Story #11783, *The September 11 Digital Archive,* August 30, 2005, http://911digitalarchive.org/stories/details/11783.

picture. Movies such as *In the Heat of the Night, American Graffiti, Psycho, The Graduate, The Exorcist, Midnight Cowboy, The Godfather, American Beauty,* and *American Pie* gave the Arab world a distorted picture of America and Americans as immoral, debased, and profane. One U.S. movie network, AMC, explored this cultural clash in a documentary in 2003:

> Muslim countries are increasingly saturated with American-produced films and television programs. These countries are struggling to cope with a cultural phenomenon that continues to seep into even the most protected markets via American movies and television. . . . As satellite television and movies invade the homes of Muslims in the Middle East, many perceive it as an insidious cultural invasion by the U.S.—overt propaganda created to undermine their religious and cultural identity. From the overt homosexuality of *Will & Grace*, to the exaggerated violence of American action films, these powerful images project a value system that can inspire, as one Egyptian television executive states, "a kind of shock and rejection and hatred."

Although most Muslims are not threatened by American culture, a radical minority violently opposes its influence. In 1979, a grassroots movement promoting fundamental Islamic beliefs and rejecting Western culture resulted in the takeover of Iran and the 444-day hostage crisis. Throughout the Middle East, terrorist camps (often with government sanction) trained young men to fight against Western insurgence into the Islamic world. Highly publicized symbolic "victories" against the West (the oil embargo, the overthrow of the shah, the hostage crisis, etc.) proved to terrorist networks that they could disrupt the American economy, influence presidential elections, and sway popular opinion.

In 1983, terrorists calling themselves Islamic Jihad attacked the U.S. embassy in Beirut, killing sixteen people. That same year a suicide bomb exploded in Beirut, killing 241 "peacekeeping" U.S. Marines in their barracks. In 1985, terrorists from the Palestinian Liberation Front hijacked the Italian cruise ship *Achille Lauro* and murdered Leon Klinghoffer, a sixty-nine-year-old American invalid. Over Lockerbie, Scotland, in 1988, a bomb attributed to Libyan terrorists exploded in a Pan American passenger jet, killing 270 people. When the United Nations (led by the United States and supported by most Arab governments) staged a war (Desert Storm) against Iraq in 1990 after its invasion of Kuwait, the presence of the Western military in sacred Islamic lands intensified the hatred of fundamentalist Muslims against the West.

The war of terrorism escalated. In 1993, a bomb exploded in the basement of the New York World Trade Center, killing six and injuring more than a thousand people. That same year in Somalia, terrorists trained by a group called al Queda and funded by the Arab millionaire Osama bin Laden killed sixteen U.S. soldiers involved in a relief mission (Restore Hope) meant to provide food for a famine-ridden population. In 1996, a Muslim fundamentalist group called the Taliban took over Afghanistan and allowed bin Laden to set up a terrorist training camp. In 1998, bin Laden made the following statement: "To kill Americans and their allies, civilians and military, is an individual duty for every Muslim who can do it, in any country in which it is possible to do it."

In 1998, after the bombing of U.S. embassies in Kenya and Tanzania, President Bill Clinton identified bin Laden as the leader of the terrorist organization that attacked the embassies. He ordered a missile strike against bin Laden's training camps in Sudan and Afghanistan, but it failed to curtail the growing movement. In 2000, a small dinghy filled with explosives and manned by terrorists from bin Laden's network attacked the destroyer USS *Cole* anchored offshore in Yemen, killing seventeen U.S. sailors and injuring thirty-nine others. The old Cold War against the Soviets may have been won, but in its place was emerging an equally disturbing divide that pitted the modern Western world against the premodern Islamic fundamentalist forces of the Middle East.

Politics in the New Millennium

Although some doomsayers warned that an apocalyptic Y2K (the notation commonly used to refer to the year 2000) disaster would occur at midnight on January 31, 1999, most Americans approached the new millennium with great hopes. America enjoyed peace, security, and prosperity. The election of 2000 focused on the future rather than the past, although the nastiness of the nineties continued to flavor the political debate. The Democrats nominated Vice President Al Gore for president and Connecticut senator Joseph Lieberman as his running mate, while the Republicans nominated Texas governor George W. Bush, the son of a former president, and Dick Cheney, a business executive and former defense secretary, as his running mate. Complicating the race was the presence on the ballot of the famous (or infamous) consumer advocate and Green Party candidate, Ralph Nader.

In the rather lackluster campaign, neither the Republicans nor the Democrats took major campaign risks. Gore reminded the electorate of the booming economy, while Bush promised to "restore dignity and honor" to the White House, a not-so-veiled reference to the sex scandal of the Clinton administration. On the issues, the Republicans called for limiting the role of government, returning American soldiers from the nation-building enterprises of the Clinton years, and partially privatizing Social Security. The Democrats, in contrast, called for an expanded federal role in education and health care. Much of the focus of the campaign centered on how the nation should spend its growing surplus. Gore wanted to use it to ensure the future solvency of

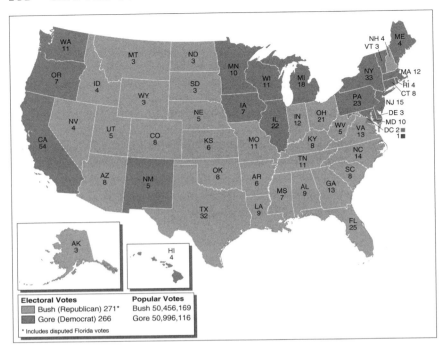

THE ELECTION OF 2000

the Social Security system, while Bush promised to return it to the nation's citizens through an across-the-board tax reduction, a plan that the Democrats charged would benefit primarily "the wealthiest one percent."

The only safe conclusion that can be drawn from the election results was that the nation was evenly divided. Gore did well among women, blacks, the poor, and urban voters; Bush performed equally well among men, Anglos, the rich, and rural voters. Jews liked Gore; evangelical and Catholic Christians preferred Bush. Middle-class Americans and suburbanites divided their votes. When all the various factions were summed, Gore won a narrow plurality of the popular vote. The results in the all-important Electoral College, however, were more controversial.

On the morning after the election, it appeared as if Gore would win 267 electoral votes and Bush 246. The remaining twenty-five electoral votes from Florida were up for grabs. Bush had a tiny lead, but there were enough irregularities at the polls to make the Democrats confident that a recount would give them the victory. The Republican Florida secretary of state certified a Bush victory, but the Democratic-controlled Florida Supreme Court ordered a recount. Bush's lawyers appealed the case to the U.S. Supreme Court. Five weeks after the election, the Supreme Court by a 5–4 decision overturned the state court's call for a recount. The next day Gore conceded defeat, and Bush emerged as president-elect. Nader underperformed nationally, although his 96,837 votes in Florida aided Bush's cause in that crucial state.

Ruling such a divided electorate would be difficult for anyone, and it proved to be especially difficult for the swashbuckling Texan. For seven months, Bush struggled. Other than pushing through Congress a tax cut priced at $1.35 trillion over eleven years and boldly rejecting the Kyoto Treaty on global warming because he deemed it detrimental to America's interests, Bush's agenda seemed unclear, and his approval ratings remained low. His presidency, and the nation, however, would change suddenly on the morning of September 11.

From Disunity to Unity and Back Again: The Attack and Its Aftermath

The horrific events of September 11, 2001, brought the escalating war of terror onto American soil. On that fateful day, when the hijacked passengers of Flight 93 contacted relatives on cell phones, they learned about the attacks in New York City. With heroic courage and the words "Let's roll," passengers Todd Beamer, Thomas Burnett, and others confronted the hijackers. What happened next remains unclear, but the plane crashed in a rural Pennsylvania field before it could reach its intended target. The courage of the passengers of Flight 93 rallied Americans to do whatever it took to end this new era of terrorism that would claim the lives of innocent people.

A new, confusing type of war emerged from the ashes of the attacks on New York and Washington. In this first war of the new millennium, nation-states did not necessarily declare war against other nation-states, but clandestine Islamic terrorist organizations issued threats against all the world powers that supported the "infidels" who rejected the sacred laws allegedly given by God through the early seventh-century prophet Muhammad. Americans knew that in distant lands enemies hiding in caves were recruiting and training men, women, and children to act as suicide bombers for their cause. What was not known was whether these enemies also were living next door, patiently waiting for an opportune time to strike America again with terror.

At no time since the news of Pearl Harbor had Americans experienced such a dramatic and heart-wrenching loss. The attack on September 11 began a new American era. In threatening times like these, concerns for security often trump demands for liberty. New phrases, concepts, and actions that affected everyday life entered into the American lifestyle. A terrorist warning system consisting of green, yellow, orange, and red levels became almost as familiar as weather forecasts. High warning levels resulted in long security lines at airports and public functions. Metal detectors and bag checks appeared in theme parks, concert halls, and sports stadiums. The Bush administration created a Department of Homeland Security to deal with the threat of terrorism on American soil. Every security agency from the FBI to the CIA escalated surveillance of suspected terrorists (some say at the expense of guaranteed personal freedoms). An antiterrorism law, cleverly dubbed the USA Patriot Act, gave law enforcers sweeping powers that included conducting searches without warrants and detaining and deporting individuals in secret. Even though only a small percentage of Arabs supported the terrorists, Muslims and people of Arabic heritage in America found themselves the target of vicious verbal and physical attacks.

After the 9/11 attack, the world community rallied together to resist the cancer of international terrorism by sharing intelligence, freezing assets of suspected terrorists, apprehending members of al Queda and other known terrorist organizations, and supporting military action against governments like Afghanistan that harbored those who claimed responsibility for the attack. Less than one month after September 11, American and British forces began strikes against the Taliban government of Afghanistan, which refused to surrender Osama bin Laden. In early December, most of the peoples of the world celebrated the collapse of the Taliban government, although many also cringed at learning that the attempts to kill or capture bin Laden had failed, leaving the mastermind of the 9/11 attacks still at large.

Although strongly behind the American efforts in Afghanistan, most nations were less enamored in 2002 when Bush announced that the long-standing U.S. foreign strategy of containment and deterrence needed to be rethought and revised. In the new age of terrorism, Bush asserted, the United States reserved the right to launch preemptive strikes against potential security threats. Around the first anniversary of 9/11, Bush told the UN that Saddam Hussein's Iraq, like the Taliban of Afghanistan, was a threat to world security. Bush insisted that Hussein must be disarmed of his weapons of mass destruction and that if the UN was unwilling to disarm him, then the United States would act alone to preserve its security.

While concerned that the Bush doctrine stressed unilateralism rather than international consensus, the UN Security Council unanimously approved a resolution that imposed new arms inspections in Iraq. Months passed and no weapons of mass destruction were found, but Hussein's lack of cooperation with the UN arms inspectors convinced Bush that the UN effort was impotent. For a number of observers, Hussein's cat-and-mouse game with the inspectors was evidence enough that he was hiding something. In his 2003 State of the Union address, Bush proclaimed,

> The United Nations concluded in 1999 that Saddam Hussein had biological weapons sufficient to produce over 25,000 liters of anthrax—enough doses to kill several million people. He hasn't accounted for that material. He's given no evidence that he has

destroyed it. . . . Our intelligence officials estimate that Saddam Hussein had the materials to produce as much as 500 tons of sarin, mustard and VX nerve agent. In such quantities, these chemical agents could also kill untold thousands. He's not accounted for these materials. He has given no evidence that he has destroyed them. U.S. intelligence indicates that Saddam Hussein had upwards of 30,000 munitions capable of delivering chemical agents. Inspectors recently turned up 16 of them—despite Iraq's recent declaration denying their existence. Saddam Hussein has not accounted for the remaining 29,984 of these prohibited munitions. He's given no evidence that he has destroyed them.

By early spring of 2003, Bush's patience wore out. On March 19, U.S. and British forces began bombing Baghdad. The brevity of this war made even America's "splendid little war" against Spain in 1898 look like a long siege. Within three weeks after bombing began, Baghdad fell, and by May 1, Bush jubilantly declared the war against Iraq over.

The postwar phase, however, did not go well. The cost of reconstruction in Iraq was great, both in money and in blood. During the eighteen months that followed the official ending of the war, America lost about a thousand more soldiers and spent $2 billion a week trying to weaken the Iraqi resistance and restore the Iraqi infrastructure that had been destroyed during and after the war. In the summer of 2004, the United States helped install an interim government in Iraq. Almost every American was glad to see Hussein's dictatorship overthrown. As months passed, however, and violence continued, American deaths mounted, and no weapons of mass destruction were found, some Americans wondered if the war against Hussein was really one and the same as the war against terrorism. Was America more secure as a result of the invasion and military occupation of Iraq? On this question, Americans remained divided. By mid-2004, the 90 percent approval ratings that Bush enjoyed following 9/11 had dropped to under 50 percent.

Complicating Bush's troubles were economic uncertainties at home. In late 2000 the fast-blooming economy of the 1990s began to wilt. As stocks dropped, jobs disappeared, and economic growth slowed, the projected budget surplus vanished. In its place was enough federal red ink to fill the Great Lakes. Between 2000 and 2004, the U.S. national debt expanded by an additional $2.5 trillion. To stimulate growth, Bush proposed another tax cut in 2003. Congress approved a scaled-down version of Bush's stimulus plan over the opposition of fiscal conservatives, who questioned the wisdom of reducing taxes while America was fighting an expensive war, and liberals, who complained that the greatest portion of the tax relief went to two groups: two-parent households with children and America's wealthiest 10 percent. While critics of the president gasped at the largest federal deficits in history, supporters insisted that the tax reductions were wise and would shorten and minimize the recession.

In the election of 2004, the incumbent Bush faced John Kerry, a Democratic senator from Massachusetts. The campaign was one of the most heated in history. Kerry accused Bush of bungling the antiterrorist fight, mismanaging the war in Iraq, and producing the worst economic record of any American president since Herbert Hoover. He adopted as his slogan a line from the African-American poet Langston Hughes, "Let America be America again."

Bush, in turn, insisted that the nation would not be safe with the "flip-flopping" Kerry as commander in chief. The Republicans called for "a safer world and more hopeful America" and "steady leadership in times of change." Both sides insisted that while all presidential elections were important, this election was especially critical. In urging Americans to vote, each side suggested that the very future of the American republic was at stake. Together, the campaigns spent more than $4 billion to win people's votes. The great portion of this vast sum was spent in about a dozen close battleground states.

What did this $4 billion buy? Some 10 million more Americans voted in 2004 than in 2000. The breakdown of the vote, however, was remarkably congruent with the results of 2000. While the Republicans picked up a few seats in the House and the Senate, 99 percent of the incumbents in Congress that sought reelection were elected. In the all-important presidential race, forty-seven states and the federal district in the Electoral College voted as they had in 2000. Bush narrowly won two states he barely lost in 2000 (Iowa and New Mexico), while Kerry narrowly picked up one new small state (New Hampshire) for the Democrats. Gaining the support of significantly more married women voters than he did four years earlier, Bush won reelection by carrying 51 percent of the popular vote and 53 percent of the Electoral College. The media, political theorists, and humorists all speculated on the long-term political impact of the separation between the "red" (Republican) states and the "blue" (Democratic) states in the presidential vote. Although critics could no longer question the legitimacy of Bush's election, the nation remained polarized, with the great heartland of America uniformly Republican and the northeast and west coast perimeters solidly Democratic.

Singing the Second-Term Blues

Among America's forty-two presidents, voters elected fifteen to a second term. It can be reasonably argued that all of these reelected presidents personally experienced rougher sailing during their second term than their first. George Washington's second term was so frustrating that he refused to seek a third term, thereby establishing the two-term presidential tradition. Similarly, Jefferson's controversial embargo policy, Madison's call for war against England, Monroe's inability to maintain party unity, and Jackson's bitter encounter with the national bank brought severe heartburn to each of these reelected incumbents. Assassins killed Lincoln and McKinley at the beginning of their second terms, scandals tarnished Grant's second administration, the Panic of 1893 plagued Cleveland throughout his second occupation of the White House, and the twice-elected Wilson experienced a debilitating stroke that destroyed both his health and his presidency. Even the ever-popular Franklin Roosevelt stumped his political toes by promoting an unpopular court-packing scheme during the second of his four terms. In more recent generations, a souring economy and scandals involving associates hurt Eisenhower's second-term popularity, the Watergate debacle destroyed the Nixon presidency, the Iran-contra scandal tarnished Reagan's legacy, and the Monica Lewinsky affair resulted in Clinton's second-term impeachment.

Coincidence can explain part of this second-term curse, but if one flips a coin that lands tails on fifteen consecutive occasions, thinking observers must ask if something other than chance is operating. Surely other factors, such as the inevitability of natural business cycles, the temptation of the powerful to overreach, the impotency of lame-duck administrations, and the short attention span of the electorate, also have contributed to the singing of these second-term blues.

After winning a noncontroversial reelection, Bush hoped to break the second-term jinx. Soon, however, like other reelected presidents before him, Bush found himself having to navigate in rough seas. The horrific event that brought his early administration to incredible heights of approval led to increasing frustration as the war on terrorism lengthened without clear victory. Even Mother Nature seemed determined to cause him trouble. On the day after Christmas 2004, for example, Americans awoke to the terrifying news that an undersea earthquake in the Indian Ocean had triggered a series of tsunamis that devastated coastal areas throughout southeast Asia. Measured at 9.0 on the Richter scale and thus one of the largest quakes in recorded history, the disaster produced massive tidal waves—some exceeding 100 feet high—that wrecked shorelines from Indonesia to East Africa. In its wake, upward of a quarter of a million people perished.

Bush promptly expressed his condolences, sent disaster experts to the region, and pledged an initial $35 million in relief assistance. As more details of the devastation became known, however, world opinion criticized the meager level of U.S. aid. Finding himself on the defensive, Bush told his critics that the United States was a "generous" nation that the previous year had provided over $2 billion in disaster relief. Within two weeks, Bush increased America's commitment to tsunami relief tenfold to $350 million, dispatched his brother, Governor Jeb Bush of Florida, and Secretary of State Colin Powell to the troubled areas to assess reconstruction needs, and asked former presidents George Bush and Bill Clinton to head an effort to raise private relief funds. Notwithstanding these efforts, however, Bush's response to this natural disaster appeared to many world citizens to be too little and too late.

Putting these criticisms aside, Bush embraced the New Year with great energy and optimism. In his second inaugural address, Bush echoed familiar themes that he would repeat in his second term. "For a half century," the confident Bush reminded the nation, "America defended our own freedom by standing watch on distant borders. After the shipwreck of communism came years of relative quiet, years of repose, years of sabbatical—and then there came a day of fire. . . . There is only one force of history that can break the reign of hatred and resentment, and . . . that is the force of human freedom." The bellicose Texan then continued with the boldness that made his supporters proud and his critics shudder:

> We are led, by events and common sense, to one conclusion: The survival of liberty in our land increasingly depends on the success of liberty in other lands. The best hope for peace in our world is the expansion of freedom in all the world. . . . So it is the policy of the United States to seek and support the growth of democratic movements and institutions in every nation and culture, with the ultimate goal of ending tyranny in our world. . . . My most solemn duty is to protect this nation and its people against further attacks and emerging threats. . . . All who live in tyranny and hopelessness can know: the United States will not ignore your oppression, or excuse your oppressors. When you stand for your liberty, we will stand with you. . . . We go forward with complete confidence in the eventual triumph of freedom. . . . History has an ebb and flow of justice, but history also has a visible direction, set by liberty and the Author of Liberty.

Just under two weeks later, in his State of the Union message, Bush expanded his focus to include other items on his second-term agenda, including the need to discipline federal spending, reduce business regulation, eliminate junk lawsuits, create an energy policy that would make America less dependent on foreign energy, reform the immigration system, support a constitutional amendment that defined marriage as a bond between a man and a woman, and, most important, fix the Social Security system by allowing voluntary personal retirement accounts for young workers. Over the ensuing months, Bush, with a Republican-controlled Congress behind him, achieved some, but not all of his goals. For example, early in his second term he signed the Class Action Fairness Act, a tort reform bill that set a cap on lawsuits and shielded drug companies from punitive damages when selling drugs approved by the Food and Drug Administration. By the end of summer, he also proudly signed into law the Central America Free Trade Agreement and an energy bill that encouraged domestic conservation, promoted greater use of nuclear energy, and funded research for the development of hydrogen automobiles.

Other items on the Bush agenda, however, proved more difficult to secure. Despite making Social Security reform a top priority, Bush's preference for voluntary personal retirement accounts rather than the meager 2-percent-beyond-inflation expected return on Social Security contributions failed to gain political traction. Timing, once again, hurt Bush's reform agenda. During the very weeks that the president was conducting a state-by-state campaign for Social Security reform, the stock market went into a funk. Between the first week of March and the first week of May 2005, the Dow Jones average dropped nearly a thousand points. During this period of stock volatility and decline, many Americans concluded that a dependable 2 percent beyond inflation looked better than the riskier alternative.

Throughout the first half year of his second term, Bush's approval ratings hovered in the mid-40s. Then Mother Nature struck again. On August 23, 2005, Katrina, the twelfth tropical storm of the season, formed in the Bahamas. Several days later, as a Category 1 hurricane with wind speeds over seventy-five miles per hour, Katrina skirted the southern tip of Florida, causing some damage, and then moved westward into the Gulf of Mexico, where for the next forty-eight hours it intensified into a Category 5 storm with winds over 170 miles per hour. Colossal in size as well as in strength, Katrina had all the markings of a catastrophic storm. When Katrina turned north and computer models predicted a landing near New Orleans, Mayor Ray Nagin of the Big Easy ordered the first-ever mandatory evacuation of the city. Hundreds of thousands fled, but tens of thousands with no available transportation remained to face Katrina's wrath. Seeking shelter, some 12,000 people poured into the Superdome, the massive indoor sports facility that served as the home of the National Football League's New Orleans Saints.

At 6:10 am on August 29, Katrina made landfall near Buras-Triumph, Louisiana, as a Category 3 storm with sustained winds of 125 miles per hour. Hurricane-force winds extended 120 miles from the eye of the storm. The dreaded nightmare became a reality when the winds, rainfall, and surges of the storm caused breaks in the levees that separated Lake Pontchartrain from New Orleans. Flowing waters rushed into the portions of the city built below sea level. Soon 80 percent of the city was underwater.

Meanwhile, Katrina continued its northeasterly drift with ripping winds and surging tides that devastated the coastal areas of Mississippi and Alabama. Population centers such as Mobile, Alabama, and Gulfport and Biloxi, Mississippi, bore the brunt of Katrina's wrath, but the storm's accompanying high winds, torrential rains, and tornado bands also brought great destruction and forced evacuations in Georgia, Tennessee, Kentucky, Ohio, and West Virginia. By the time the storm made its way into the Atlantic Ocean, 3 million Americans were without electrical power.

For the next week, Americans watching the live video reports coming out of New Orleans could scarcely believe their eyes. They saw once great neighborhoods totally submerged, marooned survivors clinging to rooftops waving for help, dead bodies lying in the streets and floating in pockets of standing water, pillaging bands wading through knee-deep waters looking for fresh water and food, looters breaking into stores and carrying away DVD players and television sets, and thousands of tired, hungry, and angry refugees stranded in the Superdome with no water purification equipment, operating toilets, or adequate medical care. Alleged eyewitnesses spoke about unconfirmed reports of rape, murder, drug dealing, and gunfights between gangs, citizens, and the city police.

The Federal Emergency Management Agency (FEMA), the U.S. Coast Guard, the Red Cross, and numerous other public and private organizations attempted to respond to the Katrina tragedy—a crisis so large that Homeland Security Secretary Michael Chertoff labeled it "probably the worst catastrophe" in U.S. history. Public reaction to the handling of the tragedy, however, ranged from lukewarm to highly critical, although Bush pledged his support to the region, promised every victimized household $2,000 in emergency disaster relief, and once again asked his father and Bill Clinton to raise private funds to assist with the recovery efforts. In time, a 600-page report prepared by a Republican-controlled Congress would chastise the president (as well as numerous others, including the heads of several federal agencies, the governor of Louisiana, and the mayor of New Orleans) both for not doing more to prevent the disaster and for the slowness and mismanagement of the government's response to it. After Katrina, and the rising gasoline prices that resulted from it, Bush's popularity began to sink to the lowest levels in his presidency.

In politics as in sports, momentum is difficult to overcome. Each new crisis provided humorists and political commentators with new material with which to pummel the administration. After the Katrina fiasco, late-night talk show host Jay Leno quipped, "President Bush said we need to rebuild Iraq, provide the people with jobs, and give them hope. If it works there maybe we'll try it in New Orleans." On an opposite channel David Letterman remarked about the prolonged Iraqi war, "President Bush is vacationing in Crawford, Texas. He will be vacationing for five weeks. That's a long time. I don't think he has an exit strategy for his vacation either."

Even as the president's approval ratings dwindled into the low 30s, his historical legacy, for good or ill, became more pronounced when retirements in the Supreme Court gave him the chance to make two potentially epoch-making appointments. Bush initially nominated John Roberts, a charismatic, well-respected, fifty-year-old judge with solid conservative credentials, to replace retiring Justice Sandra Day O'Connor, but following the death of Chief Justice William Rehnquist, Bush renominated Roberts to serve as chief justice. After the Senate confirmed Roberts, Bush nominated Harriet Miers to replace O'Connor. However, opposition from Republican conservatives who questioned her credentials forced Miers to withdraw her nomination. Bush then nominated and the Senate confirmed Samuel Alito, a savvy, Ivy League–educated, widely experienced jurist known for his sharp and penetrating mind. After having to wait for more than four and a half years for a Court vacancy, within several months Bush brought the Supreme Court into a new era with the appointment of two formidable conservative intellectuals who potentially could shape the direction of the Court for years to come.

Putting lifetime appointees on the highest court can produce profound long-term consequences, but such presidential actions generally do not create lasting front-page headlines or revive sagging poll numbers. More commonly, the electorate focuses its attention on more immediate concerns. In 2006, these concerns included the historically high, $3-per-gallon price of gasoline, the rapidly expanding national debt, the apparent inability of the nation to protect its borders from penetration by illegal immigrants, the lingering fear following the Katrina debacle that the government was still unprepared for a national emergency, the alleged ethical lapses of powerful, well-known politicians and business leaders, and the seemingly never-ending war in Iraq.

Although most Americans agreed that the Iraq war had produced some positive results, including the removal of a tyrant and the opening of democratic impulses in a former dictatorship, many felt betrayed that their national leaders had misled them about the existence and threat of weapons of mass destruction. Other Americans remained frustrated that two years after Bush triumphantly had pronounced "mission accomplished," the war in Iraq continued with no clear end in sight.

Even more alarming was the realization that while the United States needed less than three and a half years to knock out Hitler and less than four years to defeat the nation that planned the attack on Pearl Harbor, five years after the nationless bin Laden plotted the nefarious events of September 11, the mastermind of terror was still at large and many future bin Ladens were being groomed to replace him. Bush never promised that the war against terror would be easily won, but neither did the divided electorate promise prolonged patience with a war strategy that failed to produce timely results.

Looking through the Past into the Future

Looking into the future through the lens of the past does not give anyone 20/20 vision. After all, history, which it is said "often repeats itself," also can be full of surprises. In the words of political commentator George Will, "The future has a way of arriving unannounced." On numerous occasions, wise historians have attempted to prognosticate what the future holds and later looked foolish when their projections did not unfold. Still, the temptation to say "since history teaches us this, we can expect that" remains. On rare occasions, the forecasts of respected historians have even influenced the course of history itself.

In the last decade of the nineteenth century, for example, many Americans wondered what the twentieth century would be like. Eminent historian Frederick Jackson Turner offered these curious Americans a reasonable scenario of the future. Unlike many historians before him, Turner believed that American history was vastly different from European history. Although he conceded that the seeds of American ideas and institutions came largely from Europe, Turner insisted that these seeds, when transplanted into American soil, blossomed into uniquely American forms. Turner emphasized that Americans, to a far greater degree than Europeans, had always embraced principles of individualism, democracy, and egalitarianism and rejected radical ideologies like Marxism that were popular on the other side of the Atlantic. According to Turner, one great fact explained these profound differences and that fact was the presence of the American frontier.

According to Turner's frontier thesis, Americans embraced rugged individualism because in a frontier environment hard work and not heritage determined survival and status. Americans embraced democracy and egalitarian ideals because the availability of cheap land on the frontier put land ownership within reach of almost everyone, not simply the elite few. Since more Americans than Europeans owned property, the gap between the rich and poor in America was comparatively small, and the resulting creation of an egalitarian society promoted a willingness to share political power. Moreover, in America the victims of exploitation did not join radical movements that hoped to overthrow the capitalistic social order, but instead they packed their suitcases and moved to the cheap land in the West to start over again in their pursuit of the American dream.

These ideas disturbed many Americans in the 1890s, since at that moment the great American frontier seemed to be quickly disappearing. If Turner were correct, unless America found another frontier, then Americans in the twentieth century could expect to become less individualistic, less democratic, less equal, and more radicalized.

Turner's brilliant thesis influenced many politicians, including Theodore Roosevelt, who used this theory of the past to justify the need for America to find new frontiers beyond the continental United States. All of Turner's projections, however, did not materialize. More than a century after the closing of the frontier, Americans still largely remained committed to the ideals of individualism, egalitarianism, democracy, and nonradicalism. These values appeared to be even more endemic to America than Turner's thesis would suggest. They seemed to be rooted not simply in American soil, but in the heart and mind of Americans.

The moral of this story is that historians, even exceptionally gifted ones like Frederick Jackson Turner, generally are more adept at interpreting the past than in projecting the future. Readers of history, consequently, would be well advised to be skeptical of anyone who argues positions by invoking the phrase "History teaches us that . . . " Thoughtful students of the past should recognize the pitfalls in plotting the course of the past on a graph and then using it to predict specific outcomes in the future. Still, knowledge of America's recent and distant past can inform our judgments and expectations. Without enabling us to predict specific outcomes, the long lens of history can provide us with a perspective from which we can make better sense of the swirling and seemingly chaotic events of the present.

Just as Americans a century ago wondered what their future would hold, contemporary Americans also are reflective about their past and curious about their future. Most greeted the new millennium with great optimism. Although equally divided along party lines, with the economy booming, crime rates in decline, and the Cold War victoriously ended, most early twenty-first-century Americans felt secure and hopeful. They debated among themselves how the promises of "life, liberty and the pursuit of happiness" could best be extended to all citizens, but they had little doubt that the future of their nation was bright.

This optimism—some might call it complacency—evaporated in the fires of 9/11. Americans first rallied together in unity, but when the threat of terrorism did not go away and the war in Iraq did not go precisely as planned, Americans entered into their next presidential election season deeply worried about their future. Issues given high priority in less threatening times took a back seat to national and personal security. Pundits may wonder why citizens in the most powerful and protected nation on this planet felt insecure, but none should be surprised that a foremost concern of threatened people was for the safety of their children and grandchildren. This has been true of Americans since the foundation of the nation and undoubtedly applies to all threatened peoples throughout the world.

As in every wartime election when an incumbent sought reelection, American voters in 2004 returned their sitting commander in chief, although this did not happen without a fierce and often bitter and ugly fight. During the election campaign, many partisans spoke as if the future of the republic hinged on the election outcome. Some seemed to suggest that if Kerry won, the security of the nation would be endangered; others spoke as if the constitutional liberties of the people would be revoked if Bush were reelected. It remains to be seen whether this recent election was indeed a seminal election that will transform America either for good or ill. What can be said with more certainty, however, is that America has been in similar situations before and has emerged from these moments with its principles intact.

Indeed, the long story of America is largely a saga of the resiliency of diverse peoples struggling to find that delicate balance between individual freedom and security. United less by DNA than by a commitment to common principles, Americans have long celebrated Thomas Jefferson's premise: "We hold these truths to be self-evident, that all men are created equal, that they are endowed by their Creator with certain unalienable Rights, that among these are Life, Liberty and the pursuit of Happiness." For over two centuries Americans have debated the meaning of this creed, and they have disagreed, sometimes passionately, as to how it best can be applied. No one, however, has ever been successful in advocating its rejection. The values articulated in this creed defined what it meant to be an American many years ago and these values are still embedded in the hearts and souls of Americans today.

When a society feels threatened, however, the extension of liberty can be slowed. Since its beginnings, the flow of the American past has been in the direction of the expansion of liberty, but the current of this flow has never been steady. Critical turning-point moments have altered the path of this stream, but never has the flow been arrested or reversed. History may not teach us this, but the creed that established this nation affirms the truth of this promise: the future of America will be secure as long as its people hold onto its formative ideals that all people are created equal, that all people have rights that must not be taken away, and that all people should be allowed to achieve "life, liberty and the pursuit of happiness."

APPENDIXES

MAP OF THE UNITED STATES

APPENDIX II

THE DECLARATION OF INDEPENDENCE

IN CONGRESS, July 4, 1776.

*The unanimous Declaration of the
thirteen united States of America,*

When in the Course of human events, it becomes necessary for one people to dissolve the political bands which have connected them with another, and to assume among the powers of the earth, the separate and equal station to which the Laws of Nature and of Nature's God entitle them, a decent respect to the opinions of mankind requires that they should declare the causes which impel them to the separation.

We hold these truths to be self-evident, that all men are created equal, that they are endowed by their Creator with certain unalienable Rights, that among these are Life, Liberty and the pursuit of Happiness.—That to secure these rights, Governments are instituted among Men, deriving their just powers from the consent of the governed,—That whenever any Form of Government becomes destructive of these ends, it is the Right of the People to alter or to abolish it, and to institute new Government, laying its foundation on such principles and organizing its powers in such form, as to them shall seem most likely to effect their Safety and Happiness. Prudence, indeed, will dictate that Governments long established should not be changed for light and transient causes; and accordingly all experience hath shewn, that mankind are more disposed to suffer, while evils are sufferable, than to right themselves by abolishing the forms to which they are accustomed. But when a long train of abuses and usurpations, pursuing invariably the same Object evinces a design to reduce them under absolute Despotism, it is their right, it is their duty, to throw off such Government, and to provide new Guards for their future security.—Such has been the patient sufferance of these Colonies; and such is now the necessity which constrains them to alter their former Systems of Government. The history of the present King of Great Britain is a history of repeated injuries and usurpations, all having in direct object the establishment of an absolute Tyranny over these States. To prove this, let Facts be submitted to a candid world.

He has refused his Assent to Laws, the most wholesome and necessary for the public good.

He has forbidden his Governors to pass Laws of immediate and pressing importance, unless suspended in their operation till his Assent should be obtained; and when so suspended, he has utterly neglected to attend to them.

He has refused to pass other Laws for the accommodation of large districts of people, unless those people would relinquish the right of Representation in the Legislature, a right inestimable to them and formidable to tyrants only.

He has called together legislative bodies at places unusual, uncomfortable, and distant from the depository of their public Records, for the sole purpose of fatiguing them into compliance with his measures.

He has dissolved Representative Houses repeatedly, for opposing with manly firmness his invasions on the rights of the people.

He has refused for a long time, after such dissolutions, to cause others to be elected; whereby the Legislative powers, incapable of Annihilation, have returned to the People at large for their exercise; the State remaining in the mean time exposed to all the dangers of invasion from without, and convulsions within.

He has endeavoured to prevent the population of these States; for that purpose obstructing the Laws for Naturalization of Foreigners; refusing to pass others to encourage their migrations hither, and raising the conditions of new Appropriations of Lands.

He has obstructed the Administration of Justice, by refusing his Assent to Laws for establishing Judiciary powers.

He has made Judges dependent on his Will alone, for the tenure of their offices, and the amount and payment of their salaries.

He has erected a multitude of New Offices, and sent hither swarms of Officers to harrass our people, and eat out their substance.

He has kept among us, in times of peace, Standing Armies without the Consent of our legislatures.

He has affected to render the Military independent of and superior to the Civil power.

He has combined with others to subject us to a jurisdiction foreign to our constitution, and unacknowledged by our laws; giving his Assent to their Acts of pretended Legislation:

For Quartering large bodies of armed troops among us:

For protecting them, by a mock Trial, from punishment for any Murders which they should commit on the Inhabitants of these States:

For cutting off our Trade with all parts of the world:

For imposing Taxes on us without our Consent:

For depriving us in many cases, of the benefits of Trial by Jury:

For transporting us beyond Seas to be tried for pretended offences

For abolishing the free System of English Laws in a neighbouring Province, establishing therein an Arbitrary government, and enlarging its Boundaries so as to render it at once an example and fit instrument for introducing the same absolute rule into these Colonies:

For taking away our Charters, abolishing our most valuable Laws, and altering fundamentally the Forms of our Governments:

For suspending our own Legislatures, and declaring themselves invested with power to legislate for us in all cases whatsoever.

He has abdicated Government here, by declaring us out of his Protection and waging War against us.

He has plundered our seas, ravaged our Coasts, burnt our towns, and destroyed the lives of our people.

He is at this time transporting large Armies of foreign Mercenaries to compleat the works of death, desolation and tyranny, already begun with circumstances of Cruelty & perfidy scarcely paralleled in the most barbarous ages, and totally unworthy the Head of a civilized nation.

He has constrained our fellow Citizens taken Captive on the high Seas to bear Arms against their Country, to become the executioners of their friends and Brethren, or to fall themselves by their Hands.

He has excited domestic insurrections amongst us, and has endeavoured to bring on the inhabitants of our frontiers, the merciless Indian Savages, whose known rule of warfare, is an undistinguished destruction of all ages, sexes and conditions.

In every stage of these Oppressions We have Petitioned for Redress in the most humble terms: Our repeated Petitions have been answered only by repeated injury. A Prince whose character is thus marked by every act which may define a Tyrant, is unfit to be the ruler of a free people.

Nor have We been wanting in attentions to our Brittish brethren. We have warned them from time to time of attempts by their legislature to extend an unwarrantable jurisdiction over us. We have reminded them of the circumstances of our emigration and settlement here. We have appealed to their native justice and magnanimity, and we have conjured them by the ties of our common kindred to disavow these usurpations, which, would inevitably interrupt our connections and correspondence. They too have been deaf to the voice of justice and of consanguinity. We must, therefore, acquiesce in the necessity, which denounces our Separation, and hold them, as we hold the rest of mankind, Enemies in War, in Peace Friends.

We, therefore, the Representatives of the united States of America, in General Congress, Assembled, appealing to the Supreme Judge of the world for the rectitude of our intentions, do, in the Name, and by Authority of the good People of these Colonies, solemnly publish and declare, That these United Colonies are, and of Right ought to be Free and Independent States; that they are Absolved from all Allegiance to the British Crown, and that all political connection between them and the State of Great Britain, is and ought to be totally dissolved; and that as Free and Independent States, they have full Power to levy War, conclude Peace, contract Alliances, establish Commerce, and to do all other Acts and Things which Independent States may of right do. And for the support of this Declaration, with a firm reliance on the protection of divine Providence, we mutually pledge to each other our Lives, our Fortunes and our sacred Honor.

The 56 signatures on the Declaration appear in the positions indicated:

Column 1
Georgia:
Button Gwinnett
Lyman Hall
George Walton

Column 2
North Carolina:
William Hooper
Joseph Hewes
John Penn

South Carolina:
Edward Rutledge
Thomas Heyward, Jr.
Thomas Lynch, Jr.
Arthur Middleton

Column 3
Massachusetts:
John Hancock

Maryland:
Samuel Chase
William Paca
Thomas Stone
Charles Carroll of Carrollton

Virginia:
George Wythe
Richard Henry Lee
Thomas Jefferson
Benjamin Harrison
Thomas Nelson, Jr.
Francis Lightfoot Lee
Carter Braxton

Column 4
Pennsylvania:
Robert Morris
Benjamin Rush
Benjamin Franklin
John Morton
George Clymer
James Smith

George Taylor
James Wilson
George Ross

Delaware:
Caesar Rodney
George Read
Thomas McKean

Column 5
New York:
William Floyd
Philip Livingston
Francis Lewis
Lewis Morris

New Jersey:
Richard Stockton
John Witherspoon
Francis Hopkinson
John Hart
Abraham Clark

Column 6
New Hampshire:
Josiah Bartlett
William Whipple

Massachusetts:
Samuel Adams
John Adams
Robert Treat Paine
Elbridge Gerry

Rhode Island:
Stephen Hopkins
William Ellery

Connecticut:
Roger Sherman
Samuel Huntington
William Williams
Oliver Wolcott
New Hampshire:
Matthew Thornton

CONSTITUTION OF THE UNITED STATES

We the People of the United States, in Order to form a more perfect Union, establish Justice, insure domestic Tranquility, provide for the common defence, promote the general Welfare, and secure the Blessings of Liberty to ourselves and our Posterity, do ordain and establish this Constitution for the United States of America.

Article I

Section 1. All legislative Powers herein granted shall be vested in a Congress of the United States, which shall consist of a Senate and House of Representatives.

Section 2. The House of Representatives shall be composed of Members chosen every second Year by the People of the several States, and the Electors in each State shall have the Qualifications requisite for Electors of the most numerous Branch of the State Legislature.

No Person shall be a Representative who shall not have attained to the Age of twenty five Years, and been seven Years a Citizen of the United States, and who shall not, when elected, be an Inhabitant of that State in which he shall be chosen.

Representatives and direct Taxes shall be apportioned among the several States which may be included within this Union, according to their respective Numbers, which shall be determined by adding to the whole Number of free Persons, including those bound to Service for a Term of Years, and excluding Indians not taxed, three fifths of all other Persons. The actual Enumeration shall be made within three Years after the first Meeting of the Congress of the United States, and within every subsequent Term of ten Years, in such Manner as they shall by Law direct. The Number of Representatives shall not exceed one for every thirty Thousand, but each State shall have at Least one Representative; and until such enumeration shall be made, the State of New Hampshire shall be entitled to chuse three, Massachusetts eight, Rhode Island and Providence Plantations one, Connecticut five, New-York six, New Jersey four, Pennsylvania eight, Delaware one, Maryland six, Virginia ten, North Carolina five, South Carolina five, and Georgia three.

When vacancies happen in the Representation from any State, the Executive Authority thereof shall issue Writs of Election to fill such Vacancies.

The House of Representatives shall chuse their Speaker and other Officers; and shall have the sole Power of Impeachment.

Section 3. The Senate of the United States shall be composed of two Senators from each State, chosen by the Legislature thereof, for six Years; and each Senator shall have one Vote.

Immediately after they shall be assembled in Consequence of the first Election, they shall be divided as equally as may be into three Classes. The Seats of the Senators of the first Class shall be vacated at the Expiration of the second Year, of the second Class at the Expiration of the fourth Year, and of the third Class at the Expiration of the sixth Year, so that one third may be chosen every second Year; and if Vacancies happen by Resignation, or otherwise, during the Recess of the Legislature of any State, the Executive thereof may make temporary Appointments until the next Meeting of the Legislature, which shall then fill such Vacancies.

No Person shall be a Senator who shall not have attained to the Age of thirty Years, and been nine Years a Citizen of the United States, and who shall not, when elected, be an Inhabitant of that State for which he shall be chosen.

The Vice President of the United States shall be President of the Senate, but shall have no Vote, unless they be equally divided.

The Senate shall chuse their other Officers, and also a President pro tempore, in the Absence of the Vice President, or when he shall exercise the Office of President of the United States.

The Senate shall have the sole Power to try all Impeachments. When sitting for that Purpose, they shall be on Oath or Affirmation. When the President of the United States is tried the Chief Justice shall preside: And no Person shall be convicted without the Concurrence of two thirds of the Members present.

Judgment in Cases of Impeachment shall not extend further than to removal from Office, and disqualification to hold and enjoy any Office of honor, Trust or Profit under the United States: but the Party convicted shall nevertheless be liable and subject to Indictment, Trial, Judgment and Punishment, according to Law.

Section 4. The Times, Places and Manner of holding Elections for Senators and Representatives, shall be prescribed in each State by the Legislature thereof; but the Congress may at any time by Law make or alter such Regulations, except as to the Places of chusing Senators.

The Congress shall assemble at least once in every Year, and such Meeting shall be on the first Monday in December, unless they shall by Law appoint a different Day.

Section 5. Each House shall be the Judge of the Elections, Returns and Qualifications of its own Members, and a Majority of each shall constitute a Quorum to do Business; but a smaller Number may adjourn from day to day, and may be authorized to compel the Attendance of absent Members, in such Manner, and under such Penalties as each House may provide.

Each House may determine the Rules of its Proceedings, punish its Members for disorderly Behaviour, and, with the Concurrence of two thirds, expel a Member.

Each House shall keep a Journal of its Proceedings, and from time to time publish the same, excepting such Parts as may in their Judgment require Secrecy; and the Yeas and Nays of the Members of either House on any question shall, at the Desire of one fifth of those Present, be entered on the Journal.

Neither House, during the Session of Congress, shall, without the Consent of the other, adjourn for more than three days, nor to any other Place than that in which the two Houses shall be sitting.

Section 6. The Senators and Representatives shall receive a Compensation for their Services, to be ascertained by law, and paid out of the Treasury of the United States. They shall in all Cases, except Treason, Felony and Breach of the Peace, be privileged from Arrest during their Attendance at the Session of their respective Houses, and in going to and returning from the same; and for any Speech or Debate in either House, they shall not be questioned in any other Place.

No Senator or Representative shall, during the Time for which he was elected, be appointed to any civil Office under the Authority of the United States, which shall have been created, or the Emoluments whereof shall have been encreased during such time; and no Person holding any Office under the United States, shall be a Member of either House during his Continuance in Office.

Section 7. All Bills for raising Revenue shall originate in the House of Representatives; but the Senate may propose or concur with amendments as on other Bills.

Every Bill which shall have passed the House of Representatives and the Senate, shall, before it become a Law, be presented to the President of the United States; If he approve he shall sign it, but if not he shall return it with his Objections to that House in which it shall have originated, who shall enter the Objections at large on their Journal, and proceed to reconsider it. If after such Reconsiderations two thirds of that House shall agree to pass the Bill, it shall be sent, together with the Objections, to the other House, by which it shall likewise be reconsidered, and if approved by two thirds of that House, it shall become a Law. But in all such Cases the Votes of both Houses shall be determined by Yeas and Nays, and the Names of the Persons voting for and against the Bill shall be entered on the Journal of each House respectively. If any Bill shall not be returned by the President within ten Days (Sunday excepted) after it shall have been presented to him, the Same shall be a Law, in like Manner as if he had signed it, unless the Congress by their Adjournment prevent its Return, in which Case it shall not be a Law.

Every Order, Resolution, or Vote to which the Concurrence of the Senate and House of Representatives may be necessary (except on a question of Adjournment) shall be presented to the President of the United States; and before the Same shall take Effect, shall be approved by him, or being disapproved by him, shall be repassed by two thirds of the Senate and House of Representatives, according to the Rules and Limitations prescribed in the Case of a Bill.

Section 8. The Congress shall have Power To lay and collect Taxes, Duties, Imposts and Excises, to pay the Debts and provide for the common Defence and general Welfare of the United States; but all Duties, Imposts and Excises shall be uniform throughout the United States;

To borrow Money on the credit of the United States;

To regulate Commerce with foreign Nations, and among the several States, and with the Indian Tribes;

To establish an uniform Rule of Naturalization, and uniform Laws on the subject of Bankruptcies throughout the United States;

To coin Money, regulate the Value thereof, and of foreign Coin, and fix the Standard of Weights and Measures;

To provide for the Punishment of counterfeiting the Securities and current Coin of the United States;

To establish Post Offices and post Roads;

To promote the Progress of Science and useful Arts, by securing for limited Times to Authors and Inventors the exclusive Right to their respective Writings and Discoveries;

To constitute Tribunals inferior to the supreme Court;

To define and punish Piracies and Felonies committed on the high Seas, and Offenses against the Law of Nations;

To declare War, grant Letters of Marque and Reprisal, and make Rules concerning Captures on Land and Water;

To raise and support Armies, but no Appropriation of Money to that Use shall be for a longer Term than two Years;

To provide and maintain a Navy;

To make Rules for the Government and Regulation of the land and naval Forces;

To provide for calling forth the Militia to execute the Laws of the Union, suppress Insurrections and repel Invasions;

To provide for organizing, arming, and disciplining, the Militia, and for governing such Part of them as may be employed in the Service of the United States, reserving to the States respectively, the Appointment of the Officers, and the Authority of training the Militia according to the discipline prescribed by Congress;

To exercise exclusive Legislation in all Cases whatsoever, over such District (not exceeding ten Miles square) as may, by Cession of particular States, and the Acceptance of Congress, become the Seat of the Government of the United States, and to exercise like Authority over all Places purchased by the Consent of the Legislature of the State in which the Same shall be, for the Erection of Forts, Magazines, Arsenals, dock-Yards, and other needful Buildings;—And

To make all Laws which shall be necessary and proper for carrying into Execution the foregoing Powers, and all other Powers vested by this Constitution in the Government of the United States, or in any Department or Officer thereof.

Section 9. The Migration or Importation of such Persons as any of the States now existing shall think proper to admit, shall not be prohibited by the Congress prior to the Year one thousand eight hundred and eight, but a Tax or duty may be imposed on such Importation, not exceeding ten dollars for each Person.

The Privilege of the Writ of Habeas Corpus shall not be suspended, unless when in Cases of Rebellion or Invasion the public Safety may require it.

No Bill of Attainder or ex post facto Law shall be passed.

No Capitation, or other direct, Tax shall be laid, unless in Proportion to the Census or Enumeration herein before directed to be taken.

No Tax or Duty shall be laid on Articles exported from any State.

No Preference shall be given by any Regulation of Commerce or Revenue to the Ports of one State over those of another; nor shall Vessels bound to, or from, one State, be obliged to enter, clear or pay Duties in another.

No Money shall be drawn from the Treasury, but in Consequence of Appropriations made by Law; and a regular Statement and Account of the Receipts and Expenditures of all public Money shall be published from time to time.

No Title of Nobility shall be granted by the United States: And no Person holding any Office or Trust under them, shall, without the Consent of the Congress, accept of any present, Emolument, Office, or Title, of any kind whatever, from any King, Prince or foreign State.

Section 10. No State shall enter into any Treaty, Alliance, or Confederation; grant Letters of Marque and Reprisal, coin Money; emit Bills of Credit, make any Thing but gold and silver Coin a Tender in Payment of Debts; pass any Bill of Attainder, ex post facto Law, or Law impairing the Obligation of Contracts, or grant any Title of Nobility.

No State shall, without the Consent of the Congress, lay any Imposts or Duties on Imports or Exports, except what may be absolutely necessary for executing its inspection Laws: and the net Produce of all Duties and Imposts, laid by any State on Imports or Exports, shall be for the Use of the Treasury of the United States; and all such Laws shall be subject to the Revision and Controul of the Congress.

No State shall, without the Consent of Congress, lay any Duty of Tonnage, keep Troops, or Ships of War in time of Peace, enter into any Agreement or Compact with another State, or with a foreign Power, or engage in War, unless actually invaded, or in such imminent Danger as will not admit of delay.

Article II

Section 1. The executive Power shall be vested in a President of the United States of America. He shall hold his Office during the Term of four Years, and, together with the Vice President, chosen for the same Term, be elected, as follows

Each State shall appoint, In such Manner as the Legislature thereof may direct, a Number of Electors, equal to the whole Number of Senators and Representatives to which the State may be entitled in the Congress: but no Senator or Representative, or Person holding an Office of Trust or Profit under the United States, shall be appointed an Elector.

The Electors shall meet in their respective States, and vote by Ballot for two Persons, of whom one at least shall not be an Inhabitant of the same State with themselves. And they shall make a List of all the Persons voted for, and of the number of Votes for each; which List they shall sign and certify, and transmit sealed to the Seat of the Government of the United States, directed to the President of the Senate. The President of the Senate shall, in the Presence of the Senate and House of Representatives, open all the Certificates, and the Votes shall then be counted. The Person having the greatest number of Votes shall be the President, if such Number be a Majority of the whole Number of Electors appointed; and if there be more than one who have such Majority, and have an equal Number of Votes, then the House of Representatives shall immediately chuse by Ballot one of them for President; and if no Person have a Majority, then from the five highest on the List the said House shall in like Manner chuse the President. But in chusing the President, the Votes shall be taken by States, the Representation from each State having one Vote; a quorum for this Purpose shall consist of a Member or Members from two thirds of the States, and a Majority of all the States shall be necessary to a Choice. In every Case, after the Choice of the President, the Person having the greatest Number of Votes of the Electors shall be the Vice President. But if there should remain two or more who have equal Votes, the Senate shall chuse from them by Ballot the Vice President.

The Congress may determine the Time of chusing the Electors, and the Day on which they shall give their Votes; which Day shall be the same throughout the United States.

No Person except a natural born Citizen, or a Citizen of the United States at the time of the Adoption of this Constitution, shall be eligible to the Office of President; neither shall any Person be eligible to that Office who shall not have attained to the Age of thirty five Years, and been fourteen Years a Resident within the United States.

In Case of the Removal of the President from Office, or of his Death, Resignation, or Inability to discharge the Powers and Duties of the said Office, the Same shall devolve on the Vice President, and the Congress may by Law provide for the Case of Removal, Death, Resignation or Inability, both of the President and Vice President, declaring what Officer shall then act as President, and such Officer shall act accordingly, until the Disability be removed, or a President shall be elected.

The President shall, at stated Times, receive for his Services, a Compensation, which shall neither be encreased nor diminished during the Period for which he shall have been elected, and he shall not receive within that Period any other emolument from the United States, or any of them.

Before he enter on the Execution of his Office, he shall take the following Oath or Affirmation:—"I do solemnly swear (or affirm) that I will faithfully execute the Office of President of the United States, and will to the best of my Ability, preserve, protect and defend the Constitution of the United States."

Section 2. The President shall be Commander in Chief of the Army and Navy of the United States, and of the Militia of the several States, when called into the actual Service of the United States; he may require the Opinion, in writing, of the principal Officer in each of the executive Departments, upon any Subject relating to the Duties of their respective Offices, and he shall have Power to grant Reprieves and Pardons for Offenses against the United States, except in Cases of Impeachment.

He shall have Power, by and with the Advice and Consent of the Senate, to make Treaties, provided two thirds of the Senators present concur; and he shall nominate, and by and with the Advice and Consent of the Senate, shall appoint Ambassadors, other public Ministers and Consuls, Judges of the supreme Court, and all other Officers of the United States, whose Appointments are not herein otherwise provided for, and which shall be established by Law: but the Congress may by Law vest the Appointment of such inferior Officers, as they think proper, in the President alone, in the Courts of Law, or in the Heads of Departments.

The President shall have Power to fill up all Vacancies that may happen during the Recess of the Senate, by granting Commissions which shall expire at the End of their next Session.

Section 3. He shall from time to time give to the Congress Information of the State of the Union, and recommend to their Consideration such Measures as he shall judge necessary and expedient; he may, on extraordinary Occasions, convene both Houses, or either of them, and in Case of Disagreements between them, with Respect to the Time of Adjournment, he may adjourn them to such Time as he shall think proper; he shall receive Ambassadors and other public Ministers; he shall take Care that the Laws be faithfully executed, and shall Commission all the Officers of the United States.

Section 4. The President, Vice President and all Civil Officers of the United States, shall be removed from Office on Impeachment for, and Conviction of, Treason, Bribery, or other high Crimes and Misdemeanors.

Article III

Section 1. The judicial Power of the United States, shall be vested in one supreme Court, and in such inferior Courts as the Congress may from time to time ordain and establish. The Judges, both of the supreme and inferior Courts, shall hold their Offices during good Behaviour, and shall, at stated Times, receive for their Services, a Compensation, which shall not be diminished during their Continuance in Office.

Section 2. The judicial Power shall extend to all Cases, in Law and Equity, arising under this Constitution, the Laws of the United States, and Treaties made, or which shall be made, under their Authority;—to all Cases affecting Ambassadors, other public Ministers and Consuls;—to all Cases of admiralty and maritime Jurisdiction;—to Controversies to which the United States shall be a Party;—to Controversies between two or more States;—between a State and Citizens of another State;—between Citizens of different States;—between Citizens of the same State claiming Lands under Grants of different States, and between a State, or the Citizens thereof, and foreign States, Citizens or Subjects.

In all Cases affecting Ambassadors, other public Ministers and Consuls, and those in which a State shall be Party, the Supreme Court shall have original Jurisdiction. In all the other Cases before mentioned, the supreme Court shall have appelate Jurisdiction, both as to Law and Fact, with such Exceptions, and under such Regulations as the Congress shall make.

The Trial of all Crimes, except in Cases of Impeachment, shall be by Jury; and such Trial shall be held in the State where the said Crimes shall have been committed; but when not committed within any State, the Trial shall be at such Place or Places as the Congress may by Law have directed.

Section 3. Treason against the United States, shall consist only in levying War against them, or in adhering to their Enemies, giving them Aid and Comfort. No Person shall be convicted of Treason unless on the Testimony of two Witnesses to the same overt Act, or on Confession in open Court.

The Congress shall have Power to declare the Punishment of Treason, but no Attainder of Treason shall work Corruption of Blood, or Forfeiture except during the Life of the Person attainted.

Article IV

Section 1. Full Faith and Credit shall be given in each State to the public Acts, Records, and judicial proceedings of every other State. And the Congress may by general Laws prescribe the Manner in which such Acts, Records and Proceedings shall be proved, and the Effect thereof.

Section 2. The Citizens of each State shall be entitled to all Privileges and Immunities of Citizens in the several States.

A Person charged in any State with Treason, Felony, or other Crime, who shall flee from Justice, and be found in another State, shall on Demand of the executive Authority of the State from which he fled, be delivered up, to be removed to the State having Jurisdiction of the Crime.

No Person held to Service or Labour in one State, under the Laws thereof, escaping into another, shall, in Consequence of any Law or Regulation therein, be discharged from such Service or Labour, but shall be delivered up on Claim of the Party to whom such Service or Labour may be due.

Section 3. New States may be admitted by the Congress into this Union; but no new State shall be formed or erected within the Jurisdiction of any other State; nor any State be formed by the Junction of two or more States, or Parts of States, without the Consent of the Legislatures of the States concerned as well as of the Congress.

The Congress shall have Power to dispose of and make all needful Rules and Regulations respecting the Territory or other Property belonging to the United States; and nothing in this Constitution shall be so construed as to Prejudice any Claims of the United States, or of any particular State.

Section 4. The United States shall guarantee to every State in this Union a Republican Form of Government, and shall protect each of them against Invasion; and on Application of the Legislature, or of the Executive (when the Legislature cannot be convened) against domestic Violence.

Article V

The Congress, whenever two thirds of both Houses shall deem it necessary, shall propose Amendments to this Constitution, or, on the Application of the Legislatures of two thirds of the several States, shall call a Convention for proposing Amendments, which, in either Case, shall be valid to all Intents and Purposes, as Part of this Constitution, when ratified by the Legislatures of three fourths of the several States, or by Conventions in three fourths thereof, as the one or the other Mode of Ratification may be proposed by the Congress; provided that no Amendment which may be made prior to the Year One thousand eight hundred and eight shall in any Manner affect the first and fourth Clauses in the Ninth Section of the first Article; and that no State, without its Consent, shall be deprived of its equal Suffrage in the Senate.

Article VI

All Debts contracted and Engagements entered into, before the Adoption of this Constitution, shall be as valid against the United States under this Constitution, as under the Confederation.

This Constitution, and the Laws of the United States which shall be made in Pursuance thereof; and all Treaties made, or which shall be made, under the Authority of the United States, shall be the supreme Law of the Land; and the Judges in every State shall be bound thereby, any Thing in the Constitution or Laws of any State to the Contrary notwithstanding.

The Senators and Representatives before mentioned, and the Members of the several State Legislatures, and all executive and judicial Officers, both of the United States and of the several States, shall be bound by Oath or Affirmation, to support this Constitution; but no religious Test shall ever be required as a Qualification to any Office or public Trust under the United States.

Article VII

The Ratification of the Conventions of nine States, shall be sufficient for the Establishment of this Constitution between the States so ratifying the Same.

Done in Convention by the Unanimous Consent of the States present the Seventeenth Day of September in the Year of our Lord one thousand seven hundred and Eighty seven and of the Independence of the United States of America the Twelfth. In witness thereof We have hereunto subscribed our Names,

Articles in Addition to, and Amendment of, the Constitution of the United States of America, Proposed by Congress, and Ratified by the Several States, Pursuant to the Fifth Article of the Original Constitution.

Amendment I

Congress shall make no law respecting an establishment of religion, or prohibiting the free exercise thereof; or abridging the freedom of speech, or of the press; or the right of the people peaceably to assemble, and to petition the Government for a redress of grievances.

Amendment II

A well regulated Militia, being necessary to the security of a free State, the right of the people to keep and bear Arms, shall not be infringed.

Amendment III

No Soldier, in time of peace be quartered in any house, without the consent of the Owner, nor in time of war, but in a manner to be prescribed by law.

Amendment IV

The right of the people to be secure in their persons, houses, papers, and effects, against unreasonable searches and seizures, shall not be violated, and no Warrants shall issue, but upon probable cause, supported by Oath or affirmation, and particularly describing the place to be searched, and the persons or things to be seized.

Amendment V

No Person shall be held to answer for a capital, or otherwise infamous crime, unless on a presentment or indictment of a Grand Jury, except in cases arising in the land or naval forces, or in the Militia, when in actual service in time of War or public danger; nor shall any person be subject for the same offence to be twice put in jeopardy of life or limb; nor shall be compelled in any criminal case to be a witness against himself, nor be deprived of life, liberty, or property, without due process of law; nor shall private property be taken for public use, without just compensation.

Amendment VI

In all criminal prosecutions, the accused shall enjoy the right to a speedy and public trial by an impartial jury of the State and district wherein the crime shall have been committed, which district shall have been previously ascertained by law, and to be informed of the nature and cause of the accusation; to be confronted with the witness against him; to have compulsory process for obtaining Witnesses in his favor, and to have the Assistance of Counsel for his defence.

Amendment VII

In Suits at common law, where the value in controversy shall exceed twenty dollars, the right of trial by jury shall be preserved, and no fact tried by a jury, shall be otherwise re-examined in any Court of the United States, than according to the rules of the common law.

Amendment VIII

Excessive bail shall not be required, nor excessive fines imposed, nor cruel and unusual punishments inflicted.

Amendment IX

The enumeration in the Constitution, of certain rights, shall not be construed to deny or disparage others retained by the people.

Amendment X

The powers not delegated to the United States by the Constitution, nor prohibited by it to the States, are reserved to the States respectively, or to the people. [The first ten amendments were ratified Dec. 15, 1791.]

Amendment XI

The Judicial power of the United States shall not be construed to extend to any suit in law or equity, commenced or prosecuted against one of the United States by Citizens of another State, or by Citizens or Subjects of any Foreign State. [Jan. 8, 1798]

Amendment XII

The Electors shall meet in their respective states and vote by ballot for President and Vice-President, one of whom, at least, shall not be an inhabitant of the same state with themselves; they shall name in their ballots the person voted for as President, and in distinct ballots the person voted for as Vice-President, and they shall make distinct lists of all persons voted for as President, and of all persons voted for as Vice-President, and of the number of votes for each, which lists they shall sign and certify, and transmit sealed to the seat of the government of the United States, directed to the President of the Senate;—The President of the Senate shall, in the presence of the Senate and House of Representatives, open all the certificates and the votes shall then be counted;—The person having the greatest number of votes for President, shall be the President, if such number be a majority of the whole number of Electors appointed; and if no person have such majority, then from the persons having the highest numbers not exceeding three on the list of those voted for as President, the House of Representatives shall choose immediately, by ballot, the President. But in choosing the President, the votes shall be taken by states, the representation from each state having one vote; a quorum for this purpose shall consist of a member or members from two-thirds of the states, and a majority of all the states shall be necessary to a choice. And if the House of Representatives shall not choose a President whenever the right of choice shall devolve upon them, before the fourth day of March next following, then the Vice-President shall act as President, as in the case of the death or other constitutional disability of the President—The person having the greatest number of votes as Vice-President, shall be the Vice-President, if such number be a majority of the whole number of Electors appointed, and if no person have a majority, then from the two highest numbers on the list, the Senate shall choose the Vice-President; a quorum for the purpose shall consist of two-thirds of the whole number of Senators, and a majority of the whole number shall be necessary to a choice. But no person constitutionally ineligible to the office of President shall be eligible to that of Vice-President of the United States. [Sept. 25, 1804]

Amendment XIII

Section 1. Neither slavery nor involuntary servitude, except as a punishment for crime whereof the party shall have been duly convicted, shall exist within the United States, or any place subject to their jurisdiction.

Section 2. Congress shall have power to enforce this article by appropriate legislation. [Dec. 18, 1865]

Amendment XIV

Section 1. All persons born or naturalized in the United States and subject to the jurisdiction thereof, are citizens of the United States and of the State wherein they reside. No State shall make or enforce any law which shall abridge the privileges or immunities of citizens of the United States; nor shall any State deprive any person of life, liberty, or property, without due process of law; nor deny any person within its jurisdiction the equal protection of the laws.

Section 2. Representatives shall be apportioned among the several States according to their respective numbers, counting the whole number of persons in each State, excluding Indians not taxed. But when the right to vote at any election for the choice of electors for President and Vice President of the United States, Representatives in Congress, the Executive and Judicial officers of a State, or the members of the Legislature thereof, is denied to any of the male inhabitants of such State, being twenty-one years of age, and citizens of the United States, or in any way abridged, except for participation in rebellion, or other crime, the basis of representation therein shall be reduced in the proportion which the number of such male citizens shall bear to the whole number of male citizens twenty-one years of age in such State.

Section 3. No person shall be a Senator or Representative in Congress, or elector of President and Vice President, or hold any office, civil or military, under the United States, or under any State, who, having previously taken an oath, as a member of Congress, or as an officer of the United States, or as a member of any State legislature, or as an executive or judicial officer of any State, to support the Constitution of the United States, shall have engaged in insurrection or rebellion against the same, or given aid or comfort to the enemies thereof. But Congress may by a vote of two-thirds of each House, remove such disability.

Section 4. The validity of the public debt of the United States, authorized by law, including debts incurred for payment of pensions and bounties for services in suppressing insurrection or rebellion, shall not be questioned. But neither the United States nor any State shall assume or pay any debt or obligation incurred in aid of insurrection or rebellion against the United States, or any claim for the loss or emancipation of any slave; but all such debts, obligations and claims shall be held illegal and void.

Section 5. The Congress shall have power to enforce by appropriate legislation, the provisions of this article. [July 28, 1868]

Amendment XV

Section 1. The right of citizens of the United States to vote shall not be denied or abridged by the United States or by any State on account of race, color, or previous condition of servitude.

Section 2. The Congress shall have power to enforce this article by appropriate legislation. [March 30, 1870]

Amendment XVI

The Congress shall have power to lay and collect taxes on incomes, from whatever source derived, without apportionment among the several States, and without regard to any census or enumeration. [Feb. 25, 1913]

Amendment XVII

The Senate of the United States shall be composed of two Senators from each State, elected by the people thereof, for six years; and each Senator shall have one vote. The electors in each State shall have the qualifications requisite for electors of the most numerous branch of the State legislatures.

When vacancies happen in the representation of any State in the Senate, the executive authority of such State shall issue writs of election to fill such vacancies: Provided, That the legislature of any State may empower the executive thereof to make temporary appointments until the people fill the vacancies by election as the legislature may direct.

This amendment shall not be so construed as to affect the election or term of any Senator chosen before it becomes valid as part of the Constitution. [May 31, 1913]

Amendment XVIII

Section 1. After one year from the ratification of this article the manufacture, sale, or transportation of intoxicating liquors within, the importation thereof into, or the exportation thereof from the United States and all territory subject to the jurisdiction thereof for beverage purposes is hereby prohibited.

Section 2. The Congress and the several States shall have concurrent power to enforce this article by appropriate legislation.

Section 3. This article shall be inoperative unless it shall have been ratified as an amendment to the Constitution by the legislatures of the several States, as provided in the Constitution, within seven years from the date of the submission hereof to the States by the Congress. [Jan. 29, 1919]

Amendment XIX

The right of citizens of the United States to vote shall not be denied or abridged by the United States or by any State on account of sex.

Congress shall have power to enforce this article by appropriate legislation. [Aug. 26, 1920]

Amendment XX

Section 1. The terms of the President and Vice President shall end at noon on the 20th day of January, and the terms of Senators and Representatives at noon on the 3d day of January, of the years in which such terms would have ended if this article had not been ratified; and the terms of their successors shall then begin.

Section 2. The Congress shall assemble at least once in every year, and such meeting shall begin at noon on the 3d day of January, unless they shall by law appoint a different day.

Section 3. If, at the time fixed for the beginning of the term of the President, the President elect shall have died, the Vice President elect shall become President. If a President shall not have been chosen before the time fixed for the beginning of his term, or if the President elect shall have failed to qualify, then the Vice President elect shall act as President until a President shall have qualified; and the Congress may by law provide for the case wherein neither a President elect nor a Vice President elect shall have qualified, declaring who shall then act as President, or the manner in which one who is to act shall be selected, and such person shall act accordingly until a President or Vice President shall have qualified.

Section 4. The Congress may by law provide for the case of the death of any of the persons for whom the House of Representatives may choose a President whenever the right of choice shall have devolved upon them, and for the case of the death of any of the persons from whom the Senate may choose a Vice President whenever the right of choice shall have devolved upon them.

Section 5. Sections 1 and 2 shall take effect on the 15th day of October following the ratification of this article.

Section 6. This article shall be inoperative unless it shall have been ratified as an amendment to the Constitution by the legislatures of three-fourths of the several States within seven years from the date of its submission. [Feb. 6, 1933]

Amendment XXI

Section 1. The eighteenth article of amendment to the Constitution of the United States is hereby repealed.

Section 2. The transportation or importation into any State, Territory, or possession of the United States for delivery or use therein of intoxicating liquors, in violation of the laws thereof, is hereby prohibited.

Section 3. This article shall be inoperative unless it shall have been ratified as an amendment to the Constitution by conventions in the several States, as provided in the Constitution, within seven years from the date of the submission hereof to the States by the Congress. [Dec. 5, 1933]

Amendment XXII

Section 1. No person shall be elected to the office of the President more than twice, and no person who has held the office of President, or acted as President, for more than two years of a term to which some other person was elected President shall be elected to the office of the President more than once. But this Article shall not apply to any person holding the office of President when this Article was proposed by the Congress, and shall not prevent any person who may be holding the office of President, or acting as President, during the term within which this Article becomes operative from holding the office of President or acting as President during the remainder of such term.

Section 2. This article shall be inoperative unless it shall have been ratified as an amendment to the Constitution by the legislatures of three-fourths of the several States within seven years from the date of its submission to the States by the Congress. [Feb. 27, 1951]

Amendment XXIII

Section 1. The District constituting the seat of Government of the United States shall appoint in such manner as the Congress may direct:

A number of electors of President and Vice President equal to the whole number of Senators and Representatives in Congress to which the District would be entitled if it were a State, but in no event more than the least populous State; they shall be in addition to those appointed by the States, but they shall be considered, for the purposes of the election of President and Vice President, to be electors appointed by a State; and they shall meet in the District and perform such duties as provided by the twelfth article of amendment.

Section 2. The Congress shall have power to enforce this article by appropriate legislation. [Mar. 29, 1961]

Amendment XXIV

Section 1. The right of citizens of the United States to vote in any primary or other election for President or Vice President, for electors for President or Vice President, or for Senator or Representative in Congress, shall not be denied or abridged by the United States or any State by reason of failure to pay any poll tax or other tax.

Section 2. The Congress shall have power to enforce this article by appropriate legislation. [Jan. 23, 1964]

Amendment XXV

Section 1. In case of the removal of the President from office or of his death or resignation, the Vice President shall become President.

Section 2. Whenever there is a vacancy in the office of the Vice President, the President shall nominate a Vice President who shall take office upon confirmation by a majority vote of both Houses of Congress.

Section 3. Whenever the President transmits to the President pro tempore of the Senate and the Speaker of the House of Representatives his written declaration that he is unable to discharge the powers and duties of his office, and until he transmits to them a written declaration to the contrary, such powers and duties shall be discharged by the Vice President as Acting President.

Section 4. Whenever the Vice President and a majority of either the principal officers of the executive departments or of such other body as Congress may by law provide, transmit to the President pro tempore of the Senate and the Speaker of the House of Representatives their written declaration that the President is unable to discharge the powers and duties of his office, the Vice President shall immediately assume the powers and duties of the office as Acting President.

Thereafter, when the President transmits to the President pro tempore of the Senate and the Speaker of the House of Representatives his written declaration that no inability exists, he shall resume the powers and duties of his office unless the Vice President and a majority of either the principal officers of the executive department or of such other body as Congress may by law provide, transmit within four days to the President pro tempore of the Senate and the Speaker of the House of Representatives their written declaration that the President is unable to discharge the powers and duties of his office. Thereupon Congress shall decide the issue, assembling within forty-eight hours for that purpose if not in session. If the Congress, within twenty-one days after receipt of the latter written declaration, or, if Congress is not in session, within twenty-one days after Congress is required to assemble, determines by two-thirds vote of both Houses that the President is unable to discharge the powers and duties of his office, the Vice President shall continue to discharge the same as Acting President; otherwise, the President shall resume the powers and duties of his office. [Feb. 10, 1967]

Amendment XXVI

Section 1. The right of citizens of the United States, who are eighteen years of age or older, to vote shall not be denied or abridged by the United States or by any State on account of age.

Section 2. The Congress shall have power to enforce this article by appropriate legislation. [June 30, 1971]

Source: http://usinfo.state.gov/usa/infousa/facts/democrac/6.htm

ADMISSION OF STATES

Order of Admission	State	Date of Admission
1	Delaware	December 7, 1787
2	Pennsylvania	December 12, 1787
3	New Jersey	December 18, 1787
4	Georgia	January 2, 1788
5	Connecticut	January 9, 1788
6	Massachusetts	February 6, 1788
7	Maryland	April 28, 1788
8	South Carolina	May 23, 1788
9	New Hampshire	June 21, 1788
10	Virginia	June 25, 1788
11	New York	July 26, 1788
12	North Carolina	November 21, 1789
13	Rhode Island	May 29, 1790
14	Vermont	March 4, 1791
15	Kentucky	June 1, 1792
16	Tennessee	June 1, 1796
17	Ohio	March 1, 1803
18	Louisiana	April 30, 1812
19	Indiana	December 11, 1816
20	Mississippi	December 10, 1817
21	Illinois	December 3, 1818
22	Alabama	December 14, 1819
23	Maine	March 15, 1820
24	Missouri	August 10, 1821
25	Arkansas	June 15, 1836
26	Michigan	January 26, 1837
27	Florida	March 3, 1845
28	Texas	December 29, 1845
29	Iowa	December 28, 1846
30	Wisconsin	May 29, 1848
31	California	September 9, 1850
32	Minnesota	May 11, 1858

Order of Admission	State	Date of Admission
33	Oregon	February 14, 1859
34	Kansas	January 29, 1861
35	West Virginia	June 20, 1863
36	Nevada	October 31, 1864
37	Nebraska	March 1, 1867
38	Colorado	August 1, 1876
39	North Dakota	November 2, 1889
40	South Dakota	November 2, 1889
41	Montana	November 8, 1889
42	Washington	November 11, 1889
43	Idaho	July 3, 1890
44	Wyoming	July 10, 1890
45	Utah	January 4, 1896
46	Oklahoma	November 16, 1907
47	New Mexico	January 6, 1912
48	Arizona	February 14, 1912
49	Alaska	January 3, 1959
50	Hawaii	August 21, 1959

APPENDIX V

AREA AND POPULATION OF THE UNITED STATES: 1790–2006

Year	Land area (square miles)	Population	Population per square mile
1790	864,746	3,929,214	4.5
1800	864,746	5,308,483	6.1
1810	1,681,828	7,239,881	4.3
1820	1,749,462	9,638,453	5.5
1830	1,749,462	12,866,020	7.4
1840	1,749,462	17,069,453	9.8
1850	2,940,042	23,191,876	7.9
1860	2,969,640	31,443,321	10.6
1870	2,969,640	39,818,449*	13.4
1880	2,969,640	50,155,783	16.9
1890	2,969,640	62,947,714	21.2
1900	2,969,834	75,994,575	25.6
1910	2,969,565	91,972,266	31.0
1920	2,969,451	105,710,620	35.6
1930	2,977,128	122,775,046	41.2
1940	2,977,128	131,669,275	44.2
1950	2,974,726	150,697,361	50.7
1960	3,540,911	179,323,175	50.6
1970	3,536,855	203,235,298	57.5
1980	3,618,770	226,545,805	62.6
1990	3,787,425	248,709,873	65.7
2000	3,787,425	281,421,906	74.3
2006	3,787,425	300,000,000	79.2

*Revised to include adjustment of 1,260,078 for underenumeration in Southern States. Unrevised census count is 38,558,371.

APPENDIX VI

PRESIDENTIAL ELECTIONS

Year	Candidates	Parties	Popular Vote	Percentage of Popular Vote	Electoral Vote	Percentage of Voter Participation
1789	GEORGE WASHINGTON				69	
	John Adams				34	
	Others				35	
1792	GEORGE WASHINGTON				132	
	John Adams				77	
	George Clinton				50	
	Others				5	
1796	JOHN ADAMS	Federalist			71	
	Thomas Jefferson	Dem-Rep			68	
	Thomas Pinckney	Federalist			59	
	Aaron Burr	Dem-Rep			30	
	Others				48	
1800	THOMAS JEFFERSON	Dem-Rep			73	
	Aaron Burr	Dem-Rep			73	
	John Adams	Federalist			65	
	C.C. Pinckney	Federalist			64	
	John Jay	Federalist			1	

Year	Candidate	Party	Popular Vote	%	Electoral Vote	Turnout %
1804	THOMAS JEFFERSON	Dem-Rep			162	
	C.C. Pinckney	Federalist			14	
1808	JAMES MADISON	Dem-Rep			122	
	C.C. Pinckney	Federalist			47	
	George Clinton	Dem-Rep			6	
1812	JAMES MADISON	Dem-Rep			128	
	De Witt Clinton	Federalist			89	
1816	JAMES MONROE	Dem-Rep			183	
	Rufus King	Federalist			34	
1820	JAMES MONROE	Dem-Rep			231	
	John Quincy Adams	Dem-Rep			1	
1824	JOHN Q. ADAMS	Dem-Rep	108,740	30.5	84	26.9
	Andrew Jackson	Dem-Rep	153,544	43.1	99	
	William H. Crawford	Dem-Rep	46,618	13.1	41	
	Henry Clay	Dem-Rep	47,136	13.2	37	
1828	ANDREW JACKSON	Democratic	647,286	56.0	178	57.6
	John Quincy Adams	Nat Republican	508,064	44.0	83	
1832	ANDREW JACKSON	Democratic	687,502	55.0	219	55.4
	Henry Clay	Nat Republican	530,189	42.4	49	
	John Floyd	Independent			11	
	William Wirt	Anti-Mason	33,108	2.6	7	
1836	MARTIN VAN BUREN	Democratic	765,483	50.9	170	57.8
	W.H. Harrison	Whig			73	
	Hugh L. White	Whig	739,795	49.1	26	
	Daniel Webster	Whig			14	
	W.P. Magnum	Independent			11	
1840	WILLIAM HARRISON	Whig	1,274,624	53.1	234	80.2
	Martin Van Buren	Democratic	1,127,781	46.9	60	
	J.G. Birney	Liberty	7,069			

(continued)

Appendix VI *(continued)*

Year	Candidates	Parties	Popular Vote	Percentage of Popular Vote	Electoral Vote	Percentage of Voter Participation
1844	JAMES POLK	Democratic	1,338,464	49.6	170	78.9
	Henry Clay	Whig	1,300,097	48.1	105	
	J.G. Birney	Liberty	62,300	2.3	—	
1848	ZACHARY TAYLOR	Whig	1,360,967	47.4	163	72.7
	Lewis Cass	Democratic	1,222,342	42.5	127	
	Martin Van Buren	Free-Soil	291,263	10.1		
1852	FRANKLIN PIERCE	Democratic	1,601,117	50.9	254	69.6
	Winfield Scott	Whig	1,385,453	44.1	42	
	John P. Hale	Free-Soil	155,825	5.0	—	
1856	JAMES BUCHANAN	Democratic	1,832,955	45.3	741	78.9
	John C. Frémont	Republican	1,339,932	33.1	114	
	Millard Fillmore	American	871,731	21.6	8	
1860	ABRAHAM LINCOLN	Republican	1,865,593	39.8	180	81.2
	Stephen Douglas	N Democratic	1,382,713	29.5	12	
	John C. Breckinridge	S Democratic	848,356	18.1	72	
	John Bell	Union	592,906	12.6	39	
1864	ABRAHAM LINCOLN	Republican	2,213,655	55.0	212	73.8
	George McClellan	Democratic	1,805,237	45.0	21	
1868	ULYSSES GRANT	Republican	3,012,833	52.7	214	78.1
	Horatio Seymour	Democratic	2,703,249	47.3	80	
1872	ULYSSES GRANT	Republican	3,597,132	55.6	286	71.3
	Horace Greeley	Dem/Liberal Rep	2,834,125	43.9	66	
1876	RUTHERFORD HAYES	Republican	4,036,298	48.0	185	81.8
	Samuel Tilden	Democratic	4,300,590	51.0	184	

Year	Candidate	Party	Votes	Percent	Electoral	Turnout
1880	JAMES GARFIELD	Republican	4,454,416	48.5	214	79.4
	Winfield Hancock	Democratic	4,444,952	48.1	155	
1884	GROVER CLEVELAND	Democratic	4,874,986	48.5	219	77.5
	James Blaine	Republican	4,851,981	48.2	182	
1888	BENJAMIN HARRISON	Republican	5,439,853	47.9	233	79.3
	Grover Cleveland	Democratic	5,540,309	48.6	168	
1892	GROVER CLEVELAND	Democratic	5,556,918	46.1	277	74.7
	Benjamin Harrison	Republican	5,176,108	43.0	145	
	James Weaver	People's	1,041,028	8.5	22	
1896	WILLIAM McKINLEY	Republican	7,104,779	51.1	271	79.3
	William J. Bryan	Democratic-People's	6,502,925	47.7	176	
1900	WILLIAM McKINLEY	Republican	7,207,923	51.7	292	73.2
	William J. Bryan	Dem/Populist	6,358,133	45.5	155	
1904	THEODORE ROOSEVELT	Republican	7,623,486	57.9	336	65.2
	Alton Parker	Democratic	5,077,911	37.6	140	
	Eugene Debs	Socialist	402,283	3.0	—	
1908	WILLIAM TAFT	Republican	7,678,098	51.6	321	65.4
	William J. Bryan	Democratic	6,409,104	43.1	162	
	Eugene Debs	Socialist	420,793	2.8	—	
1912	WOODROW WILSON	Democratic	6,293,454	41.9	435	58.8
	Theodore Roosevelt	Progressive	4,119,538	27.4	88	
	William Taft	Republican	3,484,980	23.2	8	
	Eugene Debs	Socialist	900,672	6.0	—	
1916	WOODROW WILSON	Democratic	9,129,606	49.4	277	61.6
	Charles Hughes	Republican	8,538,221	46.2	254	
	A.L. Benson	Socialist	585,113	3.2	—	
1920	WARREN HARDING	Republican	16,152,200	60.4	404	49.2
	James Cox	Democratic	9,147,353	34.2	127	
	Eugene Debs	Socialist	919,799	3.4	—	

(continued)

Appendix VI *(continued)*

Year	Candidates	Parties	Popular Vote	Percentage of Popular Vote	Electoral Vote	Percentage of Voter Participation
1924	CALVIN COOLIDGE	Republican	15,725,016	54.0	382	48.9
	John Davis	Democratic	8,386,503	28.8	136	
	Robert LaFollette	Progressive	4,822,856	16.6	13	
1928	HERBERT HOOVER	Republican	21,391,381	58.2	444	56.9
	Alfred Smith	Democratic	15,016,443	40.9	87	
	Norman Thomas	Socialist	267,835	0.7	—	
1932	FRANKLIN ROOSEVELT	Democratic	22,821,857	57.4	472	56.9
	Herbert Hoover	Republican	15,761,841	39.7	59	
	Norman Thomas	Socialist	881,951	2.2		
1936	FRANKLIN ROOSEVELT	Democratic	27,751,597	60.8	523	61.0
	Alfred Landon	Republican	16,679,583	36.5	8	
	William Lemke	Union	882,479	1.9		
1940	FRANKLIN ROOSEVELT	Democratic	27,244,160	54.8	449	62.5
	Wendell Willkie	Republican	22,305,198	44.8	82	
1944	FRANKLIN ROOSEVELT	Democratic	25,602,504	53.5	432	55.9
	Thomas Dewey	Republican	22,006,285	46.0	99	
1948	HARRY TRUMAN	Democratic	24,105,695	49.5	304	53.0
	Thomas Dewey	Republican	21,969,170	45.1	189	
	J. Strom Thurmond	Dixiecrat	1,169,021	2.4	38	
	Henry Wallace	Progressive	1,156,103	2.4	—	
1952	DWIGHT EISENHOWER	Republican	33,936,252	55.1	442	63.3
	Adlai Stevenson	Democratic	27,314,992	44.4	89	

Year	Candidate	Party	Popular Vote	%	Electoral Vote	Turnout %
1956	DWIGHT EISENHOWER	Republican	35,575,420	57.6	457	60.6
	Adlai Stevenson	Democratic	26,033,066	42.1	73	
1960	JOHN KENNEDY	Democratic	34,227,096	49.9	303	62.8
	Richard Nixon	Republican	3,108,546	49.6	219	62.8
	Other				15	
1964	LYNDON JOHNSON	Democratic	43,126,506	61.1	486	61.7
	Barry Goldwater	Republican	27,176,799	38.5	52	
1968	RICHARD NIXON	Republican	31,770,237	43.4	301	60.6
	Hubert Humphrey	Democratic	31,270,533	42.7	191	
	George Wallace	Am. Indep.	9,906,141	13.5	46	
1972	RICHARD NIXON	Republican	47,169,911	60.7	520	55.2
	George McGovern	Democratic	29,170,383	37.5	17	
1976	JIMMY CARTER	Democratic	40,828,587	50.0	297	53.5
	Gerald Ford	Republican	39,147,613	47.9	241	
	Other		1,575,459	2.1	—	
1980	RONALD REAGAN	Republican	43,901,812	50.7	489	52.6
	Jimmy Carter	Democratic	35,483,820	41.0	49	
	John Anderson	Independent	5,719,722	6.6	—	
	Ed Clark	Libertarian	921,188	1.1	—	
1984	RONALD REAGAN	Republican	54,455,075	59.0	525	53.3
	Walter Mondale	Democratic	37,577,185	41.0	13	
1988	GEORGE BUSH	Republican	47,946,422	54.0	426	50.2
	Michael Dukakis	Democratic	41,016,429	46.0	112	
1992	WILLIAM CLINTON	Democratic	44,908,233	43.3	370	55.2
	George Bush	Republican	39,102,282	37.7	168	
	Ross Perot	Independent	19,721,433	19.0	—	
1996	WILLIAM CLINTON	Democratic	47,401,185	49.3	379	49.0
	Robert Dole	Republican	39,197,469	40.7	159	
	Ross Perot	Reform	8,085,294	8.4	—	

(continued)

Appendix VI (continued)

Year	Candidates	Parties	Popular Vote	Percentage of Popular Vote	Electoral Vote	Percentage of Voter Participation
2000	GEORGE W. BUSH	Republican	50,459,211	47.89	271	51.0
	Albert Gore, Jr.	Democratic	51,003,894	48.41	266	
	Ralph Nader	Green	2,834,410	2.69	—	
2004	GEORGE W. BUSH	Republican	62,028,285	50.73	286	60.0
	John Kerry	Democratic	59,028,109	48.27	251	
	Ralph Nader	Independent	463,647	0.38	0	

Source: All data from Federal Election Commission, www.fec.gov ~wwfec.gov/pubrec/fe2004/2004Presg~~1tml.

PARTY AFFILIATIONS IN CONGRESS, 1789–PRESENT

Congress	Senate			House		
	Major # (%)	Minor # (%)	Other # (%)	Major # (%)	Minor # (%)	Other # (%)
1. 1789–1791	Fed 17 (65%)	Op 9 (35%)		Fed 38 (59%)	Op 26 (41%)	
2. 1791–1793	Fed 16 (55%)	Op 13 (45%)		Fed 37 (53%)	Op 33 (47%)	
3. 1793–1795	Fed 17 (57%)	Op 13 (43%)		Fed 57 (54%)	Op 48 (46%)	
4. 1795–1797	Fed 19 (59%)	Op 13 (41%)		Fed 54 (51%)	Op 52 (49%)	
5. 1797–1799	Fed 20 (63%)	DR 12 (37%)		Fed 58 (55%)	DR 48 (45%)	
6. 1799–1801	Fed 19 (59%)	DR 13 (41%)		Fed 64 (60%)	DR 42 (40%)	
7. 1801–1803	DR 18 (56%)	Fed 14 (44%)		DR 69 (66%)	Fed 36 (34%)	
8. 1803–1805	DR 25 (74%)	Fed 9 (26%)		DR 102 (72%)	Fed 39 (28%)	
9. 1805–1807	DR 27 (79%)	Fed 7 (21%)		DR 116 (82%)	Fed 25 (18%)	
10. 1807–1809	DR 28 (82%)	Fed 6 (18%)		DR 118 (83%)	Fed 24 (17%)	
11. 1809–1811	DR 28 (82%)	Fed 6 (18%)		DR 94 (66%)	Fed 48 (34%)	
12. 1811–1813	DR 30 (83%)	Fed 6 (17%)		DR 108 (75%)	Fed 36 (25%)	
13. 1813–1815	DR 27 (75%)	Fed 9 (25%)		DR 112 (62%)	Fed 68 (38%)	
14. 1815–1817	DR 25 (69%)	Fed 11 (31%)		DR 117 (64%)	Fed 65 (36%)	
15. 1817–1819	DR 34 (77%)	Fed 10 (23%)		DR 141 (77%)	Fed 42 (23%)	
16. 1819–1821	DR 35 (83%)	Fed 7 (17%)		DR 156 (85%)	Fed 27 (15%)	
17. 1821–1823	DR 44 (92%)	Fed 4 (8%)		DR 158 (86%)	Fed 25 (14%)	
18. 1823–1825	DR 44 (92%)	Fed 4 (8%)		DR 187 (88%)	Fed 26 (12%)	
19. 1825–1827	Adm 26 (57%)	Op 20 (43%)		Adm 105 (52%)	Op 97 (48%)	
20. 1827–1829	Op 28 (58%)	Adm 20 (42%)		Op 119 (56%)	Adm 94 (44%)	
21. 1829–1831	D 26 (54%)	NR 22 (46%)		D 139 (65%)	NR 74 (35%)	

(continued)

APPENDIX VII *(continued)*

Congress	Senate			House		
	Major # (%)	Minor # (%)	Other # (%)	Major # (%)	Minor # (%)	Other # (%)
22. 1831–1833	D 25 (52%)	NR 21 (44%)	2 (4%)	D 141 (66%)	NR 58 (27%)	14 (7%)
23. 1833–1835	D 20 (42%)	NR 20 (42%)	8 (16%)	D 147 (57%)	AM 53 (20%)	60 (23%)
24. 1835–1837	D 27 (52%)	W 25 (48%)		D 145 (60%)	W 98 (40%)	
25. 1837–1839	D 30 (58%)	W 18 (35%)	4 (7%)	D 108 (45%)	W 107 (45%)	24 (10%)
26. 1839–1841	D 28 (56%)	W 22 (44%)		D 124 (51%)	W 118 (49%)	
27. 1841–1843	W 28 (54%)	D 22 (42%)	2 (4%)	W 133 (55%)	D 102 (42%)	6 (2%)
28. 1843–1845	W 28 (52%)	D 25 (46%)	1 (2%)	D 142 (64%)	W 79 (36%)	1 (0%)
29. 1845–1847	D 31 (55%)	W 25 (45%)		D 143 (63%)	W 77 (34%)	6 (3%)
30. 1847–1849	D 36 (62%)	W 21 (36%)	1 (2%)	W 115 (51%)	D 108 (48%)	4 (1%)
31. 1849–1851	D 35 (57%)	W 25 (40%)	2 (3%)	D 112 (49%)	W 109 (47%)	9 (4%)
32. 1851–1853	D 35 (57%)	W 24 (39%)	3 (4%)	D 140 (60%)	W 88 (38%)	5 (2%)
33. 1853–1855	D 38 (61%)	W 22 (36%)	2 (3%)	D 159 (68%)	W 71 (30%)	4 (2%)
34. 1855–1857	D 40 (67%)	R 15 (25%)	5 (8%)	R 108 (46%)	D 83 (35%)	43 (18%)
35. 1857–1859	D 36 (56%)	R 20 (31%)	8 (13%)	D 118 (50%)	R 92 (39%)	26 (11%)
36. 1859–1861	D 36 (55%)	R 26 (39%)	4 (6%)	R 114 (48%)	D 92 (39%)	31 (13%)
37. 1861–1863	R 31 (63%)	D 10 (21%)	8 (16%)	R 105 (59%)	D 43 (24%)	30 (17%)
38. 1863–1865	R 36 (72%)	D 9 (18%)	5 (10%)	R 102 (55%)	D 75 (40%)	9 (5%)
39. 1865–1867	R 42 (81%)	D 10 (19%)		R 149 (78%)	D 42 (22%)	
40. 1867–1869	R 42 (79%)	D 11 (21%)		R 143 (74%)	D 49 (26%)	
41. 1869–1871	R 56 (84%)	D 11 (16%)		R 149 (70%)	D 63 (30%)	
42. 1871–1873	R 52 (70%)	D 17 (23%)	5 (7%)	D 134 (55%)	R 104 (43%)	5 (2%)
43. 1873–1875	R 49 (67%)	D 19 (26%)	5 (7%)	R 194 (65%)	D 92 (30%)	14 (5%)
44. 1875–1877	R 45 (59%)	D 29 (38%)	2 (3%)	D 169 (58%)	R 109 (37%)	14 (5%)
45. 1877–1879	R 39 (51%)	D 36 (47%)	1 (2%)	D 153 (52%)	R 140 (48%)	
46. 1879–1881	D 42 (55%)	R 33 (43%)	1 (2%)	D 149 (51%)	R 130 (44%)	14 (5%)
47. 1881–1883	R 37 (49%)	D 37 (49%)	1 (2%)	R 147 (50%)	D 135 (46%)	11 (4%)
48. 1883–1885	R 38 (51%)	D 36 (49%)		D 197 (61%)	R 118 (36%)	10 (3%)
49. 1885–1887	R 43 (56%)	D 34 (44%)		D 183 (56%)	R 140 (43%)	2 (1%)
50. 1887–1889	R 39 (51%)	D 37 (49%)		D 169 (52%)	R 152 (47%)	4 (1%)

(continued)

51. 1889–1891	R 39 (51%)	D 37 (49%)		R 166 (51%)	D 159 (49%)	
52. 1891–1893	R 47 (54%)	D 39 (44%)	2 (2%)	D 235 (71%)	R 88 (27%)	9 (2%)
53. 1893–1895	D 44 (52%)	R 38 (45%)	3 (3%)	D 218 (61%)	R 127 (36%)	11 (3%)
54. 1895–1897	R 43 (49%)	D 39 (44%)	6 (7%)	R 244 (69%)	D 105 (29%)	7 (2%)
55. 1897–1899	R 47 (53%)	D 34 (39%)	7 (8%)	R 204 (57%)	D 133 (32%)	40 (11%)
56. 1899–1901	R 53 (61%)	D 26 (30%)	8 (9%)	R 185 (52%)	D 163 (45%)	9 (3%)
57. 1901–1903	R 55 (61%)	D 31 (34%)	4 (5%)	R 197 (55%)	D 151 (42%)	9 (3%)
58. 1903–1905	R 57 (63%)	D 33 (37%)		R 208 (54%)	D 178 (46%)	
59. 1905–1907	R 57 (63%)	D 33 (37%)		R 250 (65%)	D 136 (35%)	
60. 1907–1909	R 61 (66%)	D 31 (34%)		R 222 (58%)	D 164 (42%)	
61. 1909–1911	R 61 (66%)	D 32 (34%)		R 219 (56%)	D 172 (44%)	
62. 1911–1913	R 51 (55%)	D 41 (45%)		D 228 (58%)	R 161 (41%)	1 (1%)
63. 1913–1915	D 51 (54%)	R 44 (46%)		D 291 (67%)	R 127 (29%)	17 (4%)
64. 1915–1917	D 56 (58%)	R 40 (42%)		D 230 (53%)	R 196 (45%)	9 (2%)
65. 1917–1919	D 53 (56%)	R 42 (44%)		D 216 (50%)	R 210 (49%)	6 (1%)
66. 1919–1921	R 49 (51%)	D 47 (49%)		R 240 (55%)	D 190 (44%)	3 (1%)
67. 1921–1923	R 59 (61%)	D 37 (39%)		R 303 (70%)	D 131 (30%)	1 (0%)
68. 1923–1925	R 51 (53%)	D 43 (45%)	2 (2%)	R 225 (52%)	D 205 (47%)	5 (1%)
69. 1925–1927	R 56 (58%)	D 39 (41%)	1 (1%)	R 247 (57%)	D 183 (42%)	4 (1%)
70. 1927–1929	R 49 (51%)	D 46 (48%)	1 (1%)	R 237 (55%)	D 195 (45%)	3 (0%)
71. 1929–1931	R 56 (58%)	D 39 (41%)	1 (1%)	R 267 (62%)	D 167 (38%)	1 (0%)
72. 1931–1933	R 48 (50%)	D 47 (49%)	1 (1%)	D 220 (51%)	R 214 (49%)	1 (0%)
73. 1933–1935	D 60 (63%)	R 35 (37%)		D 310 (72%)	R 117 (27%)	5 (1%)
74. 1935–1937	D 69 (72%)	R 25 (26%)	2 (2%)	D 319 (74%)	R 103 (24%)	10 (2%)
75. 1937–1939	D 76 (79%)	R 16 (17%)	4 (4%)	D 331 (76%)	R 89 (21%)	13 (3%)
76. 1939–1941	D 69 (72%)	R 23 (24%)	4 (4%)	D 261 (61%)	R 164 (38%)	4 (1%)
77. 1941–1943	D 66 (69%)	R 28 (29%)	2 (2%)	D 268 (62%)	R 162 (37%)	5 (1%)
78. 1943–1945	D 58 (60%)	R 37 (39%)	1 (1%)	D 218 (51%)	R 208 (48%)	4 (1%)
79. 1945–1947	D 56 (59%)	R 38 (40%)	1 (1%)	D 242 (56%)	R 190 (44%)	2 (0%)
80. 1947–1949	R 51 (53%)	D 45 (47%)		R 246 (57%)	D 188 (43%)	1 (0%)

APPENDIX VII *(continued)*

Congress	Senate Major # (%)	Minor # (%)	Other # (%)	House Major # (%)	Minor # (%)	Other # (%)
81. 1949–1951	D 54 (56%)	R 42 (44%)		D 263 (61%)	R 171 (39%)	1 (0%)
82. 1951–1953	D 49 (51%)	R 47 (49%)		D 235 (54%)	R 199 (46%)	1 (0%)
83. 1953–1955	R 48 (50%)	D 47 (49%)	1 (1%)	D 221 (51%)	D 212 (49%)	1 (0%)
84. 1955–1957	D 48 (50%)	R 47 (49%)	1 (1%)	D 232 (53%)	R 203 (47%)	
85. 1957–1959	D 49 (51%)	R 47 (49%)		D 232 (54%)	R 199 (46%)	
86. 1959–1961	D 62 (65%)	R 34 (35%)		D 261 (65%)	R 152 (35%)	
87. 1961–1963	D 65 (65%)	R 35 (35%)		D 280 (60%)	R 176 (40%)	
88. 1963–1965	D 67 (67%)	R 33 (33%)		D 258 (59%)	R 177 (41%)	1 (0%)
89. 1965–1967	D 68 (68%)	R 32 (32%)		D 295 (68%)	R 140 (32%)	
90. 1967–1969	D 64 (64%)	R 36 (36%)	1 (1%)	D 247 (57%)	R 187 (43%)	
91. 1969–1971	D 58 (58%)	R 42 (42%)		D 243 (56%)	R 192 (44%)	
92. 1971–1973	D 54 (54%)	R 45 (45%)	1 (1%)	D 254 (59%)	R 180 (41%)	1 (0%)
93. 1973–1975	D 56 (56%)	R 42 (42%)	2 (2%)	D 240 (55%)	R 192 (44%)	3 (1%)
94. 1975–1977	D 61 (61%)	R 37 (37%)	2 (2%)	D 291 (67%)	R 144 (33%)	
95. 1977–1979	D 61 (61%)	R 38 (38%)	1 (1%)	D 292 (67%)	R 143 (33%)	
96. 1979–1981	D 58 (58%)	R 41 (41%)	1 (1%)	D 276 (63%)	R 159 (37%)	
97. 1981–1983	R 53 (53%)	D 46 (46%)	1 (1%)	D 242 (56%)	R 191 (44%)	2 (0%)
98. 1983–1985	R 54 (54%)	D 46 (46%)		D 269 (62%)	R 166 (38%)	
99. 1985–1987	R 53 (53%)	D 47 (47%)		D 253 (58%)	R 182 (42%)	
100. 1987–1989	D 55 (55%)	R 45 (45%)		D 258 (59%)	R 177 (41%)	
101. 1989–1991	D 55 (55%)	R 45 (45%)		D 260 (60%)	R 175 (40%)	
102. 1991–1993	D 56 (56%)	R 44 (44%)		D 267 (62%)	R 167 (38%)	1 (0%)
103. 1993–1995	D 57 (57%)	R 43 (43%)		D 258 (59%)	R 176 (41%)	1 (0%)
104. 1995–1997	R 52 (52%)	D 48 (48%)		R 230 (53%)	D 204 (47%)	1 (0%)
105. 1997–1999	R 55 (55%)	D 45 (45%)		R 226 (52%)	D 207 (48%)	2 (0%)
106. 1999–2001	R 55 (55%)	D 45 (45%)		R 223 (51%)	D 211 (49%)	1 (0%)
107. 2001–2003	R 50 (50%)	D 50 (50%)		R 221 (51%)	D 212 (49%)	2 (0%)
108. 2003–2005	R 51 (51%)	D 48 (48%)	1 (1%)	R 229 (53%)	D 205 (47%)	1 (0%)
109. 2005–2007	R 55 (55%)	D 44 (44%)	1 (1%)	R 231 (53%)	D 202 (47%)	1 (0%)

APPENDIX VIII

STATISTICS OF MAJOR U.S. WARS

War/Conflict	Duration of War	Number Serving	U.S. Military Deaths
Revolutionary War	1775–1783	?	4,435
War of 1812	1812–1815	286,730	2,260
U.S.-Mexican War	1846–1848	78,718	13,283
Civil War	1861–1865	2,250,000	618,000
Spanish-American War	1898	306,760	2,446
World War I	1917–1918	4,734,991	116,516
World War II	1941–1945	16,112,566	405,399
Korean War	1951–1953	5,720,000	36,574
Vietnam Conflict	1964–1973	8,744,000	58,209
Persian Gulf War	1990–1991	2,225,000	382
Afghanistan	2001–	?	357 (as of 1/16/2007)
Iraqi	2003–	600,000	3,026 (as of 1/16/2007)

BIBLIOGRAPHY

Code: Description:
BB   Biography at its best
CC   Critic's choice—has to be good; we know the author
DD   Dramatic days—insights into moments that changed America
EP   For entertainment and pleasure—just a good read
G   Good introductory text for general audience
GO   Golden oldie—your parents may have read it
M   For mature historians only
PC   Passionate and controversial
PP   Best of the year—won a Pulitzer Prize in history or biography
PS   Classic primary source documents

Chapter 7

Clinton, Catherine. 1984. *The Other Civil War: American Women in the Nineteenth Century*. Hill and Wang. 242 pages.   EP   GO

Dew, Charles B. 2002. *Apostles of Disunion: Southern Secession Commissioners and the Causes of the Civil War*. University Press of Virginia. 138 pages.   PC

Foner, Eric, and Joshua Brown. 2005. *Forever Free: The Story of Emancipation and Reconstruction*. Knopf. 304 pages.   G   PC

Klein, Maury. 1999. *Days of Defiance: Sumter, Secession and the Coming of the Civil War*. Vintage. 528 pages.   DD

McFeely, William S. 2002. *Grant: A Biography*. W.W. Norton. 608 pages.   BB   PP

McPherson, James M. 2003. *Battle Cry of Freedom: The Civil War Era*. Oxford University Press. 952 pages.   G   PP

Neely, Mark E. 1992. *The Fate of Liberty: Abraham Lincoln and Civil Liberties*. Oxford University Press. 304 pages.   PP

Stout, Harry S. 2006. *Upon the Altar of the Nation: A Moral History of the Civil War*. Viking. 576 pages.   CC   PC

Woodward, C. Vann, ed. 1993. *Mary Chesnut's Civil War*. Yale University Press. 892 pages.   GO   PS   PP

Chapter 8

Argersinger, Peter H. 1995. *The Limits of Agrarian Radicalism: Western Populism and American Politics*. University Press of Kansas. 312 pages.   CC   M

Blum, Edward J. 2005. *Reforging the White Republic: Race, Religion and American Nationalism, 1865–1898*. Louisiana University Press. 356 pages.   M   PC

Buck, Paul H. 1937. *The Road to Reunion.* Little, Brown. 320
pages.   GO   PP
Cherny, Robert W. 1997. *American Politics in the Gilded Age 1868–1900.* Harlan
Davidson. 167 pages.   G
Edwards, Rebecca. 1997. *Angels in the Machinery: Gender in American Party
Politics from the Civil War to the Progressive Era.* Oxford University Press. 256
pages.   M   PC
Hahn, Steven. 2005. *A Nation under Our Feet: Black Political Struggles in
the Rural South from Slavery to the Great Migration.* Belknap Press. 624
pages.   PC   PP
Hoogenboom, Ari. 1995. *Rutherford B. Hayes: Warrior and President.* University
of Kansas Press. 712 pages.   BB
Morris, Roy, Jr. 2003. *Fraud of the Century: Rutherford B. Hayes, Samuel Tilden
and the Stolen Election of 1876.* Simon & Schuster. 320 pages.   DD   PC
Woodward, C. Vann. 1991. *Reunion and Reaction: The Compromise of 1877 and the
End of Reconstruction.* Oxford University Press. 288 pages.   DD   GO

Chapter 9

Beisner, Robert L. 1968. *Twelve Against Empire: The Anti-Imperialists, 1898–1900.*
McGraw-Hill.   GO   M   PC
Cooper, John Milton. 1992. *Pivotal Decades: The United States, 1900–1920.* W.W.
Norton. 408 pages.   G
Jacobson, Matthew Frye. 2001. *Barbarian Virtues: The United States Encounters
Foreign Peoples at Home and Abroad, 1876–1917.* Hill and Wang. 336
pages.   M   PC
Keegan, John. 2000. *The First World War.* Vintage. 528 pages.   G
Kennedy, David M. 1982. *Over Here: The First World War and American Society.*
Oxford University Press. 416 pages.   EP   PC
Leech, Margaret. 1999. *In the Days of McKinley.* American Political Biography
Press.   BB   EP   GO   PP
Mead, Rebecca J. 2004. *How the Vote Was Won: Woman Suffrage in the Western
United States, 1868–1914.* New York University Press. 273 pages.   M
Merk, Frederick. 1995. *Manifest Destiny and Mission in American History.* Harvard
University Press. 286 pages.   M   PC
Trask, David F. 1997. *The War with Spain in 1898.* University of Nebraska Press.
654 pages.   G   DD

Chapter 10

Dickinson, Matthew J. 1999. *Bitter Harvest: FDR, Presidential Power and
the Growth of the Presidential Branch.* Cambridge University Press. 280
pages.   M   PC
Fass, Paula S. 1979. *The Damned and the Beautiful: American Youth in the 1920s.*
Oxford University Press. 520 pages.   GO   EP
Freidel, Frank. 2006. *Franklin D. Roosevelt: A Rendezvous with Destiny.* American
Political Biography Press. 710 pages.   BB   GO
Galbraith, John Kenneth. 1997. *The Great Crash: 1929.* Mariner Books. 224
pages.   GO

Gorn, Elliot J., Randy Roberts, and Terry D. Bilhartz. 2004. *Constructing the American Past,* vol. 2. Longman. 368 pages.   CC   PS

Knock, Thomas J. 1995. *To End All Wars: Woodrow Wilson and the Quest for a New World Order.* Princeton University Press. 400 pages.   BB   PC

Kyvig, David E. 2004. *Daily Life in the United States, 1920–1940: How Americans Lived During the Roaring Twenties and the Great Depression.* Ivan R. Dee. 350 pages.   EP

Larson, Edward J. 1998. *Summer for the Gods: The Scopes Trial and America's Continuing Debate over Science and Religion.* Harvard University Press. 344 pages.   M   PP

Chapter 11

Ambrose, Stephen E. 1991. *Eisenhower.* Simon & Schuster. 640 pages.   BB

Goodwin, Doris Kearns. 1995. *No Ordinary Time: Franklin and Eleanor Roosevelt: The Home Front in World War II.* Simon & Schuster. 768 pages.   G   EP   PP

Hixson, Walter L. 1997. *Parting the Curtain: Propaganda, Culture and the Cold War, 1945–1961.* Palgrave Macmillan. 299 pages.   PC

Klarman, Michael J. 2004. *From Jim Crow to Civil Rights: The Supreme Court and the Struggle for Racial Equality.* Oxford University Press. 655 pages.   M

La Forte, Robert S., and Ronald E. Marcello. 2001. *Remembering Pearl Harbor: Eyewitness Accounts by U.S. Military Men and Women.* Ballantine Books. 336 pages.   DD   EP   PS

McCullough, David. 1993. *Truman.* Simon & Schuster. 1,120 pages.   BB   PP

Oshinsky, David M. 2005. *Polio: An American Story.* Oxford University Press. 368 pages.   EP   PP

Rorabaugh, W.J. 2002. *Kennedy and the Promise of the Sixties.* Cambridge University Press. 317 pages.   G   PC

Rosenberg, Emily S. 2003. *A Date Which Will Live: Pearl Harbor in American Memory.* Duke University Press. 236 pages.   DD   EP

Chapter 12

Branch, Taylor 1989. *Parting the Waters: America in the King Years 1954–63.* Simon & Schuster. 1,088 pages.   PC   PP

Dudziak, Mary L. 2002. *Cold War Civil Rights: Race and the Image of American Democracy.* Princeton University Press. 344 pages.   PC

Kutler, Stanley, ed. 1998. *Abuse of Power: The New Nixon Tapes.* Touchstone.   PS

Lubin, David M. 2003. *Shooting Kennedy: JFK and the Culture of Images.* University of California Press. 341 pages.   M

McDougall, Walter A. 1986. *. . . the Heavens and the Earth: A Political History of the Space Age.* Johns Hopkins University Press. 584 pages.   PC   PP

President's Commission on the Assassination of President John F. Kennedy. 1992. *The Warren Commission Report: Report of the President's Commission on the Assassination of President John F. Kennedy.* St. Martin's Griffin. 912 pages.   PS

Roberts, Randy, and James S. Olson. 1998. *John Wayne: America.* Bison Books. 772 pages.   BB   CC   EP

Schlesinger, Arthur M., Jr. 2002. *A Thousand Days: John F. Kennedy in the White House.* Mariner Books. 1,120 pages.   BB   EP   GO   PP
Wills, Garry. 2002. *Nixon Agonistes: The Crisis of the Self-Made Man.* Mariner Books. 640 pages.   BB

Chapter 13

Balmer, Randall. 1993. *Mine Eyes Have Seen the Glory: A Journey into the Evangelical Subculture in America.* Oxford University Press. 294.   EP   PC
Brinkley, Douglas G. 1999. *The Unfinished Presidency: Jimmy Carter's Journey to the Nobel Peace Prize.* Penguin. 624 pages.   BB   PC
Farber, David. 2004. *Taken Hostage: The Iran Hostage Crisis and America's First Encounter with Radical Islam.* Princeton University Press. 224 pages.   DD   PC
Gergen, David. 2000. *Eyewitness to Power: The Essence of Leadership, Nixon to Clinton.* Simon & Schuster. 384 pages.   G
Harris, John F. 2005. *The Survivor: Bill Clinton in the White House.* Random House. 544 pages.   BB
Patterson, James T. 2005. *Restless Giant: The United States from Watergate to Bush vs. Gore.* Oxford University Press. 496 pages.   G
Podell, Janet, and Steven Anzovin, eds. 2001. *Speeches of American Presidents.* H.W. Wilson. 866 pages.   PS
Reeves, Richard. 2005. *President Reagan: The Triumph of Imagination.* Simon & Schuster. 592 pages.   BB
Shilts, Randy, and William Greider. 2000. *And the Band Played On: Politics, People and the AIDS Epidemic.* Stonewall Inn. 656 pages.   PC

Chapter 14

Brinkley, Douglas G. 2006. *The Great Deluge: Hurricane Katrina, New Orleans and the Mississippi Gulf Coast.* HarperCollins. 736 pages.   PC
Calhoun, Craig, Paul Price, and Ashley Timmer. 2002. *Understanding September 11.* New Press. 454 pages.   DD   PC
Dudziak, Mary L., ed. 2003. *September 11 in History: A Watershed Moment?* Duke University Press. 240 pages.   DD
Galbraith, Peter W. 2006. *The End of Iraq: How American Incompetence Created a War Without End.* Simon & Schuster. 272 pages.   PC
Gillman, Howard. 2001. *The Votes That Counted: How the Court Decided the 2000 Presidential Election.* University of Chicago Press. 325 pages.   PC
Gregg, Gary L., and Mark J. Rozell. 2003. *Considering the Bush Presidency.* Oxford University Press. 224 pages.   M   PC
Hershberg, Eric, and Kevin W. Moore. 2002. *Critical Views of September 11: Analyses from around the World.* New Press. 290 pages.   DD   PC

Index